## ALSO BY WENDY LESSER

# SCANDINAVIAN NOIR

# SCANDINAVIAN NOIR

## IN PURSUIT OF A MYSTERY

### WENDY LESSER

FARRAR, STRAUS AND GIROUX | NEW YORK

Farrar, Straus and Giroux
120 Broadway, New York 10271

Printed in the United States of America
First edition, 2020

Library of Congress Cataloging-in-Publication Data
Names: Lesser, Wendy, author.
Title: Scandinavian noir : in pursuit of a mystery / Wendy Lesser.
Description: First edition. | New York : Farrar, Straus and Giroux, 2020.
Identifiers: LCCN 2019055659 | ISBN 9780374216979 (hardcover)
Subjects: LCSH: Detective and mystery stories, Scandinavian—History
    and criticism.
Classification: LCC PT7083.5.D48 L47 2020 | DDC 839/.5—dc23
LC record available at https://lccn.loc.gov/2019055659

*Designed by Gretchen Achilles*

Our books may be purchased in bulk for promotional,
educational, or business use. Please contact your local bookseller
or the Macmillan Corporate and Premium Sales Department
at 1-800-221-7945, extension 5442, or by e-mail at
MacmillanSpecialMarkets@macmillan.com.

www.fsgbooks.com
www.twitter.com/fsgbooks • www.facebook.com/fsgbooks

10  9  8  7  6  5  4  3  2  1

*For the Scandinavian police officers,*
*fictional and real,*
*who made this book possible*

# CONTENTS

# SCANDINAVIAN NOIR

# CAVEAT LECTOR

This is not an Encyclopedia of Nordic Crime Fiction (though there is such a thing, indicating just how ubiquitous this genre has now become). It is instead something much more eccentric and personal: that is, my take on the three Scandinavian countries—Sweden, Norway, and Denmark—as seen through the mystery novels I've read over the past four decades or so. What I have constructed here is a map, or a portrait, or a cultural history of a place that both exists and does not exist.

You will not, I'm afraid, find Iceland and Finland in my account, even though they are both acknowledged contributors to the Nordic noir trend. While Iceland has produced a strong and much-admired cache of police procedurals, most of them happen to take place in the wild, frozen countryside. As an inveterate city person, I don't find this environment conducive to my thriller-reading pleasure—I rarely read American mysteries set in the backwoods, either—so although I gave the eminent Arnaldur Indridason and his fellow Icelanders a try, I'm afraid I quit after finishing only a couple of novels. Finland, on the other hand, has so far exported only a very limited amount of crime fiction (though it *has* yielded at least a couple of good television shows in that vein). It will no doubt catch up with the other

Nordic countries soon, but given the present scarcity, I have felt free to leave it aside.

For a long time now, my primary source of information about Denmark, Sweden, and Norway has been these novels about murders committed and murders solved. That they all contained a great deal of information on daily life *aside* from the murders is what has enabled me to construct my imaginary Scandinavia. Perhaps its sole oddity, as a realistic world, is that many of its most noticeable inhabitants are police officers. It is nonetheless a fully populated world, with its own characteristic styles of housing and clothing, its street maps and traffic patterns, its hospitals and schools and public buildings, its annual holidays and festivals, its extremes of weather, its summer and winter light, its traditions of food and drink, its poverty and wealth, its problems with drugs and alcohol, its routine and less routine interactions between men and women, its wily politicians and obstructive bureaucrats, its bridges and airports and ferries and borders and, increasingly, its migrants from other countries.

Over the course of many years this imagined place grew more and more solidly visible to me, especially as films and TV series (also focusing on murder stories) began to supplement the mental images I had derived from books. For years I never had any strong desire to visit in person the real countries that corresponded to these fictional ones; I remained satisfied with just the Scandinavia I had constructed in my mind. And then suddenly, between one day and the next, that no longer seemed sufficient. This is the story of the adventure that ensued.

# FICTION AS REALITY

S ometime in the early 1980s, I began reading a series of mysteries that featured a Swedish homicide detective named Martin Beck. I was living in Berkeley at the time, studying for a PhD in English literature as I worked at a variety of part-time jobs, and I knew a lot of people both inside and outside the academy. Being a talkative sort, I started telling everyone around me about this incredible Scandinavian cop series. Soon we were all reading it.

What I knew at the time was that it was written by a couple, Maj Sjöwall and Per Wahlöö, who had from the very beginning envisioned it as a sequence of ten books that would portray Swedish society from a distinctly Marxist perspective. Published between 1965 and 1975, the Martin Beck series grew noticeably darker as it moved toward its end—though whether this was because Sweden itself (not to speak of the world beyond it) had worsened during that decade, or because Per Wahlöö had learned in the early 1970s that he was dying of cancer, was something no one could answer. Wahlöö died, I later learned, on the exact day in June of 1975 when the tenth volume was published in Sweden, having worked like a maniac to finish it on time. (Sjöwall, who was his equal partner in many ways—they would write their alternating chapters at night, so as not to be interrupted by their small children, and would then exchange chapters for editing—has said that at the very end Wahlöö was pretty much writing everything himself.) At any rate, he left behind exactly what he had intended to produce: ten books containing thirty chapters each, which, taken together, constitute a single continuous social narrative comparable in some ways to a Balzac, Zola, or Dickens project, though clothed in the garments of a police procedural.

It would be a melodramatic exaggeration to say that the Martin Beck series changed my life, but like all such exaggerations, this one would be built on a nugget of truth. Both my idea of Scandinavia and my sense of what a mystery could do were shaped by those books. If I later became a veritable addict of the form, gobbling up hundreds if not thousands of dollars a year in Kindle purchases of Swedish, Danish, and Norwegian mysteries, that habit could no doubt be attributed to many things besides the Martin Becks: the invention of digital books, for instance, which allowed for impulse buying and virtually infinite storage; the massive and surprising success of Stieg Larsson's Lisbeth Salander series, which encouraged American publishers to bring out any and every available Scandinavian thriller; the introduction of the long-cycle police procedural on American television, including such gems as *Hill Street Blues*, *NYPD Blue*, and ultimately *The Wire*, all of which cemented my fascination with the form; not to mention dozens if not hundreds of similar behavior-shaping factors that remain, for me, at an unconscious level. We never know for sure why we read what we read. I cannot, at the moment, even call to mind who first recommended the Martin Becks to me (though I know it was a person and not, say, a bookstore display or a newspaper review). Whoever it was, in any case, deserves my eternal gratitude.

What is so special about these ten books? Or—a slightly

different question—what was it that so appealed to me back in
1981 or 1982, when I was about to turn thirty and America was
on the verge of becoming what it is today?

Ronald Reagan, remember, had just been elected president.
Many of us who voted against him (particularly among the
Californians who had suffered through his governorship) had
sworn that we would leave the country if he won. We didn't
actually carry out these threats—one never does, as I have
learned repeatedly in the years since—but in my imagination I
must have pictured Sweden, that haven for dissident Americans
since the time of the Vietnam War, as one of the ideal refuges
to which one could flee in such circumstances. That the society in which the Martin Beck novels took place represented a
form of humane, non-Soviet socialism was certainly a great part
of their appeal for me. What I failed to notice at the time was
how severely Sjöwall and Wahlöö were in fact *criticizing* the
inadequate socialism practiced in their country. Instead, what
I saw was the difference between gun-crazy, corporate-run,
murder-riddled America and this small, sensible nation where
even policemen hated guns, where crime was seen as a social
problem rather than an individual pathology, and where the
rare appearance of a serial or mass killer instantly provoked
comparisons to the well-chronicled history of such crimes in
the United States.

And then there was the specific affection I felt for Martin
Beck's team of homicide detectives. The idea of a team was itself
appealing, especially in contrast to the usual American detective, a hardboiled rogue who typically despised collective procedures and chose to work alone and unregulated. But beyond
that, I loved the individual characters in the team, who over the

course of ten volumes began to seem as familiar to me as most of my real-life acquaintances.

To begin with, there is Martin Beck himself, who exhibits rectitude, fairness, a decent sense of empathy even for murderers, a useful skepticism about the criminal justice system, a healthy dislike of stupidity, careerism, and greed, and a willingness to let those around him do their best work. His home life, perhaps, leaves something to be desired—alienated from his nagging wife and distant from his two small children, he spends as many hours as possible on the job—but this changes over the course of the ten volumes, as he and his wife divorce and as he grows closer to his growing daughter. And though Martin Beck is something of a loner, with few strong emotional ties, he does have a best friend, in the form of Lennart Kollberg, his second-in-command on the National Homicide squad.

Kollberg is one of the great characters of detective fiction. (He is almost always called simply "Kollberg" by the omniscient narrator of these books, just as Martin Beck is always called by his full name; it is only the other characters who address them as "Martin" or "Lennart.") His fame, in the years since he came into being, has so transcended his original circumstances that a recent Norwegian mystery writer, Karin Fossum, can name her chief detective's dog Kollberg and expect everyone to pick up the allusion.

It's not easy to convey what is so lovable about Kollberg. His charm and wit, though notable, don't lend themselves to brief quotation; they are cumulative, like everything else in the series. Nor is he particularly magnetic, at least in terms of looks. For one thing, he's distinctly overweight, though that doesn't prevent him from being very attractive to certain women (in particular his much appreciated and significantly younger wife, Gunnar). He doesn't have any of the special talents some of his teammates possess—the phenomenal memory of Fredrik Melander, say, or the immense physical bravery of Gunvald Larsson, or even the sheer dogged persistence of the unimaginative Einar Rönn—but his all-round intelligence and sharp, ironic sense of humor make him an invaluable collaborator and sounding board for Martin Beck. As is often remarked in this series, the two of them can understand each other without explaining themselves, which is perhaps the essential definition of a close friendship. It is also, as Sjöwall and Wahlöö must have known, the defining element of any intimate collaboration on an important and prolonged piece of work.

If Sweden, as a place and an idea, was able to colonize a permanent spot in my imagination through these books, it may have been because a certain amount of groundwork had already been laid. I was not, in other words, a complete tabula rasa in regard to all things Scandinavian. Some of my prior associations were personal; others were things I shared with my culture at large.

In the late 1950s and 1960s, and especially in the middle-class Northern California suburb where I grew up, Scandinavian design was considered the height of good taste. Moreover, it was affordable good taste, particularly in its knock-off versions, which meant that we could have it in our somewhat-reduced-circumstances, single-parent-run, money-cannot-be-wasted household. The clean lines and absence of decorative frou-frou were a good match, too, with the modern simplicity of our Eichler tract house. In fact, both the redwood-frame dwelling my parents had bought new in 1955 and the spare wooden furniture we later acquired at the local Copenhagen outlet embodied the same theory: that mass-produced designs aimed at the pocketbooks of the general population could be as beautiful and as fashionable as anything the aristocracy might have inherited. We didn't know from aristocracy in my neighborhood, but the class rebellion that the Scandinavians had consciously initiated in their furnishings happened to suit our obliviously deracinated California style just fine. So the desk on which I did my schoolwork when I was eight, like all the desks I have had since then (including the one on which I am now writing), looked like something that had come straight off the boat from Denmark or Sweden.

And then there was Ingmar Bergman. Perhaps his movies did not penetrate as deeply into the general culture as the furniture had, but in my mother's intellectual milieu, he represented the pinnacle of artistic intelligence. (My father was another matter: he found Bergman's films downright depressing and, as he often said, he didn't go to the movies to be depressed. This pronounced difference in taste may have been one among the many reasons they got divorced when I was six.) I myself was exposed to Bergman at what now seems to me a shockingly young age. I know I was taken to both *Persona* and *Shame* while I was still in high school, because when I got to college and first saw *Smiles of a Summer Night*, I was amazed to find that he could be so cheerful. Imbued with the maternal aesthetic, I continued to keep up with Ingmar Bergman's films throughout my twenties and early thirties, and I can still vividly recall passages from *Scenes from a Marriage* and *Fanny and Alexander* even though I have not seen them again since they first came out.

This amount of Scandinavian culture (along with a few other items, like Marimekko fabrics and Dansk crockery) was made available during my youth to all of America, or at least all of middle-class America. But I had a couple of private introductions as well. When my sister and I were children, a family that included an American father, a Swedish mother, and three kids moved in down the street from us. Our two families were never especially close, but my sister, who was (and still is) two years younger than I, became good friends with the oldest girl, Eva, who was exactly her age. In the summer of 1968, when I took off for three months on an Israeli kibbutz, my fourteen-year-old sister accompanied Eva, her siblings, and their mother on a family trip to Sweden. I remember being intrigued by the reports my sister brought back when we regrouped in California in the fall. Eva's grandmother, she told me, was called Mormor, because she was the mother of her mother, and the grandfather was called Morfar. When they gave you something to eat (which was often, by my sister's account), you said "Tack för maten" in response. And so on, through a list of distinctly appealing cultural eccentricities. I did not feel envious at the time—I had had my own adventures in Israel, some good, some bad—but as the years went by and I failed to get to Sweden myself, it came to seem a place that belonged to my sister in a way it never would to me.

This despite the fact that my first Berkeley boyfriend, with whom I lived for a year during graduate school, was a Swede. Christened Ulf (a common Swedish name, apparently), he had come to America to study mathematics and logic after completing his undergraduate degree in his native Sweden. He had traveled widely before getting to the States—he was particularly

fond of Latin America, I remember—and he disdained the
Swedes for being a provincial, closed, old-fashioned society,
even as he shared a number of their socialist and communitar-
ian beliefs. As a very young man he had legally changed his last
name from Jansson (a surname he shared with an excessive number of Swedes) to an entirely new, made-up name, as the government was encouraging people to do in an effort to reduce
the nearly unmanageable level of duplication. The new name,
which sounded fine in Swedish, struck him as slightly ridiculous
when pronounced in the American manner, but Ulf preferred
even that to the relative anonymity of Jansson.

Grateful as he was to escape his origins, he nonetheless cherished fond memories of a few Swedish traditions. One, I remember, was the festival of Lucia, which somehow involved candles
and took place shortly before Christmas; another was the habit of
eating open-faced sandwiches. The only other thing I recall his
telling me about Sweden was that all social arrangements were
extremely formal and planned. When our next-door neighbors
in Berkeley once invited us over for drinks on the spur of the
moment, Ulf grew strangely excited, and when I asked him what
the big deal was, he said, "In Sweden you never come at the last
minute; you have to be invited days beforehand." Like all such
generalizations that we make about the world, this may have had
more to do with the family or village he grew up in than with
his whole culture. But I, knowing nothing, took it as the truth.

Only about five years passed between my breakup with Ulf
and my first reading of the Martin Becks, but a year is a
long time when you are in your twenties, and—at least on a

conscious level—I in no way associated the series with him. Or, for that matter, with Ingmar Bergman or Scandinavian design. It was its own new world, this Sweden that I was encountering through Sjöwall and Wahlöö.

As it happens, it was something new for Scandinavia, too. In the early 1960s, when the Swedish couple were formulating their idea for a ten-volume police procedural that would mirror the whole society, nothing of the kind had ever appeared in Scandinavian literature. America may have produced Dashiell Hammett and Ed McBain by then, not to mention numerous noir detective films and even some early urban TV shows, like *Dragnet*, that edged toward this territory. But the Scandinavian tradition was different. There were mysteries, true, but they utterly lacked the broad social perspective, the insistence on some kind of realism, that Sjöwall and Wahlöö were about to introduce.

One of the existing strands, for example, descended from the book Jo Nesbø has described as the original Nordic thriller: a 1909 mystery called *The Iron Chariot*, written by Norway's Sven Elvestad under the pen name Stein Riverton. It's a readable enough work, though a bit slow and (especially compared to latter-day practitioners like Nesbø himself) grotesquely unsuspenseful. *The Iron Chariot* is basically a country-house murder mystery, set in an idyllic landscape somewhere on the southern Norwegian coast at the height of summer—a location and a season that together allow for a great deal of crepuscular light shimmering on the ocean at midnight and other effects of that sort. The mysteriously clanking and reputedly ghostly "chariot" of the title turns out to be a newfangled flying machine invented by a local professor, one of the murder victims. In the end, the murderer is revealed to be the story's narrator, a weirdly impalpable creature whose crimes and methods are exposed by the Holmes-like detective called in from the nearest city—though not before we have pretty much figured them out by ourselves. The whole novel is like a combination of Edgar Allan Poe and Arthur Conan Doyle, a narrative that is at once logical and insane, but in any case very particular and very enclosed, with an extremely limited pool of suspects and no perspective whatsoever on the society at large.

Another precedent—perhaps even farther from the Martin Becks in style and intent, though closer temporally and geographically—consisted of the various Swedish mysteries written for children in the mid-twentieth century. These included Åke Holmberg's novels about the private eye Ture Sventon, issued between 1948 and 1973, and Nils-Olof Franzén's illustrated books about the detective Agaton Sax, which came out around the same time. Those detective characters, too, were clearly modeled on Holmes, though with certain features—such as a jolly round figure and an animal associate, in the case of Sax—that would make them especially appealing to children. The most famous series in this genre, perhaps because it actually employed a child as the detective, was Astrid Lindgren's trio of mysteries featuring a schoolboy named Kalle Blomqvist (a central character who, when the books proved popular enough to export, was later renamed Bill Bergson). These three tales, which appeared in Sweden between 1946 and 1953, are somewhat reminiscent of America's Nancy Drew series, with a youthful amateur detective who, together with the necessary age-appropriate sidekicks, always succeeds in outwitting the bad guys. Even now, the books remain sufficiently well known in

Sweden so that present-day readers of the Stieg Larsson books are expected to get the joke when Lisbeth's ally, the crusading journalist Mikael Blomkvist, is nicknamed "Kalle" by his friends. (This would seem to be a joke that never stales among Swedish mystery writers, for Leif G. W. Persson brings it up again in his recent novel *The Dying Detective*.)

But here I am getting ahead of myself, for the Larsson and Persson books—not to mention the dozens of other Nordic crime novels I'll be mentioning in the forthcoming pages—did not exist until decades after the Martin Becks were first published. It took a particular pair of authors working together at a specific moment in history to create that now-dominant form, the modern-day Scandinavian mystery. And despite the fact that they were naive beginners, or perhaps in some ways because of that, their achievement in the form has never been topped.

Let's agree at the outset to dispense with any discussion about brow levels. If I happen to invoke Dickens, Balzac, or Dostoyevsky when talking about these books, it is not to insist that Per Wahlöö and Maj Sjöwall are their equals as the writers of sentences and paragraphs—though nor would I want to grant outright that they are *not* at the same level in some other way. After all, Wilkie Collins was a thriller writer of the late nineteenth century whose best novels we are still reading with enormous satisfaction today; with each passing decade, he comes to seem more and more of a Victorian classic. One could also argue that Eric Ambler is as much a twentieth-century stylist as Ernest Hemingway, along the same spare lines, and it is not yet clear, if you ask me, which we'll be reading longer. My point is not just that we can't, from our limited perspective, answer questions about longevity and importance. It's also that I don't particularly want to, for that is not really what this book is about.

What matters to me is how persuasively these mystery writers manage to create a world that one can imaginatively inhabit—for the duration of a first reading, initially, but also long after. The various features of Martin Beck's world, including his Stockholm streets, his police department colleagues, his lovers, his friends, the crimes he solves, the murderers he pities, the politicians and bureaucrats he deplores, even the apartments he inhabits, all seemed terribly real to me when I first encountered them, and all continue to seem so today, even after one or more re-readings. This is the mystery novel not as a puzzle that can be forgotten as soon as it is solved, but as an experience one is living through along with the characters. If they are sometimes "flat" characters in the manner of Dickens's grotesques or Shakespeare's clowns, that is not an absence of realism, but rather a realistic acknowledgment that in our own lives most other people remain opaque to us, often memorable mainly through their caricaturable qualities. We do not have the capacity, as George Eliot famously noted, to be fully empathetic at all times. Much of our observant life, and even much of our own experience, is conducted in a kind of shorthand.

Yet part of what makes the Sjöwall/Wahlöö books great, in comparison to most other mystery series, is precisely the opposite of this shorthand. They are oddly inclusive, with an eye for extraneous detail and a concern with the kinds of trivialities (subways ridden, meals eaten, suspicions vaguely aroused, meandering conversations, useless trains of thought, sudden bursts of intuition, random acts or events that cause everything to change suddenly) which make up not only every life, but every prolonged police investigation. This means that the timing of the books is, for some readers, excessively slow: we often have to wait for the necessary facts to surface, so we tend to find ourselves floating along rather than racing toward an increasingly visible conclusion. I always tell people that they have to wade through at least the first two volumes, *Roseanna* and *The Man Who Went Up in Smoke*, before things really get going in the Martin Beck series. Only when they reach *The Man on the Balcony* or, even better, *The Laughing Policeman* will they be able to judge how much they like the series. Patience is required of the reader, just as it is of the detective.

Nor are these the sort of "fair" mystery that lays out all the potential suspects and relevant clues (if perhaps in cleverly disguised form) early enough for you to arrive at the solution yourself. Leave that to Agatha Christie and the other puzzle-mongers. In the Martin Becks, the murderer might be someone we meet on the first page, but he equally well might not appear until nearly the end of the volume. The solution is only part of the point; it is getting there that matters.

The only other Scandinavian series that approaches the Martin Becks in having this same quality of lived, unhurried, persuasively real experience is the Kurt Wallander sequence devised by Henning Mankell. Also a Swede, and also someone with pronounced political interests (though his tended toward a kind of global progressivism rather than a locally focused Marxism), Mankell placed his lead detective in the town of Ystad, which sits along the southern coast of Sweden in the Skåne region.

Characters from Skåne who appear in the Stockholm mysteries are always portrayed as rather slow-paced and small-townish, with a distinctive regional accent and a willingness to suspend quick judgment. (Think of Frances McDormand's Marge character in *Fargo*, if you want a good American comparison.) And Kurt Wallander would certainly not deny this characterization of himself. He is a small-town policeman who happens, in the course of his own ten-book series, to solve murders that begin or end on Swedish soil but that grow increasingly complex and international in scope as the series moves forward. Partly, this is due to his moment in time (roughly 1989 to 1997, with a single follow-up volume appearing over a decade later)—a period when the Soviet Union was breaking down, South African apartheid was coming to an end, and all sorts of other global events were having a direct effect on once-isolated Sweden. Partly, though, the wide-angle view is attributable to Henning Mankell's own life, which was divided annually between Sweden and Mozambique, and which included theatrical work and journalism as well as fiction-writing.

Kurt Wallander is, in a way, like a cross between Martin Beck and Kollberg. He is overweight like the latter and emotionally isolated like the former, though with an increasingly close relationship with his daughter, Linda, who eventually becomes a police officer too. Moreover, he is as ruminative as the two of them put together—and this, in a way, is both the virtue and the flaw of the series. Much of the narrative, although it is voiced in third-person, takes place inside Kurt's mind. Instead of the back-and-forth conversations which characterize the Stockholm squad room, and which in a way define both the social nature and the low-key humor of the Martin Beck series,

Kurt Wallander's conversations and realizations are either with a dead colleague (the sainted Rydberg) or, mostly, with himself. Even as he spends a great deal of time re-reading the case notes and thinking about what he might have missed, he is also reserving the laundry room in his apartment building, checking the temperature outdoors, going to the doctor, getting his old Peugeot repaired, remembering to call or visit his father, and otherwise leading a slow, uneventful life. Thoughts flicker in the margins of his brain before they take shape fully, and it is this recognizable process—of questioning and intuition gradually transforming itself into realization and understanding—that most fully characterizes the Wallander books. Granted, they have a few moments of cinematic excitement (as when Wallander is pursued by the armed and hostile Latvian police in *The Dogs of Riga*, or engages in a gun battle with foreign assassins in *The White Lioness*), but for the most part they lack the high-wire, shoot-'em-up denouements that more commonly characterize the thriller genre. They are mysteries, for the most part, about the process of thinking.

I began reading the Kurt Wallanders in the 1990s, just as they were coming out in English translations, and by the time the ninth one had appeared, around the beginning of the twenty-first century, I had pretty much read them all. Unlike Sjöwall and Wahlöö, Mankell had not envisioned the Wallander series as a complete arc to begin with. He just kept producing them, one after another, as both the rapt audiences and the increasing seriousness of world events made their demands on him. Like many other thriller writers before him (including, notoriously, Arthur Conan Doyle), he eventually came to find his famous detective a burden, and in the belated final volume, *A Troubled*

*Man*, which came out in English in 2011, he firmly shut Kurt
Wallander down by giving him Alzheimer's.

By this time, though, the dam had burst on Scandinavian
mysteries and America was flooded with them. I can still recall
my initial encounter with Stieg Larsson's *The Girl with the Dragon
Tattoo*, which almost singlehandedly set off the whole process. It
was the summer of 2009, and I was in the hospital for a few days,
resting up after some routine orthopedic surgery. As I lay there,
intermittently pushing the button that allowed morphine to flow
directly into my body, I finished the entire first volume of Larsson's Lisbeth Salander series. (My surgeon was so impressed by
my evident fascination that he subsequently bought the book to
take on his vacation.) It was not, I thought, that the book was so
good; as a staunch mystery reader, I had plenty of objections to it
on the grounds of implausibility, superficial character creation,
and general axe-grinding. But it was, almost literally, un-put-
downable. I found this with both of the subsequent two volumes
as well. Even as I despised the cheap feminism of the books, with
their obvious approval of Lisbeth's take-no-prisoners, violent-
revenge-on-behalf-of-the-abused approach, I still couldn't stop
reading them until I got to the end of each.

And the rest of Larsson's English readership apparently felt
the same way, because from that point onward, the American
publishing industry couldn't get enough of the Scandinavian
mystery genre. That, I suppose, is how my addiction really got
started (my addiction to Scandinavian mysteries, I mean: I had
no trouble leaving behind the hospital's morphine drip). It was
a case of supply generating demand. Abetted by Amazon's algo-
rithm recommending similar books purchased by other custom-
ers, the American branch of the Scandinavian mystery industry

located my weakness and proceeded to feed my seemingly bottomless need.

Practically on the heels of Stieg Larsson, I remember, came Jo Nesbø—a Norwegian, and therefore a somewhat new taste to be added to the existing Swedish mixture. I loved the first three volumes I read in Nesbø's Harry Hole series, and even though I found that the violence and hair-raising tactics began to get old after a while, I still bought each new one as it came out. But even the best current series, in which new entries will appear at intervals of twelve or eighteen months, is not enough to feed a serious obsession. In some moods, I can consume four or five of these in a *week*. So a host of other Scandinavian detectives lined up behind Martin, Kurt, and Harry: Swedes like Mari Jungstedt's Anders Knutas, Åke Edwardson's Erik Winter, Kjell Eriksson's Ann Lindell, Arne Dahl's Paul Hjelm, Helene Tursten's Irene Huss, and Lars Kepler's Joona Linna (who is actually a Finn working in Sweden); Norwegian investigators like Karin Fossum's Konrad Sejer, K. O. Dahl's Frank Frølich, Gunnar Staalesen's Varg Veum, Gard Sveen's Tommy Bergmann, and Thomas Enger's Henning Juul; and a collection of Danes ranging from Jussi Adler-Olsen's Carl Mørck through Lene Kaaberbøl and Agnete Friis's Nina Borg to Lotte and Søren Hammer's Konrad Simonsen and beyond.

If your mind now feels like a stew of indifferentiable Scandinavian names, well, all I can say is: Welcome to my world. A steady diet of these things will cause anyone to lose track of the individual differences, and this is complicated by the fact that the three countries themselves have a great deal in common. The Swedish currency is the krona, whose plural is kronor, while in Denmark and Norway they are called kroner; as with

Canadian and U.S. dollars, they are not worth exactly the same, though all three values are in the same ballpark. The languages, too, manifest a similar "near but not the same" quality. Swedish and Danish, for instance, although often considered (even by their speakers) to be mutually understandable, are apparently different enough to cause confusion, a fact that is pointed out in a number of the novels and also in a recent television program, *The Bridge*, that is set between the cities of Malmö and Copenhagen. There are definite borders between these three countries—at times heavily enforced borders—but the criminals in these mysteries seem able to flee relatively easily from one to another, in part because of the prevalence of watery modes of transport.

Overall, the people of these three nations, though they may think of themselves as distinct nationalities, share so many cultural traits that from an American point of view they tend to come across as generally Scandinavian rather than specifically Danish, Swedish, or Norwegian. Perhaps the thing they seem to share most, in fact, is a kind of emphasis on insuperable regional differences *within* each small country, such that Stockholmers feel superior to citizens of Gothenburg and Malmö, Oslo inhabitants think of Bergen as the sticks, and citizens of Copenhagen view the rest of Denmark as a mere appendage. Or so it would seem from the mysteries these countries export to the rest of the world.

Because they are mysteries, you might expect that plot is primary. But in fact plot is the first thing to dissolve, at least in my mental reservoir. What I am left with instead is a wide-ranging but rather formless body of knowledge about the way things are done in these three Nordic countries. "Knowledge" may not be quite the right word, since what I've learned from these books could well be illusory and is almost certainly distorted. But I do have a number of remarkably clear impressions about this imaginary region, and they run the full gamut, pertaining to many different parts of the culture's daily and communal existence. I want to get some of this information across to you, but I don't want to burden you with dozens of summarized murder plots. So, in an effort to contain the chaos, I've trammeled my various perceptions into a sequence of logically arranged categories, each of which explores an aspect of how life is lived in my fictional Scandinavia—and perhaps in the real one, too.

You might well ask why you need to take in all this information (or perhaps non-information, if my assumptions prove wrong), and that is a fair question. The answer lies in the division of our responsibilities. For now, I am posing as the expert, the one who has read all these books, and as such I am attempting to transmit to you in capsule form the fruits of my ill-gotten knowledge. But later on it will be you who has to draw the conclusions about how accurate this so-called knowledge really is. That is, you will be the one responsible for testing the fictional rules I outline here against the reality they supposedly represent.

I say "you" as if it means something specific, but of course I don't know exactly who you are. In fact, I don't have any *idea* who you are, except that you have been enticed this far into a book that has something to do with Nordic crime fiction. For all I know, you've read hundreds more of these books than I have, making you the true expert and me a mere amateur. And on the other hand you could be a complete newcomer, with only a few of these mysteries, or possibly none at all, already under your belt. In that case, I must warn you that spoilers lie ahead: I couldn't really summarize my cultural gleanings without giving away a few important plot points in the course of my discussion. If that disturbs you, then please feel free to skip to the appendix, where you will find an annotated list of recommended books that you can read right now, before I have a chance to ruin the plots for you. Or, if you prefer, you can just continue to read onward here, hoping you'll have forgotten my indiscretions by the time you get around to reading the mysteries. (That's probably what I would do myself—rely on my own forgetfulness, I mean, since it's proven itself so consistently in the past.)

But whichever kind of Scandinavian mystery reader you are, a seasoned expert or a fresh-faced novice, your job from here on in will be the same. You'll need to take in my cultural assertions with both a high degree of attention and a strong element of doubt. Remember, what is true and what is not true will not be apparent yet. My arguments may sound persuasive, but this is all untested theory so far. You yourself will be doing the actual testing when we get to the second half of the book—and I sense you'll be up to the task, because I can already tell, based on our acquaintance thus far, that you too have a logical mind.

So now here's the orderly sequence of topics I've devised for that mind to absorb.

**ALCOHOL** would have to come first on any such list. It's not that the Scandinavians are all big drinkers (though a surprising number of them do appear to be), but that drunks and drunkenness feature so heavily in all the accounts. Drink lies behind quite a few of the murders, starting in the Martin Beck series and extending up to the most recent novels, and it would seem to explain a large portion of the violence in this relatively non-violent region. Murder victims, too, are often victimized when drunk, especially in the books that are set in vacation spots like the Stockholm archipelago or the island of Gotland. Festive drinking, particularly by teenagers, can easily lead to sudden death; so can hanging out at bars with one's girlfriends, if one is a young female preyed upon by a crazed killer. Drowning deaths from ferries (or supposed drowning deaths that turn out to be murders) are often linked to the excessive consumption of alcohol, which is in turn encouraged by the open bars that such vessels feature. Indeed, certain novels suggest that the main reason a Swede might take a ferry to Finland or Poland is to drink steadily at the bar on the way over and back.

Nor is the alcohol problem limited to the murderers and their victims. Many of the detectives depicted in these novels are also portrayed as enjoying their liquor. Lars Martin Johansson, the "dying detective" in Leif Persson's novel of that name, enjoys his aquavit so much that he cannot give it up even under a doctor's orders, and the resulting heart attack is his series-ending punishment. Johansson's nemesis in the Swedish police force, a total creep named Evert Bäckström, has many disgusting qualities—racism, misogyny, dishonesty, corruption, greed, just to name a few—and they all become exacerbated when he drinks (which he often does to excess, even going so far as to steal expensive liquor from a murder victim's apartment). Denmark's Carl Mørck frequently drowns his sorrows in beer, wine, and hard liquor, usually to the point where he wakes up hungover. Even Kurt Wallander and Martin Beck are likely to resort to a few too many glasses of wine or whiskey when they get home after a hard day at the office.

Perhaps the worst case, in terms of alcoholism, is Harry Hole, Jo Nesbø's hero. He is renowned in the Oslo Police Department as a hopeless drunk, and the people who can't stand him are constantly trying to get him fired on those grounds. Unluckily for them, he is also the most effective homicide detective in Norway, and since his drinking rarely if ever results in actual mistakes on the job, his departmental enemies have not to this day been successful in getting rid of him. This is partly because Harry often goes on the wagon: he starts drinking because things in his life get him down (events like the sudden death of his partner or the threats made to his lover), and then he stops drinking when he is needed in order to solve precisely those problems. His usual hangout in Oslo, Schrøder's Cafe, is a bar that attracts a rather insalubrious crowd (of whom Harry is sometimes the rattiest-looking, especially after he's been beaten up in a drunken fight), and the waitresses there tend to keep an eye on him, bringing him soft drinks instead of beer when he is supposed to be in one of his dry periods.

Harry Hole may buy his drinks retail, as most of the characters in Nesbø's novels seem to do, but in Swedish mysteries there is a great deal of reference to the "state liquor store," which apparently existed in Martin Beck's time and continues to exist today. (Something similar, called Vinmonopol, pops up occasionally in Norwegian tales, but the references to it are surprisingly infrequent, given the amount of drinking that takes place in that country.) It is not clear from the context whether Swedes frequent the state liquor store because it is the only purveyor of alcohol or because it is the cheapest, but in any case, cops and civilians can be found in its long lines, particularly on a Friday afternoon, when everyone is eager to get home to drink.

Women tend to be less heavy drinkers than men, choosing wine, say, over aquavit. But they do drink, and often it is for psychological or social reasons: either to relax themselves and forget about their anxieties, or else to ease the connection to whomever they are with. For example, in Lotte and Søren Hammer's *The Hanging*—the first and best volume in their Konrad Simonsen series—two female journalists who dislike each other, urgently needing to confer about a personal matter, meet at a café and end up drinking together at eleven in the morning. When one attempts to turn down the offered beer, saying, "I don't drink beer at this time of day," the other persuasively explains that she has brought the two beers to their table because "this is personal, and because we are Danish. We don't talk about personal things without beer, do we?"

I can't think of a single Scandinavian mystery I've read that does not, somewhere in its pages, refer to alcohol consumption, and most of them refer to it as a noticeable welfare or health problem, even when the characters themselves are happily enjoying their drinks. Tobacco has nowhere near the same prominence in the plots (though, granted, there are many pipe-smokers and cigarette-addicts among the cops, witnesses, and criminals, as well as people who regularly use something called snus, which appears to be a kind of chewing tobacco). And while cannabis and harder drugs have played an increasing role in recent mysteries—their illegality naturally means they are closely linked to crime—they are not as deeply rooted in Scandinavian life as alcohol is. Part of the reason Harry Hole's higher-ups can't fire him for his alcoholism is that they too, and *their* higher-ups, suffer to some degree from the same illness. It is a social problem that runs across classes and across occupations, afflicting both the high and the low, and that is evidently why the national governments have made so much effort to control it with bureaucratic institutions like the state liquor outlets.

**BUREAUCRACY**—including all kinds of government regulations, serious amounts of red tape, and wastefully complicated top-to-bottom command chains—is bound to be a factor in any socialist or social-democratic country, but it seems particularly pervasive in Scandinavia. American cops may hate their bosses or their colleagues, and may even at times allude to corrupt politicians whose ambitions get in the way of justice, but no American mystery series harps on the intrusive role of the entire system of police organization the way so many Scandinavian mysteries do.

This was apparently true from the very beginning of the contemporary genre. Perhaps one might say that it was even an originating *cause* of the genre, for the golden period of Swedish policing, according to Sjöwall and Wahlöö, lay in the half-decade before their series began. "It seemed to Martin Beck that the first half of the sixties had been an auspicious period in the history of the Stockholm police," his authors tell us. "Everything had seemed to be improving, common sense had been about to conquer rigidity and cliquishness, the recruiting base had been broadened, and even relations with the public had seemed to be getting better. But nationalization in 1965 had broken the positive trend. Since then, all the good prospects had been betrayed and all the good intentions laid to rest." Our sense of this structural damage to the police force is only peripheral in the earliest volumes of the Martin Beck series, but it increases gradually, and when we get to the final four books we find problems with the bureaucracy intruding heavily on the characters and the story. Beck and his team, by this point, are no longer free agents; their actions are governed by a hierarchy of careerist officials, from the National Police Commissioner on down.

Martin Beck actively deplores this increasingly bureaucratic trend, but it is Kollberg who gets angry enough to quit the police force—something he has been threatening to do for several volumes, and which he finally does at the end of *Cop Killer*, the penultimate book in the series. And that, in turn, means that the final volume, in which Kollberg puts in only a belated appearance, and in which the smarmy, obnoxious police chief Stig Malm dominates the process from the beginning, is the most depressing of them all (though also, in its dark way, the most humorous). If it were not for the voice of the oddly explicit, obliquely satiric, deeply concerned narrator, we would feel desperately lonely at this point—abandoned by Kollberg, left to the devices of Malm and his ilk. That, surely, is how Martin Beck must feel. But we, at any rate, have the ironic voice of the storyteller to keep us company in these miserable circumstances.

Per Wahlöö and Maj Sjöwall may hate the police bureaucrats more than anyone else does, but they are far from the only Swedes to target the police force's hierarchy. Even out in the relative countryside of Ystad, Kurt Wallander has to cope with unreasonable demands and poor support from the Stockholm police, the foreign ministry, the National Police Board, the Minister of Justice, and other overseers of his work. And among the

more recent Swedish novels, several involve secret collabora-
tions, if not outright conspiracies, between top-level police
officials and government departments.

Meanwhile, in Copenhagen, Jussi Adler-Olsen's "Department Q," a newly formed department headed by the rebellious
Carl Mørck and charged with solving cold cases, spends half
its time fighting off budget-grabs by the higher-ups in the police. (The hierarchy is made literal in the police building itself,
where Department Q is kept down in the basement and Carl
has to storm upstairs every time he has a complaint.) And if
things are rotten in Denmark, they seem no better in Norway. In
fact, Harry Hole's immediate boss and frequent protector is so
depressed at the state of the Oslo police administration and its
subjection to political interference that he is constantly threatening to move to quieter Bergen, as in fact he eventually does.

Even the television programs set in these countries emphasize the extent to which government ministers and legislators
control, not to say hamper, the local administration of justice.
Danish series like *The Killing, Borgen,* and *The Protectors,* Norwegian shows like *Nobel,* and the Swedish-Danish collaboration *The
Bridge* all portray societies in which police officers, soldiers, and
secret-service employees had better pay attention to what their
politicians are thinking if they want to get their jobs done. This
is not unique to Scandinavia, of course. The excellent French
series *Engrenages* (renamed *Spiral* in America) demonstrates just
how intertwined the French judicial and ministerial system is
with its cops. But in that case the connection appears to be ancient and structural, so that what we are getting is a portrait of
how French justice has been carried out for centuries. In the

Scandinavian television programs, by contrast, it all seems to be a function of battling personalities, each trying to dominate his or her turf.

Bureaucracy in these countries does not begin and end with the police, and sometimes it can have its useful side as well as its dangerous ones. To judge by Kaaberbøl and Friis's Nina Borg series, the Danish child protection services are very active and often quite humane. (This puts them in direct contrast to Stieg Larsson's take on Sweden's version, a child-welfare system which notoriously fails—and, indeed, abuses—Lisbeth Salander.) Welfare in general is of course a strong feature in all three Scandinavian countries, and though the financial resources are hardly distributed evenly, they do seem to be distributed much more fairly than in America. Apparently all that paperwork, red tape, and political grandstanding are accomplishing something good after all, at least some of the time. It's just that in the hands of the wrong people, the process can turn distinctly sour. But then, of what process is that not true?

COMPETENCE and incompetence are the two extremes that define police behavior in the Martin Beck books. Getting the job done—making the system work, however slow and laborious that process may be—lies at the heart of the exemplary detective work we encounter there. And, conversely, it is the failure to follow time-tested practical procedures, or to think through the possible consequences of one's acts, that results in the departmental disasters. There is very little overt corruption in the whole series (unless being selfishly ambitious, in the usual way

that striving professionals are, counts as being corrupt). Evil, in
this particular Scandinavian universe, is not the problem; stupidity is.

This turns out to be true from top to bottom. Chief of Police
Stig Malm and his deplorable allies may not know how to manage an effective police action, but neither do many of the police
on the ground, and throughout the ten books we meet and re-
encounter a large number of these local dumbbells. Yet not even
they are always useless. Given the important role of chance in
solving the Martin Beck mysteries, even a pair of Shakespear-
ean clowns like Kristiansson and Kvant, who are the laziest and
most idiotic patrolmen imaginable, can stumble upon the murderer at times. (It is typical of the series that, as it gets darker,
it kills off one of these two clowns—a shocking moment that
completely violates the reader's expectations in regard to comic
characters.) Part of what makes the Martin Beck series so readable, and also so humane, is that willful villainy is rarely if ever
blamed for events. Simple human idiocy, combined with bad
luck, is sufficient.

In contrast, most other Scandinavian series want to pin the
fault on a particular bad guy within the system as much as on
the criminals without. Leif Persson's Evert Bäckström, for example, is so vehemently obnoxious and corrupt that we virtually
cease to believe in him. There may indeed be real policemen in
Stockholm who are as greedy, racist, and deceitful as Bäckström,
but he is too one-dimensional for fiction: on the page, he comes
off more as an opportunity for Persson to ventriloquize foul remarks than as a credible character. A much more frightening
figure of evil is Jo Nesbø's Tom Waaler, who functions as Harry
Hole's secret opponent in the trilogy that includes *The Redbreast*,

*Nemesis,* and *The Devil's Star.* Waaler is thought by everyone else in Oslo to be an excellent policeman, whereas in reality he is a drug dealer, a weapons runner, and a cop killer. It takes three full volumes for Harry to discover, expose, and then end Tom Waaler's monstrous reign, and though they are probably the best three volumes in the series (I happily re-read them recently), they are also ludicrously implausible.

This tendency to create villains within the police force goes hand-in-hand with a desire to manufacture grotesquely clever and powerful murderers. Again, the Sjöwall/Wahlöö books are the exception: many of the criminals in this series, when not pathetic creatures to be pitied, are routinely selfish guys who have overstepped the lines, often by mistake or under sudden pressure. To someone schooled in the bizarre and intricate plots of more recent thriller writers, the crimes Martin Beck solves might even seem rather boring and run-of-the-mill. There are no monsters in these volumes, except possibly in *The Abominable Man* and *The Terrorists*—and even there the criminals' destructive behavior can always be linked to a power or profit motive.

Most of the other detectives in Scandinavia, though, seem to be up against super-villains modeled along Hannibal Lecter lines. Lars Kepler's Joona Linna, for instance, has a long-term nemesis so powerful and so frightening that, even when he is securely jailed, he can engineer people's deaths. In *The Hanging,* where Konrad Simonsen's team is faced with a ring of executioners self-righteously killing off suspected child molesters, the criminal mastermind is an incredibly brilliant alcoholic mathematician whose clever plans leave the police always one step behind. Even Kurt Wallander, who seems a calm, reasonable man, is repeatedly confronted by irreconcilable evil, whether in the form of heartless KGB officers, demonic South African politicians, or plain old deliriously crazy madmen.

One misses, in these more recent renderings, the social view of crime that motivated Sjöwall and Wahlöö. Individual pathology of the American sort seems to have seeped into virtually all of the later books, where the killers tend to share Iago's motiveless malignity rather than, say, Hamlet's melancholy confusion or Macbeth's clear desire for advancement. And this trend, in turn, sits oddly with the relative humanity of the detectives, who (again with certain exceptions) are shown as leading relatively normal, well-regulated lives. Even Joona Linna and Harry Hole are not *always* lone wolves, the way detectives in American fiction so often are, for Joona starts out with a normal family life and Harry eventually gets one.

This embrace of convention is not just psychological. It also has to do with a kind of social egalitarianism. In other words, Nordic detectives generally seem indifferentiable, as individuals and as a class, from the population they serve. Thus Konrad Simonsen, though he ends up marrying a member of the Danish aristocracy, does not live in a mansion with servants, the way an aristocratic British detective like Peter Wimsey or Thomas Lynley would. The vast majority of these Scandinavian police officers carry on their lives in much the way their readers do, occupying typical middle-class houses and doing typical middle-class things when they are not engaged in chasing murderers.

DWELLING places—whether of the police themselves, the criminals they pursue, or the peripheral witnesses they interview— seem strangely prominent in these mysteries. I wonder whether

I only notice this because there is something slightly exotic about these houses and flats, something unfamiliar to an American and therefore of special interest. Do I bother to focus on the residential details when American cops raid a rural farmhouse, a Park Avenue apartment, a New Jersey slum? Perhaps not, since I am already acquainted with such places, from movies and TV if not from my own experience. But I think the difference is something more. The Scandinavian mystery, on the whole, strikes me as weirdly domestic, with the house and household often playing an important role—not fantastically, as it does in Edgar Allan Poe's tales or Stephen King's horror stories, but routinely, in an almost offhand way. The Swedes, Danes, and Norwegians seem to occupy their interiors more particularly and perhaps more cozily than we do, even if they don't always seem aware of it themselves.

Most of these Scandinavian crime investigators, being urban types, inhabit flats rather than actual houses. (The notable exceptions are Department Q's Carl Mørck, who has his own house on the outskirts of Copenhagen, and the Swedish detective Anders Knutas, who lives in a comfortable family house surrounded by a large garden on the island of Gotland.) Harry Hole, for example, occupies a small, spartan bachelor flat on Sofies gate in central Oslo. Karin Fossum's Inspector Sejer, a widower, has a larger, nicer Oslo flat, but it is still a unit within an apartment building. Lars Kepler's Joona Linna lives in a Stockholm apartment, first with his family, then on his own (though in the later volumes of the series, after he quits the police and essentially goes crazy, he becomes homeless and stays for a time with the Roma in their trailers). Even Kurt Wallander, though his town of Ystad is far smaller than Stockholm, has an apartment rather than a house; and though his flat actually gets blown up in one volume of his series, he soon returns to it, for it is the only place he feels at home.

Martin Beck initially occupies an apartment with his wife and two little children in an outlying district of Stockholm, from which he has to take the subway into work. When he leaves his wife, he is able to move to a small, centrally located place in Gamla Stan—the Old Town—which is where, as a native-born Stockholmer, he has always wanted to live. His girlfriend, Rhea, when he eventually meets her, lives in still another neighborhood, in a different kind of flat: that is, a communal apartment she shares with a variety of tenants and guests.

Only a few extremely rich Stockholm residents seem to have whole houses to themselves, and they appear to be mainly in the northern reaches of the city. Even Östermalm, the wealthy area near the center where Beck's colleague Gunvald Larsson grew up, consists primarily of grand or in some cases not-so-grand apartments. By the 1960s and 1970s, when he is working for the homicide squad, Larsson himself has long since moved out of that prestigious neighborhood—he despises the upper class, as only a rebel from that background can—but he has not managed to leave behind his cultivated sensibility. As the narrator takes pains to inform us in one of the later volumes in the series, "His bachelor apartment bore witness to good taste and a feeling for quality. Furniture, rugs, drapes, everything, from his Italian white leather slippers to his pivoting Nordmende color TV, was first class."

For a pair of Marxists, Sjöwall and Wahlöö seem strangely obsessed by people's furnishings, especially in this particular volume, *The Abominable Man*. When two members of the

homicide team go to a small town called Segeltorp to interview
the elderly parents of the main suspect, we get a full description
of the "little wooden building" inhabited by these entirely peripheral characters, followed by a detailed account of their living-
room furniture, including "a straight-backed pine sofa and four
chairs with striped upholstered seats around a large table topped
by a massive slab of beautifully veined fir." None of this has anything to do with clues. The descriptions exist, it would seem,
entirely to give us the texture of a certain class of life.

Furnishings as the key to the murderer's personality also
come up in another Swedish series, the Gotland-based novels
written by Mari Jungstedt. In *Unseen*, the first volume in the series, Anders Knutas and one of his colleagues pay a visit to the
house that ultimately turns out to belong to the murderer, and
we get a sizeable dose of interior design: "A dark brown wall-to-
wall carpet lay on the floor. The walls were covered with dark
green wallpaper. Paintings clustered thickly on three of them,
mostly scenes of animals in a winter landscape . . ." And so on,
through the "heavy curtains" and "dark and ungainly" furniture.

This is certainly not the kind of interior decor that I associated with Sweden during my California childhood. But then,
there is very little sign of what we Americans would call "Swedish modern" or "Danish modern" in any of the mysteries—and
that goes for the Norwegian thrillers as well. It would appear
from these books that most Scandinavian country houses, and
indeed many of the urban ones, are decorated in a much older
style, with floral upholstery, dark wood, and heavy antiques.
Harry Hole's girlfriend, Rakel, for instance, lives up in Oslo's
Holmenkollen neighborhood in a "dark-timbered" house that
sounds decidedly old-fashioned, both inside and out.

Occasionally a modern interior surfaces in a hotel room, as when Harry investigates the high-rise SAS in downtown Oslo and notices that the Danish-modern furniture is designed by Poul Henriksen. But even in hotels, what we foreigners are used to thinking of as Scandinavian design remains unusual. Much more typical is the intricately furbeloved, distinctly old-fashioned Savoy in Malmö, which makes a sustained appearance in Sjöwall and Wahlöö's *Murder at the Savoy.*

In the vacation land of the Stockholm archipelago, where Viveca Sten's Sandhamn mysteries are set, Sten's heroine—a lawyer named Nora Linde—spends a remarkable amount of time worrying about real estate. Apparently only the wealthy can afford to buy a summer house in the Stockholm archipelago now, though decades earlier, in the late 1960s, Martin Beck and his wife found a cheap summer rental there. Nora, who is faced with various life choices that might pressure her into leaving Sandhamn, can't bear the thought of giving up her childhood summer home. Nor can she bear to part with another, even grander house she inherited from her murderous-old-lady neighbor in the first volume of the series. (Like *Midsomer Murders,* that ridiculous British TV series in which, week after week, a dead body is discovered at the village fête, the Sandhamn mysteries seem to have an excessive number of killings for such a small, upscale place.) Sten, as might be expected, is fond of giving us details about home decor, and it was in her volumes that I not only noticed the constant recurrence of the paint color "Falun red," but also became aware of the ubiquitous "tile stove" that both decorates and warms a variety of Scandinavian dwellings, including those of the wealthy as well as the very poor.

The focus on domestic life, in all of these Nordic mysteries, seems to go along with the sense of decorum that surrounds even the most importunate police visits to someone's home. In American thrillers, when the cops come calling, the residents eye them with emotions ranging from anxiety to resentment to sheer hatred, and the visit is concluded as quickly as possible. In Scandinavia, by contrast, the police who arrive to interview witnesses or take statements are invariably welcomed in with coffee and cakes. And when they come in the door, many of these officers take off their shoes, or at least offer to—the implication being that this is a standard courtesy in Swedish, Danish, and Norwegian households. Perhaps such courtesies (we Americans might view them as intimacies) explain why more than one of these detectives ends up in a relationship with a witness he has met on the job.

EROTIC life is a central aspect of the police officers' stories in these Scandinavian mysteries. While there may be a few characters—Gunvald Larsson leaps to mind—about whose sex lives we know absolutely nothing, for the most part we are given extensive details. These include, but are not limited to, the names, physical descriptions, and occupations of the men's wives or girlfriends. (With the exception of the protagonist in the recent Norwegian TV show *Borderliner*, there are no gay policemen, apparently, in all of Scandinavia, and even lesbian cops barely exist outside of Anne Holt's Hanne Wilhelmsen series.) Beyond this, the information often extends to sexual desires, preferred sexual practices, and individual sexual experiences.

In fact, a featured detective or even amateur sleuth rarely goes to bed with someone in these novels without our getting the full description.

I am not kidding about the tendency to get involved with witnesses. Martin Beck meets his eventual lover, an intelligent, forthright social worker named Rhea Nielsen, when he goes to talk to her about the solitary fellow who dies mysteriously in *The Locked Room*. Kurt Wallander's Latvian girlfriend, Baiba Liepa, is the chief witness in his investigation of her husband's death. Crime reporter Johan Berg, who visits Gotland to cover each of the murders chronicled in Mari Jungstedt's series, falls in love with practically the first woman he interviews and ends by breaking up her marriage. Frank Frølich, the hero of K. O. Dahl's Norwegian cop series, has a torrid and ultimately dangerous affair with a pretty bystander he protects during an armed robbery. It would seem that a Scandinavian police officer can barely speak to a woman without wanting to make a pass at her. The most extreme example, I think, comes up in one of the Sjöwall/Wahlöö novels, where Kollberg, before interviewing an attractive witness, actually makes a quick trip home to have sex with his wife as a prophylactic measure against infidelity.

There is something very odd, in fact, about the role of sex in these novels. A male friend of mine, recently reading the Martin Beck series for the first time, commented that every volume seemed to include a gratuitous mention of women's nipples. I hadn't really noticed this myself, but when I went back to check, I found that this preference, or fetish, or call it what you will, afflicts many other series as well. An enormous number of these Scandinavian mysteries presume that men are always looking at women hungrily. And the women often seem to return the favor.

Two healthy young officers of opposite sexes (or so it would seem from the Hammer series) can hardly even do a house search without trying out the beds.

Of course, Americans have historically viewed Swedes, and especially Swedish women, as sexy. Some of this probably has to do with pornography, and the fact that much of it was generated or distributed by the Scandinavian countries in the late twentieth century. Some of it may involve the link between sixties youth culture and Scandinavia, including the popular idea, possibly promulgated by draft resisters and deserters fleeing the Vietnam War, that "free love" was already the norm over there before it ever reached our shores. But if you look closely at these mysteries, and not just the older ones, what you find is generally not a meeting of two sexual equals, happily embracing their inner desires. Instead you may well detect a deep fear of, and in some cases overt resentment about, the unleashed sexuality of women. Quite often, the motive for the mad killer's crime turns out to be some kind of hatred of "loose" women—and this is as true in Jo Nesbø's recent *The Snowman* as it is in Wahlöö and Sjöwall's *Roseanna*, written nearly half a century earlier.

"Nymphomania" is not a word I have heard recently in America, but the idea if not the term is sprinkled all through the Martin Beck books. What the men in those volumes seem to fear—particularly but not only the murderous men—is a raging female desire they can't satisfy. It's hard to figure out whether these novels are shrewdly commenting on this aspect of Scandinavian culture or simply exemplifying it. Granted, both Martin Beck and Kollberg eventually get involved with women who desire sex as much as they do, and they are both happy with that.

But that there *are* women who are oversexed, and who can't stop having sex with numerous partners, seems to be a given in these stories. The excess is not just in the imagination of the killers.

A vast number of the crimes investigated in Scandinavian novels have to do, in one way or another, with sex. Often children are involved (childhood sexual abuse appears to be a Scandinavian preoccupation), but even adult women are disproportionately raped and killed in these mysteries—disproportionate, I mean, in relation to the other kinds of murders that frequently take place in big cities. And because sex itself is a big business in Scandinavia, the profit motive and the antagonism-toward-women motive become intertwined. Especially in more recent novels, sex trafficking and prostitution, mainly involving African or Eastern European women, have become central issues for the police to investigate, and this in turn has led to discussion of the roles of both men *and* women in allowing these things to take place. That is especially noticeable, for example, in *The Lake*, the 2017 volume in Lotte and Søren Hammer's series, where the authors pointedly observe that only in Denmark is prostitution completely legal. (The Swedes, they approvingly note, levy punishment on the men who patronize prostitutes, while in Norway brothel-owners can apparently be prosecuted even though prostitution itself is allowed.)

One might conclude from these novels that Scandinavia is a region where feminism has yet to make a full impact. This fictional rendering contrasts oddly with the other kinds of reports we get from these countries—all the news about advanced social policies like extended parental leave for both fathers and mothers, marriage equality for gays and straights, and the political and economic advancement of women. Perhaps the mysteries, for reasons of their own, are misrepresenting reality. Or maybe the vaunted public benefits have not yet seeped down to the personal level. The television series *Borgen*—which features a woman who becomes prime minister, but only at the expense of her marriage to a rather likeable and fair-minded man—suggests that even the most enlightened Nordic male has trouble allowing a woman to take control. And if the characters in thrillers are at all representative, that problem afflicts police departments as much as it does the bedroom, the boardroom, and the legislature.

**FEMALE** cops are scarce on the ground in the older detective fiction, and they aren't excessively common even in the most recent mysteries. Whether this is because women still don't join the police force in large numbers, or don't get promoted to detective grade all that easily—or whether it's that mystery writers have trouble imagining more than one strong female character at a time—is something I have not been able to answer in the course of my reading. Often enough, the Scandinavian policewoman is introduced merely as a helpful sidekick to the male leader of a squad. The problem is somewhat less pronounced in the better TV shows, which feature gripping female characters like Sarah Lund from *The Killing* or Saga Norén from *The Bridge*. But unlike, say, Detective Chief Inspector Jane Tennison of Britain or Harry Bosch's LAPD boss, Lieutenant Grace Billets, even these exemplary female detectives don't head up their respective murder squads. Each reports, at least initially, to a male homicide chief, and both suffer (though in different ways) from a sense of isolation.

Still, things have improved slightly in the past half-century.

In the course of the ten-book Martin Beck series, only one woman joined the force and worked her way up from the vice squad to the murder squad; another two or three were introduced as peripheral figures along the way. But no woman was an important, fully participating member of Martin's team. It was not until Kurt Wallander's era that this began to change. There were no women in his squad room at the beginning of the series, except, inevitably, the faithful secretary. But by the mid-1990s Wallander had come to rely on Ann-Britt Höglund, the newest recruit, more than on any of his male colleagues. By this time, too, female prosecuting attorneys, female pathologists, and female chiefs of police had entered the picture. Eventually Henning Mankell even turned Wallander's erstwhile rebellious daughter, Linda, into a police officer, and then gave her a starring role in her own book.

Anders Knutas, from the beginning, has a right-hand female officer, Karin Jacobsson, on whom he depends heavily, but his series does not begin until 2010, significantly after the Wallander series. Similarly, Harry Hole (also a twenty-first-century figure) notably relies on a female helper: first on his partner, Ellen, with whom he trades questions in a curious game that helps them solve crimes, and then, after Ellen dies, on Beate Lønn, a singular woman who, due to an enlarged *fusiform gyrus*, can recognize any face she has ever seen. These fantastical creatures are portrayed as more intelligent than any of the male officers around them, but also—crucially for their collaboration with Harry—as people who are able to tolerate erratic male behavior.

There are a few female police officers (including, for example, Kjell Eriksson's Ann Lindell and Helene Tursten's Irene Huss) who are charged with singlehandedly, or nearly singlehandedly, carrying the plots of their respective series, but even they are in the minority on their respective squads. If there happens to be another woman on the same team, they often do not get along well: female solidarity, it would appear, has not become central to their professional ethic. And in their private lives, which tend to revolve around unreliable, overly demanding, or absent men, they are more likely to resemble the heroines of romances than the hardboiled figures we might expect to find in a police procedural.

As a way of evading the gender imbalance they attribute to the police force, some mystery writers have decided to draw in women from other professions, so we get amateur sleuths like Denmark's Nina Borg, a Red Cross nurse, or Sweden's Nora Linde, a corporate lawyer. Still, neither of these women is exactly an admirable female role model, especially when one compares them to their British or American counterparts. Nora is a neglected wife who finds little satisfaction in her legal work and leans heavily on a childhood friend—a policeman—in investigating the murders that take place around her. Nina, though more independent as a crime-solver, is also much more neurotic, with a tendency to run off and abandon her husband and children every time some stranger's plight catches her fancy. It is in this context, I think, that one has to consider Lisbeth Salander's remarkable success as a thriller character.

In the Stieg Larsson series, the police are not in charge. Lisbeth, a computer hacker, and her sometime ally Mikael Blomkvist, an investigative journalist, are the people who primarily solve the crimes, and if anyone is the sidekick in this situation, it is Mikael. But if the success of *The Girl with the Dragon Tattoo* and its sequels is largely attributable to their overt feminism, this attitude also constitutes their chief flaw, in that it excuses horrific—and horrifically illegal—behavior. As someone who was sexually and psychologically abused as a child, a genius repeatedly mistaken for a lunatic, and a social misfit proud of her alienation from the society in which she dwells, Lisbeth is presented as a heroine who can do no wrong. Whether she is torturing fatuous harassers or attacking murderous bullies with her bare hands, she is always in the right, and we are always meant to approve of her outlandish behavior. She is like a female Harry Hole, only more so, in that she operates completely outside the law. And like Harry, she appears to be indestructible. When one episode ends with Lisbeth shot in the head and actually buried in the ground, the next begins with her scrambling out of the premature grave—a sure way to sell books, granted, but hardly a fair approach to thriller-writing, and also a serious departure from the socially, morally aware genre that Sjöwall and Wahlöö invented.

One might expect the fact that so many Scandinavian mysteries have been written by male/female teams to show up in the characterizations of women—but again, this seems not to be the case. The Martin Becks are definitely presented from a masculine point of view; one searches in vain for Maj Sjöwall's independent voice, particularly in the sex scenes. Lotte and Sören Hammer, the brother-sister pair who write the Konrad Simonsen series, have invented a strong female character in the Countess, but she definitely plays second banana to Simonsen, and the only other woman on the homicide team, the younger Pauline, starts out courageous if unruly but ends—after a terrifying experience of imprisonment—by being just nuts. The married couple Alexander and Alexandra Ahndoril, who write under the joint name Lars Kepler, employ mainly male officers and male perspectives in their Joona Linna series. When they do bring in a woman, like the incredibly beautiful and remarkably talented Saga Bauer, they describe her as looking like "a princess from a fairy tale," with long blonde hair cascading down her back. The crimes in the Lars Kepler series, too, are almost always sex crimes directed at women, portrayed with the kind of lovingly detailed viciousness one has learned to expect from the Scandinavians.

Not that I am complaining, since I am evidently drawn to such details and such plots. No one is forcing me to read these things in the first place, or to gobble down the next and then the next in a series, each one more purposefully shocking than the last. If I am nostalgic for the relative humanity of the society portrayed in the Martin Beck series, that is no doubt due to the fact that the real world, mine as well as Scandinavia's, has become more brutal since the late 1960s. It turns out that the realities of one's own time penetrate even the most flagrantly fictional escapist literature, so complete escape is rarely possible. And perhaps this is especially true in close-knit Scandinavia, where the actual physical act of escaping—the process of fleeing from pursuit—can be fraught with the unexpected.

GOING from one Scandinavian country to another used to require a certain amount of effort. Passports had to be shown when crossing borders, and you sometimes had to cross them even before you started your trip, since Copenhagen's Kastrup airport was the likeliest departure point for Swedes or Norwegians traveling south. If you were a fleeing criminal, Denmark became an even more important destination because of its geographical link to the rest of Europe: once you got to Denmark, you could escape from Scandinavia by car or train, without alerting airport security. Still, unless you had a little boat of your own or had privately hired one from a willing accomplice, you had to rely on one of the major crossing points to get between these watery countries, and that was where the police would line up to get you.

In Martin Beck's time, a murderer escaping from Stockholm and wanting to avoid Swedish airports had three likely options. He could take the train to Oslo and fly out from there. He could go by surface transport to Helsingbörg and cross over to nearby Helsingør (the Danish name for Hamlet's Elsinore) by ferry. Or he could get himself to Malmö by train, car, or bus and then take the hydrofoil or the slower ferry to Copenhagen. In *The Terrorists*—the final and longest volume in the Sjöwall/Wahlöö series—Martin Beck posted members of his team at all three of these locations and was therefore able to capture the dangerous killer he'd been seeking throughout the last hundred pages of the book.

In the first decade of the twenty-first century, all this changed with the construction of a gigantic bridge linking Copenhagen and Malmö. It is this bridge that forms the eponymous subject of the excellent television series *The Bridge*, in which the Danish and Swedish police work together through the whole first season to catch a vengeful and clever murderer who publicizes his deeds online. The killer's up-to-date methods somehow match the novelty and high-tech quality of the Øresund Bridge itself, and the strangely touching relationship between the autistic

Swedish officer, Saga Norén, and her earthy Danish counterpart, Martin Rohde, mimics the wary closeness of the two nations cemented together by the new structure.

Oslo is a different matter, as the Harry Hole stories repeatedly indicate. There may be troves of Eastern European and other criminals flooding into Norway, but their exit routes from the country are distinctly more limited. In order to get to Copenhagen from Norway by train, one would have to pass through Sweden—and again, the necessary crossing point at Helsingbörg provides an excellent place for a police ambush. Most of the perps in Jo Nesbø's books choose instead to fly in and out, and Harry is constantly having to get on the airport express (which apparently leaves central Oslo every twenty minutes) in order to get himself out to Gardermoen Airport, either to capture an escaping criminal or, just as often, to visit Bergen, which is apparently only an hour or so away by air.

Flying, in fact, appears to be the most common way of getting around *within* Sweden and Norway as well as between them. When the journalist Johan Berg has to get out to Gotland to cover each new murder in the Mari Jungstedt books, he usually flies from Stockholm to Visby, a trip of less than an hour, rather than taking the much slower ferry. Martin Beck always flies from Stockholm to Malmö and back; so does Kurt Wallander, in reverse, though he makes the trip much less often, since his cases are mostly confined to his own Skåne region. Because of this frequent resort to air travel, I almost feel I know more about Scandinavia's airports than I do about most of the airports in America. I've become acquainted not just with their names (Arlanda, Bromma, Sturup, Gardermoen, Kastrup) but also with some of their distinctive qualities: the foggy landscape around Sturup, the brightly lit restrooms at Gardermoen, the easy efficiency of Bromma.

Denmark, because it is notably smaller, is the exception to the airport rule. Most of its police officers drive to the scenes of their crimes and the homes of their witnesses, even when these are located in another jurisdiction. And driving appears to be the most common form of Danish transport even *within* the city: if Copenhagen has an underground train system, one barely hears about it, especially compared to the equivalent subway systems in Oslo and particularly Stockholm. The hub of public transportation in Copenhagen is evidently the Central Station, but if that location is often cited, it is not so much because of the buses and trains that go in and out, but because it is a gathering spot for all the sleaze and crime that afflict the city. The Central Station is where Nina Borg actually finds the titular boy in a suitcase, for example; it is also where Carl Mørck's and Konrad Simonsen's team members go to check out drug dealers and drug users.

Stockholm may be less grungy than Copenhagen, but that does not prevent Martin Beck from complaining about the crowded subways, the traffic-riddled streets, and the air pollution caused by Sweden's numerous cars. Despite or perhaps because of his hatred of automobiles, they loom large in several of the novels—particularly *Cop Killer*, where the solution to the central mystery revolves around a stolen car and its license plate. Cars and traffic also come up in *The Laughing Policeman*, where the narrators, writing in 1967 or early 1968, happened to comment on the fact that Swedes had recently switched from the right-hand drive to the left. This sudden transformation is historical fact, not fiction, yet the idea that a whole nation could, on a dime, turn instantaneously from British-style to American-style driving strikes me as even more improbable than that mysterious murders always have solutions.

Aside from getting police officers from home to work and supplying clues to murderers' whereabouts, automobiles serve yet another important function in Scandinavian novels, and that is to allow the routine escape from the city that every citizen seems to make at least once during the year. Here again Martin Beck is the rarity: he prefers to remain in Stockholm during the empty summer months, and when he does leave—for a few weeks in the Stockholm archipelago, for instance—his chosen mode of transport is a boat rather than a car. But for the vast majority of characters in these books, civilians as well as cops, the auto is what takes them on their vacations, which are likely to strike an American as both excessively lengthy and extraordinarily frequent.

HOLIDAYS and seasonal festivals are strewn with abandon across the Scandinavian calendar, especially in Sweden. All the major holidays that we celebrate in America—Christmas, New Year's, Easter—naturally get celebrated there, but whereas our Easter is generally confined to the Sunday, theirs takes up a full four days, from Good Friday to Easter Monday, a period which everyone (including most members of the police force) seems to spend at home. Again, the Christmas to New Year's period finds the police stations barely staffed: even the most hardworking detectives generally take at least a week of vacation then.

Nothing, however, can match the time these people have off

during the summer. Even a low-paid janitor, in one of the Martin Beck novels, gets a full two months off, and it does not seem unusual for policemen, lawyers, and other busy professionals to spend five weeks or more at their summer cottages. Who is minding the shop (or the public welfare) during these long summer breaks? Fewer people than usual, it would seem. The cities empty out during this time—something which gratifies the somewhat anti-social Martin Beck, "for despite everything he loved his native city and liked being able to move around it without being hustled, or having to hurry, or being pushed about, or feeling threatened by the increasingly dominating traffic and half-suffocated by its poisonous fumes."

Not all Swedish detectives cling to the city as tightly as Martin Beck does. Even during his work week, Kurt Wallander is always driving out to the southern coast to sit and contemplate the waves, or to his father's relatively isolated house, or to Sten Widén's horse farm, or to other rural locations not far from Ystad. In Viveca Sten's Sandhamn novels, Nora Linde regrets every brief moment she has to spend in her Stockholm law office during her long summer vacation in the archipelago. And in Mari Jungstedt's Gotland series, Anders Knutas is *already* in a vacation spot, even when he's on the job. His town of Visby is apparently so pleasantly uncrowded that he can celebrate a huge familial Midsummer's Eve in his own house and garden.

It took me ages to figure out that Midsummer's Eve is not a fixed date, but a moveable feast somewhere in the vicinity of June 21. The holiday is scheduled so that it always lands on a Friday, which can range from June 19 to June 25—meaning that Midsummer itself is always a Saturday, giving people ample time off to recover from the festivities of the night before. These

include a vast amount of drinking plus the consumption of herring and other specially prepared Scandinavian foods (new potatoes, sausages, open-faced and toasted sandwiches, special egg
dishes—only crayfish, it seems, are missing from the menu, and
that is because they have their own "season" later in the summer). Midsummer's Eve also involves some kind of activity surrounding a maypole, though whether this means dancing and
singing or just the twining around of ribbons has never been
quite clear to me. It's a huge national holiday in Sweden, celebrated by just about everyone—so much so that it completely
outshines the official national holiday, June 6, which is called
Sweden Day and is equivalent to America's July 4. Neither a religious holiday nor a governmental one, Midsummer's Eve offers
an opportunity for Swedes to throw off their innate restraint,
or so it would seem from the amount of drunkenness and petty
crime—not to mention murders—that the few cops remaining
on duty have to deal with during the Midsummer holiday. It is
the most intensely celebrated pagan holiday on the calendar,
even more so than Walpurgis Night (also an occasion for excessive drinking), which falls on the last day of April.

I'm not sure whether Ulf's fondly remembered Lucia should
be categorized as pagan or Christian. According to Henning
Mankell, who has Wallander reflect on the forthcoming Lucia
as he is waiting for an important break in his murder case, this
December 13 holiday is a time when "all of Sweden would be
occupied with blond girls wearing a crown of burning candles
on their heads, singing 'Santa Lucia' and celebrating what used
to be thought of as the winter solstice." That is certainly having it both ways, though the saint does appear to be winning
out over the pagans here. In general, the Christian saints come

across as a mainstay of the Swedish calendar, manifesting themselves in people's so-called name days as well as in the more
common religious holidays.

Denmark and Norway, on the whole, seem a bit more secular
than Sweden, at least to judge by the holidays that make their
way into the mystery books. One of the few commemorative
dates Jo Nesbø mentions is May 17, Norwegian independence day,
an occasion for the Crown Prince of Norway to mingle with
his subjects in Oslo's vast Palace Gardens (and therefore an opportunity for a sharpshooting criminal to attempt an assassination). Then again, the absence of reported festivals in the Nesbø
books may be partly attributable to the character of Harry
Hole, who—as a loner, an alcoholic, *and* a workaholic—is not
big on celebrating anything and never seems to take a vacation
at all. Denmark's Carl Mørck is almost as much of an anti-social
grump as Harry, so his novels don't have much about the regular
holidays either. The two holidays that do noticeably come up
in Jussi Adler-Olsen's plots are May 1 (when a huge May Day
demonstration takes place in Copenhagen) and September 19,
the date on which the Danish police were interned by the Germans during World War Two.

All three countries celebrate Christmas, of course, but this
makes them no different from most other countries in Europe,
North America, and South America. As in the United States,
what was once a religious holiday has become mainly an opportunity for shopping, and the stress of buying presents on time,
not to mention struggling through the terrible traffic, comes up
over and over in these books. Granted, it's still an occasion for
cooking and eating special festive foods. A strange dish called
Jansson's Temptation is often cited in the Swedish accounts,

along with roast meats, roast potatoes, and rich, heavy desserts, while the Norwegians are more likely to mention *lutefisk* (an acquired taste, it seems) as well as baked goods such as *krumkaker*, *sandkaker*, *gorokaker*, and *serinakaker*. But aside from these opportunities to stuff oneself in the traditional manner, Christmas does not appear to be a particularly pleasant time in Scandinavia. Those who have families quarrel with them; those who are on their own feel abandoned by the culture at large. In fact, the Christmas season, there as here, seems designed to point out to the lonely how very much alone they are.

ISOLATION and its concomitant risks, including the ever-present danger of suicide, are central to Scandinavia's view of itself. This is not, as I had imagined in the 1960s and 1970s, simply a rumor manufactured by the Cold War right-wingers in America, who wanted us to believe that socialism led to suicide. Nor, apparently, is it merely the result—as we left-wingers were fond of asserting—of the better crime statistics kept in Sweden. Apparently there really is something about Scandinavian culture, at least at the present moment, that is conducive to self-murder. One instantly thinks of the long, cold, dark winters as a contributing factor, but this does not seem a sufficient explanation. Other places close to the Arctic Circle (Russia, Alaska, northern Canada) don't seem to be saddled with suicides to the same degree. Moreover, the suicide rates in the far north rural regions, which are the darkest and snowiest parts of Scandinavia, do not appear to be any higher than in the urban areas. If anything, the towns and cities are where these kinds of deaths prominently take place.

As many of these mysteries acknowledge, there is a certain form of loneliness that only comes into being when you are surrounded by crowds of strangers. One author, in an aside, happens to note that fully sixty percent of Stockholm's residents are singles living alone, and that statistic appears to hold generally true for the police officers, witnesses, and victims in Scandinavian novels as a whole. Kurt Wallander is constantly contemplating his wretched solitude from his apartment in the middle of Ystad. Karin Fossum's Inspector Sejer, a melancholy widower, lives alone in Oslo, and so does Harry Hole, before he marries Rakel. All three detective figures in Copenhagen's Department Q—Carl Mørck, his assistant Assad, and their helper Rose—are extremely isolated figures, and this is true even though Carl lives with two or three other people. Assad is a solitary by virtue of his political and historical position: a refugee from some unspecified Arabic-speaking country, he has no fixed place of residence and no known associates. Rose, who was psychologically abused as a child, is so unstable that she occasionally drops into psychotic dissociated states, in which she often contemplates and sometimes attempts suicide. And that's just among the police. For victims and criminals, the sense of isolation conveyed in these books can be even more profound.

In Kurt Wallander's world, self-murder has apparently become such a common problem that the police respond with a kind of black humor, calling the victims "do-it-yourselfers." A similarly offhand attitude prevails in at least one Martin Beck volume, where those charged with clearing away the bodies of suicides seem to have emerged straight out of *Hamlet*'s gravedigger scene. "In their beautiful city," the narrator informs us (before launching into a three-page sequence of dark comedy involving these characters), "these men had a special and rather important function. Their daily task was to remove suicides and other unattractive persons."

These sentences come from *The Locked Room*, a volume which is itself centrally about the loneliness and isolation afflicting Stockholm's residents. The book also, of course, includes the usual mystery to be solved—two mysteries, in fact, one entailing a dead body in a locked room and the other focusing on a fatal bank robbery. With its intertwining plots and its joking references to classic mysteries, *The Locked Room* is in many ways the most tightly constructed of the Martin Beck books. (Its construction is so tight that, unlike all the other volumes, it ends after twenty-eight chapters rather than thirty.) But if it is especially pleasing in terms of plot, it is also one of the darkest volumes, perhaps because its writing coincided with the period during which Per Wahlöö found out he had cancer.

At the beginning of the book, we learn that our old friend Martin Beck has become even more solitary since we last saw him. Felled by a serious gunshot wound at the end of *The Abominable Man*, he has been on leave for months, recuperating in his lonely city apartment and feeling increasingly isolated. Though he's finally brought back to active duty, he gets sidelined from the major bank-robbery case, which is being directed by a blowhard incompetent named Bulldozer Olsson. So Martin is left to pursue the locked-room mystery on his own.

In the course of his investigation (during which he meets Rhea, the woman who ultimately releases him from his solitary confinement), he makes an explicit comparison between his own lonely life and the locked-room mystery he is attempting to solve. He also brings up his elderly mother, whom he visits at one point in her retirement home, as further evidence of a typically Scandinavian form of solitude. "To grow old alone and in poverty, unable to look after oneself, meant that after a long and active life one was suddenly stripped of one's dignity and identity," thinks Martin Beck (or his authors, since the two perspectives are never firmly separated). Sweden's old-age pensioners, he feels, have been turned into the equivalent of locked-up criminals "by a so-called Welfare State that no longer wished to know about them. It was a cruel sentence, and the crime was being too old."

By the volume's end, both the bank robbery and the locked-room mystery have been solved, but only we and Martin Beck are aware of that. The official solution, endorsed and carried through by Bulldozer Olsson, assigns the bank robbery to a man who had nothing to do with it, though he *did* kill the victim in the locked room, by a means too ingenious and complicated to summarize here (as is always true of locked-room mysteries). Meanwhile, Martin, the only person who has correctly figured out both solutions, gets mocked ever after for his one "unsolved" case. Such is the discrepancy, Sjöwall and Wahlöö suggest, between the actual nature of crime in Sweden and the workings of the country's justice system.

JUDICIAL processes, on the whole, are nearly invisible in most of these Scandinavian thrillers. The relative absence of courtroom drama in Swedish, Danish, and Norwegian mysteries seems particularly odd to an American reader, and especially to an American television-watcher. Our long crime-show tradition, from *Perry Mason* to *Law & Order* and beyond, has repeatedly

featured attorneys as an essential part of the mystery's resolu-
tion. Even in its written form, the American thriller could not do
without lawyers and judges. Michael Connelly's Harry Bosch,
for example, would barely be able to function these days without his half-brother and lawyer Mickey Haller to resolve the
more ticklish cases for him. Or consider Scott Turow's thrillers, which from *Presumed Innocent* onward have focused more on
lawyers than on detectives (though both, obviously, are essential
to the mix). Most Americans, I think it's fair to say, have notions
about our own legal system that come to us largely through the
mysteries we have seen or read.

Even Sjöwall and Wahlöö, though eager to criticize a variety
of Swedish institutions, seem hesitant to take on the courts. It
is only after nine volumes without any courtroom scenes whatsoever that the justice system finally comes to the fore in *The
Terrorists*, the tenth and last book in their series. It is here that
we first get to witness a lengthy trial—in this case, the ludi-
crous prosecution (conducted by that same Bulldozer Olsson)
of a young woman who was naive enough to walk into a bank
and simply ask for money. That her crime was merely innocence
verging on simple-mindedness, and not a vicious and reck-
less disregard for the country's laws, only becomes apparent
when her pro bono lawyer calls Martin Beck and other crucial
witnesses to the stand.

This detailed account of a trial is one of the very few presented in the whole of Scandinavian crime literature. In contrast, we get lots of inside views of jails—usually when the
police go to visit criminals who are already locked up, but sometimes when our hero or heroine has unfairly been imprisoned.
It makes a certain amount of sense that prisons are integrated

into the mystery plots in this way, because Swedish jails are not the permanent holding-tanks such institutions are in America. With rare exceptions (Jurek Walter, Joona Linna's death-dealing nemesis, comes to mind), the criminals in these novels, like the criminals in real-life Scandinavia, do not get life sentences. In the Martin Beck series, for instance, there are at least two cases where murderers arrested in early volumes are re-encountered in the later books as free, law-abiding citizens, having served their six or seven years and been released. Even murder, it seems, is a debt that can be paid off with prison time.

If jailbirds can at times be admirable, lawyers almost never can. When attorneys do show up in the Swedish or Norwegian or Danish plots, they tend to be shadowy, grave figures charged with supervising police procedures. Thus Kurt Wallander has to report his findings to Per Åkeson, the prosecutor who is most often assigned to his Ystad cases. It is the prosecutor, apparently, who gets to decide how much police time should be spent on a particular crime, so he or she can opt to close down an investigation if it seems to be going nowhere; and it is the prosecutor who issues search warrants and otherwise keeps the police within the bounds of legality. Wallander stays on good terms with his prosecutors (*too* good terms, one might say, in regard to one prosecutor, Annette Brolin, with whom he has a brief affair), and in Skåne, at least, there is little sense of unwanted judicial interference with police procedures. But the relationship can become extremely antagonistic elsewhere. In the Roslund & Hellström series, for example, detective Ewert Grens and his primary judicial overseer, Chief Prosecutor Lars Ågestam, despise each other so much that they can barely communicate civilly. At one point Ågestam is even referred to as "the man Grens hated most." Perhaps this series' intense resentment of the prosecuting figure can be attributed to the fact that the late Börge Hellström, one of the two authors, always described himself in his author note as a "former criminal"—but that authorial peculiarity, though interesting, does not explain why the legal profession as a whole has mainly been shunted aside in the Scandinavian thriller genre.

One of the few exceptions to this pattern can be found in the Lisbeth Salander series, in the person of Annika Giannini, Mikael Blomkvist's sister. A lawyer who routinely defends the oppressed (including immigrants, violated women and children, and Lisbeth herself), Annika is presented as the soul of rectitude and an effective advocate for those entangled in the Swedish justice system. She gets one big courtroom scene in the third volume of the series, where, like the pro bono attorney in *The Terrorists*, she cleverly rescues her client from the boorish and manipulative representatives of the law. But aside from this and one or two other instances, we are hardly ever allowed to see defense lawyers in court. Perhaps the Danes, Swedes, and Norwegians have decided that their justice system is irrelevant to their mystery stories because it is too boring, or too complicated, or too unconnected to daily life. Or perhaps they think that winning a court case would imply that all the problems have been solved, whereas the real problems lie too deep to be dealt with at that practical level.

The rare mystery novel that violates the usual rule—a book which takes place almost entirely in the courtroom, as well as in flashbacks about the case at hand—is also the one that most strongly suggests the limitations of a legal victory. *Quicksand*, by Malin Persson Giolito, gives us a blow-by-blow account of the prosecution of Maria Norberg, a Swedish teenager, for the shooting deaths that took place in her school. Throughout most of the trial Maria cannot remember the events of which she is being accused, and therefore her lawyer is forced to dig up as much exculpatory evidence as he can on his own. In the end he vindicates her: someone else, it turns out, was the gun-toting murderer, and she only handled the gun in an attempt to protect her friends. But in the course of freeing her, he also frees up her traumatized memory, and Maria realizes not only that one of her childhood companions was a killer, but also that she herself was responsible for the accidental death of her best friend. The book ends at the moment when the trial does, and Maria Norberg is allowed to go home, back to her normal life. But we can't help sensing that the irreversible damage has already been done. Though proven innocent of the crimes for which she was arrested, this young girl will probably never shed her enduring sense of sorrow and guilt.

**KIDS** evidently have a hard time of it in Scandinavia. In almost every series, and generally more than once in a series, some child or teenager is sexually or psychologically abused by adults. From *The Hanging* to *The Dying Detective*, from the latest Department Q mystery to the earliest Inspector Sejer book, childhood sexual abuse, with or without murder, is a problem that all three countries appear to be consumed by. In America, at any rate, the percentage of child abductions by strangers is extremely low, and parental fears of such crimes tend to be fed mainly by salacious TV programs and aberrant news stories. Can the situation in Scandinavia really be so much more dangerous for children?

The novels certainly suggest that it is. The list of terrible abuses they present is practically unending. Stolen or borrowed children get used in pornographic films or sold to pederasts. Toddlers are kidnapped from public parks and brutally murdered. Foreign-born children, valued only for their body parts, get shipped into Denmark whole so that their kidneys can be removed and transplanted into rich but ill Danish children. Underage girls from the Baltic countries or the African nations find themselves imprisoned by pimps and subjected to unspeakable lives as prostitutes. Foster children are rejected by their new parents and made to feel worthless. Disturbed girls placed in the care of various social-service entities are repeatedly violated by the psychiatric professionals who control their lives from positions of trust. High-school students die in classroom shootings, and small children are murdered along with their parents. Cold cases are especially likely to involve lost little girls, who rarely if ever turn up alive, and such investigations are the ones that most clearly haunt the cops assigned to them, sometimes for decades after the initial crime.

Even among functioning adults—including those who function as crime-solvers in these mysteries—there is a level of remembered or repressed childhood trauma that seems unusual by American standards. In virtually every team of police officers, a devastating childhood memory lurks behind at least one officer's zealous pursuit of crime. Two or three Swedish policewomen were raped as teenagers. Two Danish women—Nina Borg and Department Q's Rose—witnessed their own fathers' deaths and as a result carried a heavy load of guilt into adulthood. At least one Swedish policeman, Ola Haver in Kjell Eriksson's books, underwent something similar with *his* father. More often than not, an unhealthy family background lurks behind the desire to solve crimes. In fact, Martin Beck and Kurt Wallander are unusual, among detectives, in having had relatively unscathed childhoods. The Lisbeth Salander experience—a criminal father, a beaten-up mother, a cruelly exploitive child psychiatrist, and a whole slew of other problems—seems far more typical, if exaggeratedly so.

Nor are the children of the police safe from attack. Kurt Wallander's daughter, Linda, and Harry Hole's stepson, Oleg, are both used as pawns by murderers their fathers are trying to capture. Joona Linna sends his own family away after the wife and children of his partner, Samuel Mendel, are kidnapped and killed on the orders of a recently jailed master criminal. In the initial season of the TV show *The Bridge*, the final and most poignant victim is the teenage son of the Danish policeman, Martin Rohde. It's as if the Scandinavian writers feel they can't generate enough concern on behalf of the cops alone; they need to put a child at risk if we are to feel sufficiently anxious. It all becomes a bit too much to take, so that as a reader you learn to harden your heart and close your ears against the desperate cries of small children, because in Scandinavian fiction they are everywhere.

All this mistreatment of children has another aspect as well—namely, that the murderer in a Scandinavian mystery may also turn out to be an abused child. The maltreatment that deforms the killer's psyche can take different forms, from incestuous rape by an evil father (in Stieg Larsson's *The Girl with the Dragon Tattoo*) to abandonment by a birth parent (in Karin Fossum's *Hell Fire*) to bullying by classmates (in Malin Persson Giolito's *Quicksand*) to the primal discovery of a mother's infidelity (in Jo Nesbø's *The Snowman*). Perhaps the most extreme example of a wounded and therefore murderous child appears in Henning Mankell's *Sidetracked*. The complicated plot, alternating between the murderer's consciousness and that of his pursuers, has Wallander looking for the serial killer of several seemingly unrelated and mainly wealthy men, only to discover that they were all killed by a fifteen-year-old boy whose sister they had sexually exploited. In this case, the chief exploiter and prime murder victim turns out to be the boy's own father, a man who not only sold his daughter into prostitution, but also terrorized his wife and other kids with repeated beatings and threats. When we learn that this man's youngest son, a boy of four, actually tried to poke out his own eyes in order to avoid seeing his father again, we begin to sense the desperation that led to the teenage killer's behavior. Even total blindness was preferable to the sights that confronted the children in this family, who all, in one way or another, chose the dark world of madness over the fierce light of sanity.

LIGHT and darkness may exist on the level of metaphor in Scandinavian mysteries, but in these books they also carry another meaning as well. They are states of mind that the whole culture understands because they are something more than states of mind. In short, they are realities that occur not only diurnally (as they do for most of us) but seasonally, in a particularly intense way. The light of summer and the dark of winter are extremes from whose effects no Norwegian, Dane, or Swede ever fully escapes.

The impact may be a bit less noticeable in the southernmost cities. As Sjöwall and Wahlöö point out near the beginning of

*Murder at the Savoy*, Malmö is noticeably different from the rest of Sweden, for it "is closer to Rome than to the midnight sun, and the lights of the Danish coast twinkle along the horizon." Copenhagen and Malmö, at least in terms of light and climate, share more with, say, Edinburgh than with Oslo or Stockholm. But this does not prevent Kurt Wallander, whose Ystad lies as far south as Malmö, from complaining about the bitter cold or deploring the encroaching winter darkness. In fact, the Wallander series probably contains more reports on the outdoor temperature, as measured from Kurt's flat, than all of the rest of Europe's mysteries combined. Weather is a daily and therefore significant feature of his life, and the need to plan around it is a sign of his methodical thinking.

Copenhagen, too, clearly manifests its own form of the general winter gloom. *The Killing*, whose great initial season is set entirely in and around that city, is probably the darkest television series ever made. From the opening scene of the victim running through the woods, in which we can hardly see what is going on, to the many plot sequences that take place at night, black is the predominant color on the screen. Even during the day, the investigators and their prey seem to spend the vast majority of their time in heavily curtained or windowless rooms, dark abandoned warehouses, or dank basements; there's barely half an hour of sunlight in the whole twenty hours. All the bleak elements in the story—the dead teenager, her grieving parents, the corrupt politicians, the squabbling police, the disintegrating life of the heroine herself—become even more disturbing against this gloomy background. Clearly there will be no light at the end of this tunnel, for them *or* for us.

As you move northward, the all-enveloping winter darkness

gets compounded by the extreme cold. In Jo Nesbø's *The Snow-man* (which, by the way, is an infinitely scarier, smarter, and more suspenseful novel than the ghastly film made from it would suggest), the bleak Oslo climate is central to the plot, which mainly takes place in the days just before Christmas. There needs to be snow, of course, for the murderous villain to build his threatening snowmen in front of his victims' houses. But the references to winter weather go far beyond that. We are repeatedly reminded that December temperatures often drop below zero Fahrenheit, so that those who do not have heavy jackets are likely to freeze outdoors. Nesbø also stresses the shortness of the winter days, with darkness closing in early and the lights in homes and offices going on by three o'clock.

The effect this has on the population's spirits comes through in the work of another Norwegian writer, Gard Sveen. At one point he shows us his central character, Tommy Bergmann, standing in an empty apartment and thinking that "everything seemed completely hopeless. As if this winter would be the last one, that there would never be another summer." Somewhat later in the same novel, *Hell Is Open*, Tommy contemplates the people huddled on a subway platform beneath Oslo's wintry streets and observes that "Resignation was written on their faces, as if they thought they wouldn't survive another winter. Bergmann had never thought of Oslo as the sort of city that stroked your cheek and whispered seductive words in your ear, but the past few weeks had been so fiercely cold that the city resembled a bombed-out war zone."

The Stockholm winter can be just as bad, it seems. "In spite of the fact that it was twelve noon, it was so dark in the room that Martin Beck had to turn on his reading light," we are told in *Roseanna*. This is at a time when the "first snow of winter had begun to fall. It flew against the windows in large, white flakes which melted immediately and ran down the window panes in broad rills. It murmured in the rain gutters and heavy drops splashed against the metal window sills." Here, in the very first book of the Sjöwall/Wahlöö series, the weather becomes almost a separate character, like the Dickensian fog at the beginning of *Bleak House*. Throughout the series, the gloomy weather often matches Beck's dour moods, and the situation is not helped by the fact that in every volume—sometimes twice in a single volume—Martin comes down with a cold.

It is against this background that the summer light and heat shed their blessings on the Scandinavian population. Over and over in these novels, the citizens greet the arrival of the warm months with incredible glee. They sit out at cafés until well after midnight, savoring the long, warm evenings. They dress in light clothes and loll about in their many urban parks, snatching up the rare rays of the northern sun. Occasionally they even complain about the excessive heat, but then they rapidly retreat from that position, congratulating themselves, perhaps, on the fact that it is temporarily warmer in Stockholm than it is on the Costa del Sol.

Yet even the long summer light does not necessarily forecast relief from the daily despair. The third Martin Beck book, *The Man on the Balcony*, starts with the sentence "At a quarter to three the sun rose." This cheerful fact does not, however, signal any kind of comfort or safety, for the man standing on the balcony and witnessing the summer sunrise will turn out to be a serial murderer of children. Actual light is not the same as moral light, and the police need to be as vigilant in the summer season as in any other: *more* vigilant, possibly, since the criminals as well as the civilians will feel free to roam the city at all hours. Nor does the long light necessarily make it any easier for the exhausted cops to do their jobs, since they, like the population at large, may well have trouble getting a full night's sleep during these months.

I make it all sound so obvious, this business of light and dark. Yet despite the frequent mentions in these books, I never really focused on this aspect of Scandinavia until I began watching Swedish, Norwegian, and Icelandic thrillers on TV. To see the cops conducting a helicopter search for the fleeing criminal at eleven o'clock at night, with broad daylight everywhere, is to understand for the first time what is really entailed in living like that. For those of us in the more temperate latitudes, who never experience a day or a night that lasts longer than fifteen hours, the idea of a pale darkness that barely endures from midnight to 3:00 a.m. is almost inconceivable, while its inverse—a shadowy day less than six hours long—is nothing short of terrifying.

Surely such an environment, one would think, produces people who are seriously unlike us. And yet that turns out not to be the case. On the contrary, the Scandinavian thriller often speaks directly to readers from the United States in a way that the books set closer to our own clime do not. When we read mysteries that take place in Japan or even in England, we are likely to come up against a relatively enclosed and distinctly self-involved culture. But when we look at the Scandinavians, we often find our own faces reflected back at us.

**MIRRORING** America was not, at least overtly, part of Sjöwall and Wahlöö's original intent in reinventing the crime novel.

Their stated aim was to create a mirror for their own society, a comprehensive picture of Sweden's inadequate socialism. And they achieved that. But what they also achieved, for those of us reading from across the Atlantic, was a strangely distant but no less accurate view of our own country.

America, in the Martin Beck novels, is a weird and relatively inaccessible place to which Swedish emigrants occasionally go and from which their descendants sometimes return, but which is mainly known through television programs and films. Communicating with America, too, is a complicated process in this era before the internet and Skype. In *Roseanna*, for example, when the victim turns out to be American, Beck's team engages in a lengthy discussion with the police from her home city of Lincoln, Nebraska—a process that entails mailed letters and documents, brief telegrams, and expensive long-distance phone calls.

On my most recent re-reading, I couldn't help noticing how closely Beck's transatlantic communication with the Nebraska cop (who happens to be named Kafka) paralleled my own discovery of Sweden through the Sjöwall/Wahlöö mysteries. We were each going on too little information, each imagining the other place in the only way our limited knowledge allowed. When he first reached Detective Lieutenant Kafka on the phone, Martin wondered "how he looked, and if the police station where he worked resembled the ones people saw on television . . . It struck him that his knowledge of the geography of North America was rather poor. He didn't know where Lincoln was at all and the name Nebraska was just another name to him. After lunch he went to the library and took a look at a world atlas." As I came to this sentence, I glanced aside at my recently acquired stack of Scandinavian city maps, where Martin Beck's apartment and Martin Beck's workplace could be plotted in my two-dimensional version of Stockholm. He and I were doing the same thing, from opposite geographical locations and at opposite ends of a fifty-year time period (not to mention our opposite placement on the fiction-to-reality spectrum).

That first volume, it turns out, is unusual. For the most part, America's role in the Martin Beck series is not to provide victims and collaborating colleagues, but to offer more general information about the crime of murder. "They have as many murders in New York in a week as we have in the whole country in a year," remarks a Central European police officer in the second volume of the series, and in *The Laughing Policeman*—the fourth volume—this attitude toward the United States gets codified in a presentation made by the punctilious, detail-minded Melander. His teammates on the homicide squad have been immersed in what they initially believe to be a random shooting of nine people on a city bus, a crime that provokes newspaper headlines like "Mass murder. Mass murder in Stockholm. Mass murder in a bus in Stockholm." Melander points out that because the local profilers had no Swedish precedents for such a crime, "they've had to base their research on American surveys that have been made during the last few decades."

> He blew at his pipe to see if it was clear and then began to fill it as he went on. "Unlike us, the American psychologists have no lack of material to work on. The compendium here mentions the Boston strangler; Speck, who murdered eight nurses in Chicago; Whitman, who killed sixteen persons from a tower and wounded many more; Unruh, who rushed out into a street in New Jersey and

shot thirteen people dead in twelve minutes, and one or
two more who you've probably read about before."

He riffled through the compendium.

"Mass murders seem to be an American specialty,"
Gunvald Larsson said.

"Yes," Melander agreed. "And the compendium gives
some plausible theories as to why it is so."

"The glorification of violence," said Kollberg. "The
career-centered society. The sale of firearms by mail order. The ruthless war in Vietnam."

The policemen who are speaking may be fictional, but the
names and facts they recite are recognizably real, and the situation in America has not improved in the decades since then. We
may no longer have Vietnam—a background factor in all the
later Martin Becks, and the implicit cause behind the events in
the final volume, *The Terrorists*—but we have plenty of ongoing
wars to replace it, and the rest of the cited problems seem only
to have worsened since the late 1960s.

Nor did such critiques of the United States end with Sjöwall
and Wahlöö. In Arne Dahl's 1999 novel *Misterioso* (whose title
and central musical theme are both borrowed admiringly from
the African-American jazz musician Thelonious Monk), a different and later Swedish homicide squad is treated to much the
same kind of lecture. Here it is Söderstedt, the team's intellectual,
who is telling his teammates what they need to know about the
difference between *their* string of serial killings and America's:

"It's easy to be led astray by American perversities. That
madman Jeffrey Dahmer was sentenced to life in prison

for having killed, dismembered, and eaten seventeen black youths... Sympathizers, some of them from South Africa, have sent him money in prison, and plenty of magazines in the United States make heroes out of serial killers. It's related to the fact that their society is on the verge of collapse. A widespread feeling of general frustration makes it possible for an entire nation to sympathize with extremists and sick outsiders."

*Misterioso* is far from the only novel to focus on the bifurcated American influence: on the one hand great jazz, and on the other hand serial killers. Something similar comes up in Jo Nesbø's Harry Hole novels, where serial murder is explicitly alluded to as an American phenomenon rarely seen in Norway. Yet even in Nesbø's novels, where American culture is repeatedly faulted for its murderous side, it is also praised for its music and its films. Harry Hole, like other characters in the series, is deeply familiar with American pop music (perhaps because his author, Nesbø, has had a side career as a musician), and another Harry in the novel, the surveillance expert who calls his company Harry Sounds, has explicitly named his business after Harry Caul, the Gene Hackman character in *The Conversation*. Obviously, sophisticated and even not-so-sophisticated Scandinavians are expected to be up on American culture.

The villains, too, regularly observe this principle. In the Danish novel *The Hanging*, the cluster of murderers who jointly kill a string of suspected pederasts decide to publicize their deeds in America because that is where they will have the greatest impact. "We can be sure that hundreds of warped minds or strange groups will forward the message, and naturally from their own perspective as the incontestable truth, which can only be doubted by complete idiots or dubious state-sanctioned leaders," one of the Danish collaborators shrewdly points out. He goes on to observe that "what happens in the USA sets the agenda in our media, and whatever garbled rumors have taken hold there will be much more long-lived than fifty thousand pieces of junk mail in Danish letter boxes."

But even with the American model before them, Scandinavians can never manage to achieve our level of crime, and that is largely, I suspect, because of the role of guns in the two cultures. Perhaps the most remarkable thing to me, in this body of work extending from 1965 to last year, is how infrequently the Swedish, Norwegian, and Danish police are seen using or even carrying firearms. Time and again, we are told that this officer has left her gun locked in the car, or that one has forgotten to strap his holster on. Numerous arrests are made without gunfire, and many of the most rebellious and ornery-minded cops—people who in American series would carry *two* guns and perhaps an ankle-knife—rarely rely on firearms of any kind. Even when police officers get shot, as Martin Beck does at the end of the seventh novel in his series, the result is not an increased dependence on or preference for guns. If anything, Sjöwall and Wahlöö become more adamantly anti-gun after that, waiting until the ninth volume to go into detail about why Kollberg never carries a gun.

Nor do the murderers in Scandinavian mysteries seem particularly attached to guns as their mode of destruction. Harry Hole's partner Ellen, for instance, has her head bashed in with a blunt instrument, while his girlfriend, Rakel, is threatened with a bizarre mode of strangulation-cum-decapitation that involves an electrified wire. If anything, Scandinavian authors go to great lengths to devise methods of killing that do *not* involve guns. It is as if they are purposely defining their difference from America in this way, obliquely commenting on a society that is being destroyed by its own vocally championed Second Amendment.

Violent as it is, though, America retains a special place in the minds and hearts of these writers. Or perhaps it's that they simply cannot escape our culture's wide reach. For whatever reason, American books, music, films, and television come up over and over again in Scandinavian thrillers. One of the most striking examples comes near the beginning of *Misterioso*, where two policemen who have been brought together from different Swedish districts are assigned to work as partners. Paul Hjelm and Jorge Chavez are not yet sure they will be able to get along, but at the end of their initial hour in the office together, as they are about to go out on their first joint exploration, they have a moment of communion:

> Chavez slapped the file folder against the desktop a few times. "Let's roll," he said, and then raised his index finger. "And hey—"
> "Let's be careful out there," they both said foolishly, in unison.

Arne Dahl is so confident we will recognize this line that he doesn't even bother to cite the source. The charm of this exchange lies not just in its presumption of their *and* our acquaintance with *Hill Street Blues*, but also in the way it makes a point about the layers of imitation. These are not just Swedish cops mimicking American cops. They are also a couple of literary characters who are in some way asserting their own reality—their existential kinship with their readers—by jokingly quoting a line spoken by a patently fictional TV character, just as we might do.

**NARRATIVE** game-playing is not normally seen as a feature of police procedurals. It is something we associate with more self-consciously highbrow novels, especially the kinds of mannered, self-referential works that have been published in large quantities in the past few decades. Never mind that the tradition is as old as the novel itself (appearing as it does in the second volume of *Don Quixote*, when the Don comments on the alleged printer's error that has taken away Sancho Panza's donkey in the preceding volume); and never mind that it has continued to infuse each century of English literature, from Shakespeare through Sterne through the wry authorial comments of Henry James. Among twentieth-century authors, Norman Mailer practiced it with particular wit and panache, I think. And though I deplore the blatantly self-congratulatory form it takes in certain contemporary authors, I am not above using the strategy myself.

Scandinavian mystery writers, it turns out, are just as likely as any other authors—including, I should add, other mystery authors—to break down the fourth wall separating readers from writers, giving us a companionable wink about the dubious reality of their fictions. The Arne Dahl sample is typical, in that many instances of the strategy involve placing the Nordic mysteries within the context of other (usually American) made-up crime stories. Scandinavian witnesses might, for example, suggest to visiting cops that they have seen such-and-such done on

*CSI*, and the police officers are then forced to say, yes, well, that is television and this is real life. At such moments, the page is slyly attempting to assert its superiority over the screen, even though we readers doubtless remain aware that both forms are equally unreal.

Structurally and stylistically, most of these novels are delivering on the promise inherent in the mystery genre: that we will be fooled into believing the story sufficiently to enjoy its suspense, but not so much that we forget the rules governing the author's obligation to us. In other words, Scandinavian mysteries, like most other mysteries, understand that we want the plot delivered whole, the loose ends tied up, the uncertainties banished—in short, all the bagginess of real life shaped into something that resembles a chess game or a mathematical proof. However much these novels allow the realities of daily life in Sweden, Norway, or Denmark to color the stories in the background, they do not for one minute mistake themselves for documentary productions. They know they are fictional, and they let us know that they know.

But in the Martin Beck series—as always, the exceptional element in the group—something even more complicated is going on in the game between author and reader. Like its successors, the series includes the standard references to mysteries-within-the-mystery. In *The Fire Engine That Disappeared*, for example, Martin Beck reads Raymond Chandler's *Lady in the Lake* in the bathtub, and in *The Man Who Went Up in Smoke*, Kollberg refers to the way murderers are portrayed in American movies. Yet that is the least of it. Perhaps because they visualized their project as a completed ten-book whole from the very beginning, or maybe because they consciously understood that they were breaking new ground in the form, Sjöwall and Wahlöö repeatedly alluded to the literary aspect of their enterprise—as when they made the volume called *The Locked Room* at once a real locked-room mystery and a commentary on the implausibility of such gadgetry.

About two or three volumes in, you may begin to notice that the titular phrases are doing a lot more work than the average mystery-book title. For one thing, they sometimes give away the plot, as in *The Man on the Balcony*, where the title tells us who the murderer is, or *Roseanna*, which gives us the name of the victim long before the cops discover it. For another, many of them carry a double meaning. *The Man Who Went Up in Smoke* refers to a character who has mysteriously vanished but also, as we learn at the end, to the fact that his corpse was burned up in a house fire. And *Cop Killer*—perhaps the most darkly ironic of these duplicitous titles—seems at first to allude to the criminals in the case (who have in fact *not* killed the cop they were accused of killing) but instead describes Kollberg, whose overwhelming guilt at accidentally causing a colleague's death early in his career has resulted in his refusal ever to carry a gun again.

One of the reasons the Martin Beck series excels at clever narrative exploits is that it so pointedly *has* a narrator, in the way that few other series do. This voice is not quite Martin Beck's, not quite Kollberg's, not quite Gunvald Larsson's, though it partakes of all of them, and of some of the murderers whose minds it inhabits, too. He—or they, or it, since the narrator has no distinct bodily personality—often hints at things before they happen, sometimes with vague foreshadowing and sometimes much more explicitly. ("She was wrong there," the narrative voice says after one character makes a remark that will be disproven by the end of the book.) That voice remains in our ear throughout each volume, guiding us in ways we are not even fully aware of and telling us its opinions as if they were established facts.

Still, part of the charm of the Martin Becks lies in how understated this narrative self-consciousness is. In fact, I never noticed any of it during my first time through the series, when I was reading primarily for the plots and the characters. Unlike the equivalently self-referential strategies in American mystery fiction (Harry Bosch's and Mickey Haller's occasional mentions of their own movie and television deals, for instance, or David Loogan's role as an editor of a mystery magazine in Harry Dolan's books), the Sjöwall/Wahlöö approach is subtle to the point of invisibility. Each volume may call attention to itself as a fictional artifact, but it does so in a way that never feels arch or arty. The narrator, and indeed the authors, are effaced by the strength of the characters they have brought into being. It is finally through the earthy realism of these stolidly persistent police officers, who come across as the very opposite of authorial creations, that we are led to appreciate the novels' artistic originality.

ORIGINAL art takes on a more concrete form in many of the more recent Scandinavian mysteries, where it appears as paintings (or drawings, or sculptures, or weavings, or ceramics) that hang on the walls or sit in the homes of everyone from sleuths to witnesses to murder victims. The number of artworks by named artists, either real or fictional, that appear in these books is likely to strike an American reader as weird to the point of obsessiveness. Offhand, I can think of a few of our own thrillers that

focus on visual art—Kenneth Fearing's *The Big Clock* importantly
features the work of a female painter in its plot, while Brian De
Palma's *Dressed to Kill* has a memorable pickup scene set in an
art museum—but there is nothing on our side of the Atlantic
to match the profusion of original wall art in Swedish mysteries. It would seem that everyone there, from the wealthy on
down, views art collecting as an important social and domestic
function.

Among the paintings that appear in these stories, the most
prominent are probably those done by Kurt Wallander's father,
a man who has always made his living as a painter of landscapes.
Old Mr. Wallander paints only two kinds of pictures—sunsets
with a grouse in the foreground, and sunsets without—and Kurt
duly labels them "kitsch," at least in his own mind. But the fact
that, over the course of the old man's working life, an estimated
seven thousand Swedes have wanted to buy one of these "original" paintings to hang in their homes does seem to indicate
something about the culture at large, and it is something that
Henning Mankell is clearly interested in telling us. Within the
novels, the paintings are only important for what they say about
Kurt's father, and Kurt's relation to him, and the society they
both inhabit; that is, unlike the Kenneth Fearing paintings, they
have no plot function whatsoever. But not a single Wallander
novel passes without some mention of them, however small, and
one can't help feeling that Mankell is offering some kind of anal-
ogy between that kind of artistic repetitiveness and the literary
kind associated with a mystery series.

Kurt Wallander's father is of course a fictional painter, but
other Swedish mysteries abound with real ones, and it is often
much less clear in those cases what these pictures are even

doing in the story. When we venture inside a murder victim's apartment in *Misterioso*, for example, we find that "On the walls hang genuine examples of modern Swedish art, three paintings by Peter Dahl, two by Bengt Lindström, two by Ola Billgren." Though I had never heard of any of these painters, Google reveals that all three were noted Swedish artists of the twentieth century—but that doesn't explain why their names are being recited to us in this talismanic fashion. A similar thing happens in the third volume of the Lars Kepler series, in which a wealthy woman named Ellin has a large salon in her house that includes not only the ubiquitous tile stove but also "an oil painting by Erland Cullberg." Even the distinctly undomestic Mikael Blomkvist has "two watercolors by Emanuel Bernstone" hanging on the walls of his bachelor flat.

A few instances like this occur in Danish and Norwegian novels (at least two of the Norwegian authors, for instance, mention Munch, and one of them, Gard Sveen, also cites Christian Krohg, Nikolai Astrup, and Lars Hertervig), but for the most part it is the Swedes who seem preoccupied with their painters. Is this because the country produced more painters than the other Scandinavian nations did? Are middle-class and upper-class Swedes, in general, more avid collectors of original art than their counterparts in the other countries? I haven't a clue: both things could be true, or neither. It could all be a coincidence, I suppose. But it is at any rate a noticeable one.

It is especially noticeable because the characters in these novels so rarely indulge in any other form of art appreciation. Kurt Wallander, it is true, listens to opera on his home stereo and in the car; Harry Hole and his colleagues know something about pop music; and Paul Hjelm, in *Misterioso*, becomes obsessed with jazz in the course of the investigation. But rarely if ever do any of the characters in these mysteries take time off from their busy crime-stopping lives to go to an art museum or see a play or hear any kind of live performance. And the same, one guesses, is probably true of the authors and readers of these books. It is only visual art, hung inside a private house, that can function as a recognizable cultural touchstone. Paintings, it would seem, are common currency because they can be brought into the home—can be owned, domesticated, and made part of the cozy household life—whereas venturing out, even just to go to a movie, entails the risk of encountering strangers.

That this can indeed pose a real risk, and not just the vague anxiety that hovers over all murder mysteries, is borne out by an actual event in Swedish history. On February 28, 1986, Prime Minister Olof Palme made a spur-of-the-moment decision to go see a movie at a cinema near his home in central Stockholm. Eluding, for once, his bodyguards, he and his wife decided to walk to the movie theater and back. It was as they were walking home, on familiar city streets and not very late at night, that a lone gunman suddenly approached, shot them both, and then disappeared. The wife survived, but Palme died on the spot.

**PALME'S** assassination is not mentioned by name in every Swedish mystery, but it looms over just about all of them. This sudden act of violence was a terrible shock to the society at large, a violation of all its conventions and expectations. There had not been a killing of a Swedish governing figure since King Gustav III was assassinated while attending a masked ball in

1792. For twentieth-century Swedes, such events lay even further in the past than Lincoln's assassination now does for us, and the murder of prominent public figures such as JFK and Martin Luther King, Jr., must have struck them—like murder in general—as a particularly American phenomenon. Yet here it was, suddenly in their midst.

For writers and readers of mystery novels, and perhaps for the general public as well, the crime took on an even greater significance because it was never solved. It remained for decades the chief example of police incompetence, an example which every subsequent investigation tried strenuously not to follow. As the prosecuting attorney says to Kurt Wallander in Mankell's 1994 *The Man Who Smiled*, "What we need least of all is a Palme situation here in Ystad." And Wallander knows exactly what he means:

> The unsolved assassination of the Swedish prime minister, a mystery now almost ten years old, had not only stunned the police but had also shocked nearly everyone in Sweden. Too many people, both inside and outside the police force, were aware that in all probability the murder had not been solved because at an early stage the investigation had been dominated and mishandled in a scandalous fashion by a police district chief who had put himself in charge despite being incompetent to run a criminal investigation. Every local force discussed over and over, sometimes angrily and sometimes contemptuously, how it had been possible for the murder, the murderer, and the motive to be swept under the rug with such nonchalance.

The same impression is conveyed by Arne Dahl's 1999 *Misterioso*, where a character says of the newly created A-Unit within the National Criminal Police: "You might say it's structured to be the antithesis of the Palme Assassination Investigation Squad. No big names, no constant changing of bosses, no fussing around with hierarchies." The attribution of causes may vary from book to book, with individual ambition and incompetence sometimes replaced by structural failures in the bureaucracy, but either way the blame falls squarely on the police department. The murderer, meanwhile, remains a mysterious entity, and although Palme's widow reported that only one man fired the gunshots, the assassination plan itself is sometimes attributed, in the wilder thrillers, to a whole group of plotters.

Even Danish and Norwegian mysteries will occasionally allude to the failed Palme investigation, but the habit is of course more common among the Swedes. Of these, the writer who most pointedly focuses on the subject of the assassination is Leif G. W. Persson. Persson, a former member of the Swedish National Police Board, has not only written a trilogy devoted almost exclusively to events surrounding the Palme murder (beginning with his 2002 *Between Summer's Longing and Winter's End* and ending with the 2007 *Falling Freely, as if in a Dream*), but has also alluded to the assassination in most of his other, seemingly unrelated mysteries. He simply cannot let go of it; more to the point, he is filled with a desire to give us his own inside theories about it.

Persson's Palme trilogy may well be among the most unsuspenseful mysteries ever composed. All three books contain wads of undigested historical information, with real spy records interlarded among made-up characters, so that in the end we haven't a clue about what is plausible conjecture and what is arrant nonsense. Moreover, we are aware of exactly how the story will end each time (and we are taken through the assassination itself at least twice, if not in all three books), which means the normal mystery satisfactions are few and far between. We know in advance who the murder victim will be, and it's also a given that the murderer will never get captured or brought to justice. The main thrust of the novels lies in the construction of an elaborate conspiracy theory, with Palme's CIA connections, a set of oozily ambitious officials, and the convenient availability of a gun-for-hire hit man all coming into play. It is an approach to fiction that might succeed in the hands of a Norman Mailer or a Don DeLillo, but it risks coming off as unpersuasive guesswork when practiced by ordinary mortals.

In all of Scandinavian fiction, perhaps the strangest reference to the Palme assassination is not a historical reference at all, but an uncanny prediction. The final volume of the Sjöwall/ Wahlöö series, completed and published in 1975, features a pathetic young woman who ends up shooting the prime minister of Sweden while the cops are essentially looking the other way. The title of the volume is *The Terrorists*, and as the plurality makes clear, the term refers not just to this singular assassin, but to the cabal of international players who have been planning to blow up a visiting American senator (closely modeled on Barry Goldwater) during his official visit with the Swedish king. Martin Beck's team members have been so focused on preventing that disaster—an effort at which they are successful—that they have not had time to keep an eye on the Clod Squad, an assembly of all the moronic officers who have appeared throughout the series, grouped together by Gunvald Larsson and carefully assigned to busywork to keep them away from the main action.

It is because a higher-up mistakes the designation "C.S." for "Commando Squad" and brings them in to protect the prime minister that the assassination occurs.

The prime minister in this volume is no one we get to know personally. He is never named, and even his half-crazed young assassin doesn't know who he is when he is first mentioned to her as "the most important person in the country." But if you look up your Swedish history, you will discover that the prime minister of Sweden in 1975, the year *The Terrorists* appeared, was Olof Palme. That he was the official leader of the Social Democratic Party would not have been enough to put Per Wahlöö and Maj Sjöwall on his side, for they too, like the oddly sympathetic assassin they create, appear to feel he could have been doing more for the oppressed of his society. It is one of the many ironies built into their final volume that the cops were focused solely on guarding the king—the descendant of the man who had suffered Sweden's most recent assassination, two centuries earlier—when the real threat was to their elected officials.

QUAINT traditions like royalty and aristocracy may seem at odds with modern Scandinavia's advanced political habits, but they nonetheless remain very much a part of the culture. All three countries, amazingly, are still officially monarchies, with a King, a Queen, or at least a Crown Prince available for public display as needed. The royals are mostly used as attractive window-dressing in these mystery books, and the only critiques ever leveled against them tend to be individual and idiosyncratic, as in the attitude of the crazed right-wing would-be assassin portrayed in Jo Nesbø's *The Redbreast*. One rarely if ever encounters in Scandinavian mysteries any sign of the saner anti-monarchical sentiments that occur in, say, the nearby British Isles. In Sweden, Norway, and Denmark, the monarchs, when not completely ignored, appear to be loved or at least respected.

There is, however, plenty of resentment of the hereditary aristocracy to be found here. Those of us on the outside can't necessarily recognize Swedish or Danish aristocratic names—they aren't always marked with a "von" or a "de," the way the German or French aristocracy is—but the insiders who live in these countries, and particularly the cops, seem to know them on sight. Rare is the encounter between an aristocrat and a police officer that does not entail a certain amount of class resentment, however hidden. (The Countess in the Hammer series, who is herself both an aristocrat and a police officer, might be the sole exception, and even she comes in for a certain amount of mild joshing from her colleagues, as is evident in her nickname.) And when the aristocrats allude to or call upon their connection with the monarchy, in an act of either willful or oblivious self-assertion, the resentment comes closer to the surface. There is clearly a huge difference between the sort of person who belongs to the Royal Swedish Yacht Club in Viveca Sten's Sandhamn mysteries and the commoners like Martin Beck who simply love boats. The former look down on the latter, if they bother to think of them at all, while the latter quietly deplore the former; and since most of us readers are not aristocrats, we tend to take sides accordingly. If class in the modern Scandinavian world is defined in large part by money, there is nonetheless an elusive area of entitlement that is linked to heritage and family connection, and it becomes as much a part of these contemporary mysteries as any other kind of local color.

This may, incidentally, shed some light on the earlier question about art collecting. Just as heavy mahogany and rich upholstery defined the furnishings of the age-old aristocracy, only to be upstaged in twentieth-century households by the sparer, cleaner lines of Scandinavian design, the collecting of old masters, an activity that was once the province of inherited wealth, seems to have given way in recent times to the collecting of new masters, or at least new *potential* masters, whose works are still affordable by the prosperously self-made.

That there is in the Scandinavian imagination a connection between visual art and aristocratic class, whether disruptive or affirmative or both, is cleverly suggested in a recent film, Ruben Östlund's witty and disconcerting *The Square*. Set largely in a Stockholm contemporary art museum which just happens to occupy the old Royal Palace, the movie skewers the pretensions of everyone in the middle-to-higher reaches of Swedish society. The well-off chief curator is shown constantly trying to seem a man of the people, even as he indulges in babyishly demanding behavior that only the entitled would consider acceptable, and by the end of the film his repeated acts of bad faith have led to the collapse of his comfortable life. Nor is he alone in being portrayed as a moral idiot. Ad campaign designers, museum board members, personal assistants, academic art critics, television journalists—all end up with mud on their faces or worse.

*The Square* is not a thriller in any normal sense (except to the extent that it involves threats of violence, fake stagings of terrorist attacks, and a substantial dose of real anxiety), but it does address many of the same issues that surface in the Scandinavian mysteries. Small children at risk, confusion surrounding female sexuality, elegantly furnished apartments versus ugly

tower blocks, prejudice against recent immigrants, patently un-
successful attempts at egalitarian family life: these themes and
more surface in miniature and are duly dispatched with a mock-
ery that partakes of something more serious. What lies at the
root of Östlund's film is something that also infuses the novels
I inveterately consume. It is a sense that the key social problem
in Sweden—and Denmark, and Norway—is not crime or violence itself, but the perception on the part of the vast majority
of people that they are not in any way to blame. *We are essentially
good people*, the Scandinavians insist, often with some justification.
But that very insistence may be the thing that blinds them to
their own moral culpability.

**RELIGION** can, I think, be held responsible for some of this.
Norway, Sweden, and Denmark are all predominantly Christian
nations, with a branch of evangelical Lutheranism playing the
part of the official state church in both Denmark and Norway,
while a looser but still prominent allegiance to the same religion
characterizes most of Sweden's inhabitants. A central principle
of Lutheranism is the doctrine of justification by faith alone,
which means that all salvation comes directly from God. Human
beings, in this view, are by definition born with original sin; they
cannot redeem themselves through their actions (or through
the actions of any intermediaries, like priests), but can only be
saved by the grace of God and his son, Jesus Christ, in whom
they must place complete faith. Though not every Scandinavian
Lutheran would necessarily be conscious of these underlying
principles, the loss of agency implied by them—the sense that
only God can really do anything about sin, or crime, or poverty,

or violence—can't help but instill in people the sense that they are not personally to blame when something goes wrong with society.

Such mind-your-own-business doctrines sit oddly with the rigorous social safety nets that operate in these countries. But then, in addition to being heavily Christian, the populations of Sweden, Denmark, and Norway are also extremely secular, and these contradictory aspects of the culture somehow manage to live on side by side. As one of the police officers in a Lars Kepler mystery reflects: "Considering that Sweden is the most secular country in the world, she can't help thinking that there are an awful lot of priests and preachers." Her team, searching for a serial killer known as the "unclean preacher," has now accumulated a list of "almost five hundred people with direct connections to various faith organizations in the Stockholm area who match the general profile." And that's just one city. If we add in all the religious figures who come under investigation in Gothenburg, Malmö, Uppsala, Copenhagen, Oslo, and Bergen, not to mention the small towns and countrysides in all three nations, we are left with the sense of a region riddled with occasionally kooky Protestant beliefs.

Secular or not, the countries of Scandinavia are underpinned by their shared Christianity—not only in the religious holidays (Lucia, Easter, Christmas) that are observed by the state, and the name-days that people celebrate along with birthdays, but also in the general assumption that everyone is basically Christian. In the entirety of Scandinavian mystery literature, I can think of only two Jews: Inspector Bublanski, who intermittently appears in the Stieg Larsson books, and Samuel Mendel, Joona Linna's dead partner in the Lars Kepler series. We are reminded

of Samuel whenever Joona recalls the tragedy that led to his suicide or else visits his grave in "the ancient Jewish burial ground"
that lies within walking distance of the police station. On one
such visit to the cemetery, "Joona places a small pebble on the
top of the gravestone and stands there with his eyes closed for
a moment." Then, as if from on high, we get a sudden historical
digression: "Samuel Mendel was a direct descendant of Koppel Mendel, who opposed Aaron Isaac, the founder of Sweden's
Jewish community, and bought this land for use as a cemetery
in 1787. Although the cemetery has not been actively used since
1857, the descendants of Koppel Mendel are still buried there."
This glaring intrusion manages to suggest that Jews in Sweden
are essentially a thing of the past, not an active presence in the
twenty-first century, and that therefore most readers will have
to be informed about their history in the country.

If Jews are scarce, Muslims abound in these novels, but always as the outsiders, the recent invaders, the pathetic or perhaps dangerous and certainly widely despised refugees. Even
children born in Scandinavia, if they have Muslim last names
and Muslim parents, are not fully viewed as "Swedish" or "Danish" or "Norwegian"; they are outsiders unto the nth generation.
Only rarely do these immigrants surface within police departments, and when they do, they are likely to be set apart in some
way. Perhaps the most extreme example is Assad, Carl Mørck's
assistant in the Department Q series. On the page, Jussi Adler-
Olsen presents him as an almost Tonto-like figure next to Carl's
Lone Ranger. This mysterious Arab has no last name, comes
from no designated country, can only speak fractured (and frequently mocked) Danish, and repeatedly indulges in annoying foreign habits like brewing up undrinkably strong tea or

praying in his office multiple times every day. Things are much improved in the Danish TV version of the series, where Assad, who is played by a tall, handsome actor, speaks the language perfectly and comes off as the better policeman of the two. And even Adler-Olsen's Assad, while silly, is at least technically a good guy, as opposed to, say, the Bosnians and other Eastern European Muslims in Jo Nesbø's books, who are likely to be drug smugglers or killers-for-hire.

Often, it is true, Nesbø introduces these prejudices only to attribute them to Norwegian right-wingers, who tend to be the true villains in his books. And Christianity, in Nesbø's hands, does not come off too well either. In *The Devil's Star*, he structures the plot and its clues around a Satanic-ritual pentagram, leading Harry Hole, and us, to believe at first that devil-worshippers are the source of the serial murders. Bizarrely, this is exactly the red herring used in Helene Tursten's Gothenburg novel *The Glass Devil*, published the same year as Nesbø's Oslo tale. Evidently this obsession with Satanism, the evil twin of evangelical Christianity, crosses national boundaries. I suppose it is the natural corollary of having all those strange little self-governing congregations—though America, which contains as least as many evangelical offshoots as Scandinavia, rarely focuses on devil-worship in its non-supernatural thrillers.

It turns out, in both the Irene Huss and Harry Hole cases, that the true killers are only pretending to be Satanists in order to throw off the police investigation. But for Nesbø, at least, the pentagram provides a useful basis for his killer's complicated and carefully constructed scheme, in which the five murders in Oslo—located on the city map at the five points of a star—take place every five days at 5:00 p.m. on the fifth floor of their respective buildings, with a different digit of the victim's hand severed each time. That this involves implausibility carried to its extreme, not to mention a high degree of motiveless malignity (since four innocent people must die so that the killer can conceal the reason behind the fifth murder), is typical of the Nesbø series, which repeatedly pulls us in through a clever combination of admirably tight plotting and intense sadism.

SADISTIC tendencies occur in all murder mysteries, of course. Part of the reason we read these books is to be appalled, or scared, or perhaps titillated by our own secret passion for violence. As Walter Benjamin remarked in an entirely different context, we warm our shivering lives with the deaths we read about. And if the thriller form makes masochists of us all, inflicting ugly sights and events on us, it also reassures and soothes us, by making sense of all the apparent mayhem through the detective's eventual solution.

Still, I am more conscious of the sadism in my cherished Scandinavian mysteries than I am in any other nation's output, including our own. We Americans have a few writers that excel at the method (Thomas Harris would come high on any such list), but given the relative amount of violence in our country, we fall far behind the Scandinavians' authorial cruelty when it comes to putting violence on the page. Whether this is to their credit or not is something I have yet to figure out, but I am always aware of the moments when it becomes a bit too much even for me.

If pressed, I would rank the Norwegians highest on the sadism scale, followed by the Danes, followed by the Swedes. Granted, my generalization about the Norwegians is not all-

encompassing. But at least three of them—Jo Nesbø, Thomas
Enger, and Karin Fossum—excel at making us, not to mention
their characters, feel terrible in one way or another. And overt
violence, though present in all three, is perhaps the least of their
sadistic strategies.

The worst sadist in all of Scandinavian literature is Karin
Fossum. I have actually had to stop reading her books, I find
them so disturbing—not disturbing in a grand, useful way, in the
manner of Dostoyevsky or Kafka, but manipulatively, personally, intentionally pain-inducing. It is not just that the crimes
detailed by Fossum are so horrible (though they are often gruesome, and generally involve the deaths of innocent women and
children), but that she lingers so over their revelation. Sometimes, as in *The Indian Bride*, the denouement involves a delayed,
particularly upsetting murder, the one we were hoping could
be averted from the start. But just as often the sad deaths occur
right at the start and then are lovingly recapitulated in slow mo-
tion. This is particularly true of her latest, *Hell Fire*, with its two
interwoven plot strands: one in which Inspector Sejer, faced with
the brutally slashed corpses of a single mother and her small
son, attempts to solve the murder; and the other, beginning
farther back in time, in which the murderer himself progresses
slowly toward the moment of the killings. Because we know exactly where this is going to end up, we suffer the whole thing
in anticipation as well as in the moment, and Fossum sharpens
the knife, as it were, by showing us in detail the cheerful, loving
interaction between mother and son just before they are killed.

Such writerly behavior might be defended on the grounds
that it makes murder more real and less of a game—that it returns the horror to a horrifying crime. But something about the

delight Fossum takes in her drawn-out rendition of the crime belies this moral stance. She is in it for the pain, and it is *our* pain that most interests her, not that of her fictional characters, in whom she doesn't really believe. Sometimes years pass and I begin to forget the effects of a Karin Fossum novel, but when I am silly enough to buy another, they all come roaring back at me. This, I would maintain, is authorial sadism in its most classic and unadulterated form.

Enger and Nesbø are milder in their effects, and they also offer more in the way of recompense. But they, too, are interested in making us squirm. Each of them—independently, I presume—has adopted a strategy in which they convey a scene through pronouns, allowing us to believe that our hero or his beloved has been killed, and only revealing much later that in fact someone else was the victim. There is at least one Harry Hole novel that ends with our presumption of Harry's death, and the revelation that he is still alive is delayed well into the sequel. As for Thomas Enger, he has titled his five-volume series with single words (*Burned, Scarred, Cursed,* etc.) that all clearly apply to his main character, Henning Juul; the final book in the series is called, tellingly, *Killed.* Enger encourages us, in the book's opening scene, to believe that we are witnessing Juul's murder, and we are duly given a funeral service toward the end of this largely flashback novel. It is only *after* the ceremony, in the last few pages of *Killed*, that we learn the dead person was someone else, not Henning, who was apparently saved at the last minute by a collection of unbelievable *dei ex machinas*.

I'm not sure why I rank the Danes second—based, admittedly, on a relatively small sample—except that there is a general air of heartlessness in the novels set in that country.

Copenhagen's urban landscape is often described in terms of its harshness and grunge, and the crimes taking place there, though horrific, do not seem to shock the people investigating them. Once again, the investigators themselves, and particularly the women among them, are likely to come in for sadistic treatment. Prior to her ultimate removal from the Lotte and Søren Hammer novels, the unfortunate Pauline is held hostage, nearly killed, and essentially driven insane, while Jussi Adler-Olsen's Rose slowly devolves into a psycho with a split personality. Though their colleagues express lip-service sympathy, these sad fates are actually treated less as tragedies than as annoyances hampering the investigative solutions: neither Pauline nor Rose can safely be sent out on a mission anymore, because of their mental instability, so their colleagues have to pick up the slack. Perhaps it is wrong to call this kind of thing sadism, in that the authorial cruelty is too casual to be piercing.

With the distinct exception of the Lisbeth Salander series (where violence, especially by and against Lisbeth herself, is the rule), the Swedes on the whole seem milder than their neighbors. Heinous crimes occur, and the detectives are left to deal with their results, but we are rarely tortured with the details as experienced by the victims. There is a thin line between fear-generated suspense and outright distress, and the Swedes tend to stay on the safer side of that border. Even when we find ourselves inside the mind of a murderer—as in certain episodes of the Martin Beck and Kurt Wallander novels—the purpose is not so much to put us through the killing at first hand as to create sympathy with the fragile mental state of the killer.

No murder mystery, of course, can be completely exempt from the charge of sadism, and women and children do die even in the exemplary Sjöwall/Wahlöö series. But there the particularly upsetting murders tend to happen offstage, and we do not learn anything about the victims until after they are dead. We are not dragged through the details of the deaths as they happen, nor are we acquainted with the living figures beforehand.

The one major exception to this, in the Martin Beck volumes, involves the murder of a policeman. The fourth book in the series, *The Laughing Policeman*, opens with a scene in which Martin Beck and Kollberg are playing chess at Kollberg's house to while away a rainy evening. After Martin leaves, Kollberg puts on a blue raincoat and tells his wife he is going out. In practically the very next scene, Beck is called to the location of a recent killing spree in which nine people have been shot to death on a city bus. One of them is a policeman wearing a blue raincoat, and naturally we assume at first that it is Kollberg, as does Martin. In the event, the victim turns out to be another colleague of theirs, a young man we didn't get to know well in the first three volumes, though now we learn what a good policeman he was. Still, the mild sadness we feel at his murder is vastly outweighed by our relief at the discovery that it is not Kollberg. Is this sadism, or its opposite? Have we been briefly tortured by Wahlöö and Sjöwall, or have they shielded us by trading one death for another? And is it reasonable, in any case, for us to tolerate without difficulty the murders of all these civilians, when we can't bear the thought of having our treasured Kollberg removed from the team?

**TEAMWORK** of a particularly collaborative and intense kind is one of the more salient qualities of the Scandinavian mystery.

You might almost say that the better the series is, the more it depends on the personalities and functions of the whole squad-room ensemble. In that respect, these Nordic novels have a greater affinity with the long-form cop shows that have been appearing on American TV over the past few decades, from *Hill Street Blues* onward, than they do with our printed mysteries, which tend to focus on a single detective. The spectacular star-player, it seems, is neither lauded nor needed among Swedes, Danes, and Norwegians. A Scandinavian thriller series may cite the name of its lead police officer in its advertising or even its individual subtitles, but he (or, more rarely, she) almost always solves crimes in collaboration with a fully delineated team.

There are exceptions to this, of course, most notably in the case of Harry Hole, who is more of a loner than any police-man I can think of in our own (or any other) national literature. But for the most part the homicide squads in these thrillers function as a multi-character unit, with each member having his own strengths or weaknesses, her own special part to play. Anders Knutas could not solve his crimes without his primary colleague, Karin Jacobsson, as well as the other members of his Gotland-based squad. Carl Mørck would be useless without the enterprising inventiveness of Assad and (when she is functional) the vigilance of Rose. Konrad Simonsen's entire squad—including his wife, the Countess, as well as various individual officers drawn from different regions of Denmark—is necessary to the solutions of the crimes he is successively faced with. And the group Arne Dahl initially pulls together for *Misterioso* and then reuses in subsequent volumes is described precisely as that: a hand-picked investigative team of formerly disparate officers, labeled by its conveners "the A-Unit." Even Lisbeth Salander, though she exemplifies the rogue outlaw in other ways, is dependent not only on her official helpers (a journalist, a lawyer, a cop, a psychiatrist, and her sometime employer in the security business), but also on a shadowy network of fellow hackers who step in to assist her when she calls upon their aid.

Neither Martin Beck nor Kurt Wallander would be able to function at all without the police officers who work under each of them, supplementing and at times questioning their guiding efforts. Over the course of the ten Martin Beck volumes and the ten or so Kurt Wallanders, we watch the personnel of these squads evolve and change. Characters who were initially seen as pains in the ass become allies, and presumed allies sometimes become backstabbers. Occasionally a policeman dies or is transferred, and his place is taken by someone who may be worse or better. (In the Wallander series, where the replacement is a woman, Ann-Britt Höglund, she turns out to be significantly better.) Sometimes the local team is supplemented by an officer from afar, as when Beck collaborates repeatedly with the Malmö police chief or when Wallander reaches out to a colleague from Helsingbörg. But the core team itself remains crucial, not only because we have come, over the course of multiple volumes, to know each member personally, but also because each brings a special set of talents to the solution of crimes.

This is especially true in the Martin Becks, where, for instance, one member of the team has a phenomenal memory, another is a persistent researcher, still another is especially good at finding lost things, and yet another terrifies the bad guys with his overwhelming physical presence. Even the seemingly colorless Einar Rönn, whom Martin Beck himself fails to appreciate for nine volumes, plays a crucial role in the tenth and final book of the series, where he personally carries out the underground activity required to foil the terrorists. And although we lose Kollberg as a police officer when he quits the force at the end of volume nine, even he returns to us at the end. He and Martin have remained friends if not colleagues, and in the final scene of the entire series, the two of them plus Gun and Rhea are gathered at Kollberg's house, playing a word game that somewhat resembles Scrabble. "My turn to start?" says Kollberg, in the very last line of the book. "Then I say X—X as in Marx." And with that closing word, Maj Sjöwall and Per Wahlöö lay down their pens for good, as if to say: We have shown you what Swedish life is like. Now it's up to the rest of you to take up the cause and make it into what it *can* be.

URBAN life, observed at close range in the city of Stockholm, is what gave Sjöwall and Wahlöö their perspective on society as a whole, and this viewpoint turned out to be a central portion of their legacy. With a few exceptions, Swedish mystery writers continue to set their novels in cities and comment on the nature of those cities, and this is often true of the Danes and Norwegians as well. Because these are crime novels, they inevitably portray the darker aspects of urban living, but they also describe numerous everyday features of their respective towns. The cities themselves, as much as the police and other investigators, become a part of the story, and I venture to guess that by reading the crime novels set in Oslo, Stockholm, or Copenhagen (or even in smaller towns like Uppsala, Visby, and Ystad), you can get a fuller sense of these places than most guidebooks have to offer.

Perhaps because its authors are the most jaundiced, or maybe because it is actually crummier in reality, Copenhagen comes off as the dirtiest and most difficult of the capital cities. We do get glimpses, in the Danish mysteries, of the normal tourist sites: Tivoli Gardens, the Folketing in Christiansborg, H. C. Andersens Boulevard, and the like. And there still seems to be a certain amount of leisurely café life in the city. Individual squad members in the Hammer series are likely to have "a favorite café . . . a secret hideaway" where they can savor "a half hour's retreat from death, murder, and the more bestial aspects of human nature." But on the whole the urban environment is forbidding and modern, the very opposite of the quaint locations the tourists flock to.

"Nørrebro was a war zone," we learn in one Adler-Olsen novel. "Concrete tenements knocked up overnight had provided ideal conditions for a complex of social problems, spawning crime, violence, and hatred." Elsewhere in the same novel, Carl Mørck refers mournfully to the recent destruction of Vesterbro, once a vital working-class neighborhood and now a soulless place "where talentless architects had deluded brainless local politicians into plastering the streets with ugly concrete blocks not even social class 5 could think of as home."

The Jo Nesbø books, by contrast, present an Oslo filled with cozy neighborhoods, appealing street names, and grand cultural locations. That Harry Hole is the very opposite of a cozy character only makes the charming setting more noticeable. The profusion of parks and squares—Palace Gardens, Tøyen Park, Frogner Park, the Ekeberg Ridge—all sound lovely and picturesque. Views are everywhere, not only from up on wealthy, hilly Holmenkollveien (where Rakel lives, and from which one can see the Oslo fjord), but also from a high floor in a downtown hotel: "From here they could see everything that was worth seeing: the Town Hall, the National Theatre, the Palace, the Norwegian Parliament—the Storting—and the Akershus Fortress." One Nesbø novel refers to the Munch Museum; another, written in 2005, mentions the forthcoming opera house, to be built right next to the harbor in a place previously occupied by shipping containers. It would seem that tourist Oslo and murder-story Oslo are mingled together in a way that would be unfathomable to Copenhagen's cops.

If Oslo comes across as a placid idyll and Copenhagen as a dirty pit, Stockholm—to judge by the thriller accounts—falls somewhere in between. (That is true, at least, in the Swedish accounts; outsiders tend to give it a distinctly higher ranking. As an old saying reproduced in one of the Norwegian mysteries puts it: "God built Stockholm, the king built Copenhagen, and City Hall built Oslo.") The Swedish capital clearly has its own distinct kind of beauty, but it is also a true metropolis, with standard urban problems such as poor neighborhoods, overcrowded subways, and traffic-riddled streets, not to mention its particularly heinous variations on the theme of modern architecture. Martin Beck is always deploring the ugly new complexes put up by city planners, and thirty or forty years later the characters in Arne Dahl's novels display the same combination of bitter nostalgia and architectural critique. "The street names—*flax, corn, hemp, oats*—were like a textbook on agronomy," Paul Hjelm and his partner notice as they drive through streets named Linvägen, Kornvägen, Hampvägen, and Havrevägen. "Everywhere loomed the antithesis of the agrarian society, the brutally unimaginative

facades of the identical tall apartment buildings from the sixties
and seventies."

While exacerbating the sense of isolation felt by modern
urban Swedes, these impersonal structures also echo the way
the nation's various bureaucracies have lumped the citizenry
into large, faceless categories. Granted, this overall impression
of uniformity is not helped by the culture's traditional nam-
ing habits. What worked in a small agrarian society, where a
local boy could be known as Sven's son, or Erik's son, or Ander's
son, becomes unmanageable in the metropolis. "There are three
hundred and ninety thousand people in Sweden called Anders-
son," we learn in one of the Martin Beck novels, when the team
is trying to locate a particular but as yet unknown Mrs. Anders-
son. "The Stockholm telephone directory alone lists ten thousand two hundred subscribers with this name, plus another two
thousand in the immediate environs." No wonder my old boyfriend Ulf wanted to replace his all-too-common surname with
a newly invented moniker of his own.

Yet Stockholm has not, it would appear, been utterly destroyed by the forces of depersonalization. It still comes across
as a lovely old city, walkable for the most part, with bridges and
ferries taking one across the water as needed. Attractive central
neighborhoods like Gamla Stan, Riddarholmen, Östermalm,
and Södermalm are filled with beautiful old buildings and surrounded not only by the frequent waterways but by a wealth of
city parks; indeed, one whole island, Djurgården, seems to be
practically *all* park.

This sense of an urban paradise ends, however, at the police
station. According to Maj Sjöwall and Per Wahlöö, the old police

headquarters, located on Kungsholmsgatan, was merely undistinguished, but the new one being built next to it in the early
1970s promised to be a monster. From his window in the old
building, one of Martin Beck's team members "had a view out over
an immense hole in the ground—out of which the gigantic showy
building of the National Police Force would in due course rise
up and obscure the view. From this ultramodern colossus in the
heart of Stockholm the police would extend their tentacles
in every direction and hold the dispirited citizens of Sweden
in an iron grip. After all, they couldn't all emigrate or commit
suicide."

In Denmark, too, the central police building looms over the
capital as a sign of law enforcement's power. "The police station in Copenhagen was a powerful and monumental building,"
Lotte and Søren Hammer tell us. "From the outside it appeared
hard and forbidding, with its gray, dirty walls of rough plaster
and mortar and its lack of adornment, if one didn't count the
entrance, where two solid iron cages flanked the colonnades."
On top of these cages sit two "oversized golden morning stars,"
the only decorative element in a building that otherwise runs
"in straight lines along the streets with window after window
after window that all opened inward in order not to break the
strength of the facade."

"Iron grip." "Iron cages." There is something deeply unpleasant and indeed frightening about these architectural rep-
resentations of the Swedish and Danish police forces. (Oslo may
have its share of police problems, but, at least as described in the
novels, they are not manifested in the physical headquarters.)
And yet, to an American, the portrayal of the Scandinavian police force is likely to seem particularly humane and thoughtful.

Perhaps it is *because* they fear police power, and the social ravages it can cause in its extremes, that the Scandinavians have been able to keep their forces so well in check. Or perhaps the dire descriptions of the police buildings are themselves examples of a Scandinavian duality: a recognition that the forces of good are not always fully distinguishable from the forces of evil, so that sometimes it can be hard to tell, in any given situation involving criminals and cops, what would count as the right side winning.

**VICTORY** and defeat are never as clear-cut in these mysteries as they are in most American thrillers, where the police normally play the role of the good guys and the murderers are the designated bad guys. Obviously there are exceptions to this national rule. Patricia Highsmith violates it completely with her Ripley novels (where Ripley, the murderer, always outwits the police and goes on to kill again), and Richard Price's later novels, which borrow some of the trappings of police procedurals, are as murky and ambivalent as anything one can find in Scandinavia. American television shows, too, tend to be more radical in this regard than our written mysteries: from *Hill Street Blues* and *NYPD Blue* to *The Sopranos* and *The Wire*, television writers have offered us complicated relations between partially corrupt police forces and partially (or even wholly) sympathetic perps. But on the page, American mysteries tend to hew to a more conservative line. Even when they locate the battle between good and evil *within* police departments—as, for instance, in Michael Connelly's Harry Bosch series—there is always the sense that the murderers are nonetheless the worst scum of all, and that bringing criminals to justice is still a worthy cause.

That conviction is lacking in Swedish, Danish, and Norwegian crime fiction. Figures like Martin Beck and Kurt Wallander carry on through their decades-long series, holding up their end as responsible police officers, but they do so with an increasing degree of discouragement, an ever-mounting feeling that the job is not what it once was, and that efforts to contain or punish crime are doing as much harm as good. They are reinforced in these beliefs by the close colleagues—Kollberg in the Beck series, Per Åkeson in the Wallanders—who decide to leave the enforcement business entirely and make a living in some other, less compromised manner. It is not just the corruption or incompetence of the higher-ups in their own profession that bothers these extremely moral police detectives; it is their whole sense that the larger society is unfair in the first place, and that the true criminals are escaping unpunished.

With the exception of an outlier like Karin Fossum (who seems to agree that murderers are indeed pure scum), the average Scandinavian novelist takes what an American cop like Harry Bosch might view as a pantywaist social-worker attitude toward criminals. Their mental derangement, their violent and abused childhoods, their jettisoning by the social system, and sometimes even their subordination to higher-up criminal masterminds are often invoked—not in a courtroom, but by the police officers handling their cases, who then transmit these attitudes to us. Crime, in Scandinavia, is rarely seen as the bad action of a single bad actor. It is nested in the social arrangement, viewed as the inevitable underside of the comfortable, oblivious lives led by the more fortunate. If nobody is totally guilty in these novels, no one is completely innocent either: the peaceful members of society share a certain amount of responsibility for the crimes, whether they are aware of it or not. Even in a social-welfare state, it is implied, there are haves and have-nots, and the former are benefiting at the expense of the latter. So when we reach the end of a Scandinavian mystery, with the crime exposed and punished, we may feel the satisfaction of a puzzle solved, but we rarely get any sense of moral satisfaction—or if we do, it is the kind that comes of having our doubts shared and clearly expressed by our author.

No murder mystery, given its premises, can be a completely victorious tale. After all, the instigating event is a death, and no discovery of the causes or arrest of the perpetrator can reverse that initial tragedy. But most mysteries are constructed to make us forget that problem—to ignore the sorrow inherent in the loss of life, and to look for our pleasure in the process of discovery and revenge. Defeat, in these terms, would consist of not solving the mystery, and very few novelists care to go that route. (With good reason, since it would violate the implied contract they have with their readers, and the readers would vociferously object.)

Many Scandinavian mysteries, however, begin and end with a level of defeat that can never be overcome. The central detective figure has already suffered too much to recover his spirits, even if he manages to solve the problem at hand. Occasionally the death that has caused his sorrow is the murder he is seeking to solve. This is true, for instance, of Henning Juul's five-book odyssey, in which he pursues the people responsible for the fire that killed his small son. Even there, though, the ending is not a real solution to the emotional problem, which means that the final volume in the series, *Killed*, is the least satisfying: it leaves us with nothing else to hope for, not even suspense. Knowledge does not, it turns out, alleviate the pain of loss, and Juul is as lonely (and as scarred, and as cursed) as he was at the beginning, if not more so.

Other detectives turn out to be even worse off, for they already know the source of their sorrow and can do nothing about it. Roslund & Hellström's Ewert Grens, for instance, is burdened with an overwhelming depression that stems from an accident his wife suffered decades earlier. When he and she were both young officers, a failed police operation resulted in her being yanked out of the police van, which then ran over her head; Grens was the unwitting driver. He never gets over this. For years he faithfully and lovingly visits her pale, mindless remnant every week in the rehab hospital, and when she dies, he transfers those visits to the cemetery. His own life has stopped cold with her death, and only the solutions of the ongoing mysteries keep him (and us) going, though not very happily.

Joona Linna has lost a wife and daughter early on in his series—not to death, but to banishment, in an attempt to keep them safe—and much later, though he reunites with his daughter, it is too late for his wife, who has sickened and died in the interim. Like Grens, Linna never overcomes his own sense of guilt, though he really had no choice if he wanted to preserve their lives. Guilt is also an ever-present factor for Carl Mørck, who has been cast out of the regular force and assigned to Department Q after an operation *he* was managing resulted in the shooting death of one partner and the permanent paralysis of another. In an act of remorse and goodwill, Mørck takes the quadriplegic former officer into his own house after the man's wife refuses to take care of him anymore—a constant reminder of his own negligence and his own better luck. Against this background, none of his Department Q successes can make a serious emotional dent.

Harry Hole is a more complicated case, in that he too always feels in the wrong, though for less specific reasons. People die around him (his partner Ellen, for instance, or the young male officer he trains later in the series), and other people he loves are constantly put at risk (his girlfriend, Rakel; her son, Oleg). He drinks to forget all this, and also to harden himself against the various unfairnesses—corrupt politicians and police bureaucrats, pathetic Eastern European refugees dragged into crime against their will, complacent Nazi sympathizers among the Norwegian upper classes—that surround him on his cases. His sense of guilt, which is somehow linked to that very notion of complacency, seems larger than a merely personal feeling. What Harry is struggling with and rebelling against is not just the self-satisfaction of contemporary Norway, a rich country filled with selfishly comfortable citizens. It also has something to do with that nation's history. As a novel like *The Redbreast* makes clear, that collective sense of guilt dates back all the way to the Second World War, and to Norway's collaborationist role in it.

**WORLD** War Two looms larger in Norwegian mysteries than elsewhere, perhaps, but its remnants and inheritances can be found all throughout Scandinavia, and this is true whether the books were written many decades ago or much more recently. Even in the mysteries that are set in the 1990s and onward, a sense of the Europe that emerged during and after the war is often embedded in the plots. Unlike America—where mid-twentieth-century history is already, as we say, History—the three Scandinavian countries appear to have preserved their wartime memories and to be dwelling among them still.

The Martin Becks, though they are set in the late sixties and early seventies, are clearly postwar novels, filled with characters who were young men in the 1940s and actively recall those years. One of the volumes, *The Man Who Went Up in Smoke*, even alludes to "the Raoul Wallenberg affair" (the mysterious 1945 disappearance of the famous Swedish savior of the Jews) as if it were still in recent memory. Or consider the Leif Persson novels, which, in investigating the causes behind the assassination, take Olof Palme's history back to the Second World War and the period immediately after the war, when he was allegedly hand-in-glove with the American secret service.

Sweden was, of course, notoriously neutral in the Second World War (though to be a neutral purveyor of munitions material when one of the competing buyers was Hitler is hardly much of a claim to moral worth). And while Sweden was at least a safety zone for the Jews and other refugees in its care, Norway and Denmark fared much worse. Denmark was in fact overrun by the Nazis, as the "Remembrance Yard" in the Copenhagen police station affirms: the location and its name commemorate the September 19 date on which Danish police officers were interned by the Nazis. There was some degree of internal resistance, and apparently individual Danes managed to save ninety percent of Denmark's Jews from deportation (or so claims a recent Christian Jungersen thriller, *The Exception*), but they did so primarily by smuggling them out of occupied Denmark into Sweden.

If Denmark was demonstrably victimized, Norway proved embarrassingly cooperative with the Germans—so much so that Quisling, the Norwegian military officer who became the nominal leader under the Nazi regime, has lent his name even in English to the definition of a traitor. As Jo Nesbø's novels make clear, the country held divided opinions even at the time. It had its Resistance members as well as its collaborators, and among Nesbø's own grandfathers he can number one of each. It is this personal background, in part, which led him to explore in his fiction the continuing effects of that wartime history on the Norway of today.

Nor is he the only Norwegian mystery writer to have done so. Gard Sveen's 2013 novel, *The Last Pilgrim*, has a dual time scheme that alternates between the period of the Second World War and the present-day investigations carried on by Tommy Bergmann. That even the most heroic Resistance figures were consumed by the violence, the deception, and the disturbing degree of collaboration required of them is perhaps the strongest theme of the novel. Guilt does not begin to cover the feeling they carry forward; it is something much closer to anger or hatred, including self-hatred. One of the most exemplary Resistance figures in *The Last Pilgrim*, for example, finds himself looking at the face of a Swedish friend in 1945 and noting "the hint of boyish optimism in his eyes, a look that suggested he was utterly unaffected by the innate evil in people." The Norwegian almost wants to "smash his handsome face with a sledgehammer, just to watch it dissolve into a mess of bone, blood, and brain matter, and then to dump the pulverized man on his wife's doorstep, so that she would understand what had taken place on the other side of the border." If this fantasy once again illustrates the Norwegian penchant for sadism, it also implies that the roots of this aggression might lie in a particular cultural experience.

The novels suggest that in failing to face up to the impli-
cations of that complicated history, Norway in particular and
Scandinavia in general have contributed to their own postwar
problems. Unlike Germany, say, which has made a huge effort to
educate its younger citizens in the horrific nature of its own past,
the Scandinavians persist in viewing themselves as innocent, or
victimized, or, in the worst cases, nobly attached to a lost cause.
As far as I can discern from these mysteries, there is very little
if any regret expressed for the national obliviousness to, and in
some cases active involvement in, Hitler's crimes.

This in turn has caused those historic memories to fester,
dispersing a kind of nearly invisible infection among the population at large. The postwar generations in Norway, Denmark,
and particularly Sweden have been very good at critiquing the
military involvements of others (they were on the Americans'
case, and quite commendably so, from early in the Vietnam
War), but they have been a bit less scrupulous about examining their own responsibilities. Granted, they currently make an
effort to justify their wars in humanitarian terms: one episode
of the TV series *Borgen*, for instance, contains perhaps the only
good argument for invading a Taliban-controlled region that I
have ever heard, while the show called *Nobel* points to the extreme differences between the cautious Norwegian troops in
Afghanistan and the carelessly violent American troops. But the
Scandinavians' unquestioned confidence in themselves as essentially good people may well have become an insidious character
flaw, blinding them at times to their own potential shortcomings
and violations.

One way in which the problematic attitudes of World War Two
have persisted into the present surfaces in the attitude toward

immigrants. As early as the Sjöwall/Wahlöö series, Swedish-born citizens were making disdainful references to Yugoslavs and Turks, the two ethnic groups that had already begun to infiltrate the local population by the late 1960s. As immigration increased, with the influx coming from ever poorer and more distant countries of origin, the Aryan-based resistance to this invasion solidified. A number of the more recent mysteries have focused explicitly on vicious Danish attitudes toward African prostitutes and Arab housekeepers, or Swedish secret societies aiming to revive the principles of Nazism, or Norwegian racists deploying their hoarded German guns, or just plain prejudice on the part of lily-white Scandinavians toward their more recently arrived fellow citizens. Some of the more political television shows, too, hinge on the growth of anti-immigrant nationalist parties, which are in turn opposed by left-wing coalitions that include immigrants or the children of immigrants among their elected officials. This may be the story of Europe writ large, but it also has a very particular Scandinavian flavor.

XENOPHOBIA is nothing new in this quarter of the world, but for a long time it had very few objects to focus its fears upon. The Sweden of the Martin Beck mysteries possessed a largely homogeneous population—so much so that if someone came in for an ethnic slur, it was more likely to be a southern Swede viewed disdainfully by a Stockholmer than any actual outsider. Casual racism against Turks and dark-skinned Americans (particularly the African-American soldiers who deserted to Sweden during the Vietnam War) prevailed in the general population, but since there were so few immigrants to fear, the expressions of such hatred were neither animated nor widespread. They were, on the whole, simply the routine prejudices of ignorant or provincial people.

By the time of the Kurt Wallanders, though, in the 1990s, things had started to heat up. Refugees were not yet pouring into Scandinavia—that didn't happen until the twenty-first century—but the sense of national boundaries threatened and breached was on the upsurge. Early on in the series, a boat that lands on the Skåne shore with two corpses in it is eventually traced to Eastern European drug peddlers, and Wallander himself is forced to travel to Latvia (depicted in all its Cold War dankness and scariness) to help resolve the mystery. A later episode involves evil doings in South Africa, including a trainee assassin on Swedish soil—but even here, the visiting black South African, though a rare sight in Sweden, doesn't seem to suffer from much overt racism, except on the part of his ex-KGB instructor.

The frightening country in this and other late-twentieth-century series is not located in the Mideast, Africa, or even southern or central Europe, but right next door. It is the former U.S.S.R. that provides many of the criminals Wallander and his ilk find themselves combatting. This fear of an unleashed Russia is also manifested in television shows such as *Bordertown*—set, as its name implies, on the boundary between Finland and its eastern neighbor—and *Occupied*, which postulates a complete takeover of Norway by Russian troops and officials. The latter show (credited to an idea of Jo Nesbø's) in many ways recapitulates the problems experienced by the Norwegians during World War Two, with "quisling" prime ministers submitting to Russian control and "Free Norway" resisters operating from the relative safety of Sweden.

For the most part, though, hatred of a specific outside nation has been replaced, since the turn of the century, by a more concerted fear of the enemy that has slipped inside the borders. Anti-immigrant feelings of one kind or another form part of the general atmosphere of most recent Scandinavian mysteries, even when they do not constitute the basis of the plot. And that bias can prevail within the police department, among the central heroes of the series, as easily as it can in the population at large. In the Department Q novels, Carl Mørck's superior attitude toward his Islamic assistant Assad might be tossed off as a humorous attempt to portray prejudice, but it is nonetheless a thorn in the side of the reader, who may begin to wonder just how a man with no last name ever got a position in the police department to begin with. And in Arne Dahl's *Misterioso*, it is Paul Hjelm's alleged racial prejudice (against an Albanian, in this case) that gets him thrown off the regular police force and into the specialized A-Unit. There he is paired with a self-described "blackhead," a Swedish-born cop of Chilean descent, Jorge Chavez, who is constantly announcing that he is *not* a foreigner, despite the way other Swedes treat him. That the narrow-minded Paul ultimately comes around to sharing Jorge's perspective, as well as to a love of African-American jazz, is part of the moral education of this main character.

A number of recent Danish novels focus on "racial purity" as the motivation of the killers. In Adler-Olsen's *The Purity of Vengeance*, for instance, a cabal headed by a crazy doctor named Curt Wad aims to sterilize any dark-skinned women seeking abortions, as a way of secretly reducing (and, its members hope, ultimately eliminating) the minority populations of Denmark. Perhaps most shocking to me, because of their matter-of-factness, were the references to Danish immigration law implied in Lotte and Søren Hammer's *The Lake*, the fourth book in their Konrad Simonsen series. I knew, from watching several seasons of *Borgen*, that Denmark's far-right political parties had been gaining power. But what I did not realize is how deeply embedded their anti-immigrant policies have become in current law. According to *The Lake* (which focuses on the importation of African women as nannies so that they can then be used as prostitutes), no African who is temporarily resident in Denmark can obtain permanent residency *under any circumstances*, including by marrying a Dane. In fact, even legal employees cannot get permanent resident status: they need to constantly renew their temporary permits. Paired in the novel with a kind of casual racism that is taken for granted among cops and TV journalists (the use of the term "nignog," for example, to describe a murdered African prostitute), these conditions make Denmark seem much less enlightened than I had previously imagined.

To a certain extent the racist attitudes in all three Scandinavian countries appear to be age-related, so one might expect them to die out, or at least die down, as time goes on. It is the older cops, the older doctors, the older farmers, the older ex-army retirees who are likely to be most virulent in their anti-immigrant attitudes. But as the Jorge Chavez situation shows, even the children of immigrants are often viewed as foreigners in these previously all-white countries. And the situation is exacerbated, at least from a police point of view, by the fact that there are demonstrable links between poverty and crime. If minority groups within the larger population are barred from the privileges accorded to full citizens, they are naturally more likely to be the ones causing social problems.

The familiarity of this vicious circle to American readers makes it no less disturbing; on the contrary, it puts us under the spotlight, too. In fact, it is by reflecting and at the same time differing from our own society, in ways that make the oddities and effects more noticeable, that Scandinavian novels allow us to see our own situation more clearly. They suggest that these problems need to be looked at with a steady eye and a firm will, for the cultural schisms are not just going to disappear. The younger generations may be more flexible and open than their elders, at least in some respects, but they will not be able to solve problems like xenophobia and racism—or, for that matter, crime—on their own. And in some cases the young may even be part of the problem.

"YOUTH culture," as it was called in my youth, first surfaces in the Martin Beck tales as something rather innocent and even appealing. The communal living, the tie-dyed clothing and long hair, the vehement protests against the Vietnam War, the agitation about the unfairness and rigidity of society—all this, from a distance of fifty years, comes across as a needed poultice applied to the body politic. Even the drug-taking and the slacker unemployment seem fairly unthreatening, though the links to heavier-duty crime are already apparent in the casual friendships between naive hippies and lifelong thieves. *Cop Killer*, the ninth novel in the Beck series, is the one in which these connections first get explored thoroughly, and by the tenth and last volume, *The Terrorists*, we are faced with a pathetic and rather likeable hippie girl who later turns into a murderer. Yet all along Martin Beck's own sympathies are increasingly drawn to the young—through his daughter, Ingrid, the only member of his immediate family he gets along with, but also through his girlfriend, Rhea, a social worker who lives and works with younger people and shares some of their habits and beliefs. The sense at the end of the series is not exactly optimistic (one would never expect anything but darkly humorous perspectives from Wahlöö and Sjöwall), but nor is it dire: things may be getting worse in many ways on the police force, but that is not to say that they are getting worse in society at large.

By the time we have reached the Kurt Wallander books, in the decade of the 1990s, the results of the so-called youth revolution have become more apparent. Drugs are rampant in the society (though this can be blamed on Eastern European gangsters as much as on pot-smoking teens); families are falling apart right and left, turning children into victims and criminals; and even the police force is increasingly divided between its younger, computer-savvy generation and its older, more traditional one. This last is not necessarily a bad thing, but it can be hard on the senior staff, as Wallander himself realizes when he considers his relationship to the very able Ann-Britt Höglund. "It seemed to Wallander that their differing views indicated something he had been thinking for a long time, that the police force was being split by a generation gap," the narrator muses from inside Kurt's head. "It wasn't so much that Höglund was a woman, but rather that she brought with her quite different experiences. We are both police officers, but we do not have the same worldview, Wallander thought. We may live in the same world, but we see it differently."

As one moves into the twenty-first century, more and more of the crimes that take place in the Scandinavian countries involve or circulate around drugs. In fact, drug-related activities would probably have overwhelmed the mystery genre if they didn't offer such repetitive plot elements—a literary rather than a social problem, and one that has forced authors to invent other and more interesting crimes to augment the basic story. Illegal drug sales cannot lie behind every murder if we are to keep reading with any degree of fascination. So the murders committed in the novels of Jo Nesbø, Lotte and Søren Hammer, Mari Jungstedt, and other talented writers feature multiple motives and a variety of complex methods—not in order to simulate reality (as was the case in the Martin Becks), but to keep us turning the pages. Still, even though they have reduced drug sales to a fraction of the total number of stories, these authors have had to acknowledge the heavier and heavier use of drugs by the ordinary citizenry, and especially its younger members. When Harry Hole's much-loved stepson, Oleg, gets caught up in drug usage, he becomes emblematic of the many teenagers hanging around the Plata in Oslo (or the Central Station in Copenhagen, or Sergels Torg in Stockholm), all living from one fix to another and causing untold pain to their parents.

It's a far cry from the young people who were trying to save the world by protesting Vietnam and capitalism in 1970, and some novels actively remark on this loss. In Steffen Jacobsen's 2014 novel *Trophy*—a clever recent addition to the Danish crime tradition—the main character, Michael Sander, contemplates the behavior of younger people who have joined the Danish military, as he too had in his youth. Part of the difference lies in the wars they are now being asked to fight, in Afghanistan and elsewhere. "Going off to fight was easy, but coming home could be impossible, especially to a country divided in its views on the necessity of the war," the narrator points out. The malaise discerned by Jacobsen (or at least by his character Sander) has as much to do with the Danish situation at home as with the battleground, for these young people seem to him to have grown up in a world without adult authority figures, and therefore without any discipline or limits. On top of that, their perceptions have been utterly distorted by the technology that surrounds them. "Until they witnessed their first real-life fatality," he concludes, "they believed that everyone would get up again, without a scratch, the moment someone restarted the computer."

To solve murders in a world of this sort—even to write or read murder mysteries in such a world—has a new and different flavor. Death is not something real, but an entertainment on a screen (even if that screen is sometimes a page of digital text rather than a video game). The intensity, the *reality* of the project that Maj Sjöwall and Per Wahlöö undertook no longer seems possible in such an environment, where everything can be manipulated or simulated. It was not just their skill as writers and their clear perceptions as social thinkers that made the Martin Beck authors able to do what they did. It was also their moment in history. They lived in a time when the forces at work were simpler, or at any rate easier to point to, and when the worst obstructions a policeman had to fear in his daily work came from his superiors, on the one hand, and the public—as represented, most conspicuously, by the ever-baying press—on the other.

ZEALOUS journalists used to be the bane of the homicide squad's existence; now they are the leading investigators themselves. Characters like Mikael Blomkvist (the crusading

left-wing journalist in the Stieg Larsson series) and Henning
Juul (Thomas Enger's crime-reporter-turned-grieving-father)
simply did not exist in the Scandinavia of the 1960s and 1970s.
When Martin Beck and his colleagues ran into print or TV journalists, such figures were always caricatures—opportunists out
to get the most outrageous news, liars who mangled every quote,
corporate employees eager to sell papers and unconcerned about
anything else. The one exception to this pattern was a journalist whom they themselves arrested for murder at the end of the
second volume in the series. When he reappeared in the ninth
book, having served his prison time and returned to his former
profession, he turned out to be the only reasonable fellow in the
journalistic pack, and they duly took him into their confidence.

Journalism as a morally suspect profession persists well into
the early years of the twenty-first century. In *The Hanging*, for
example, Konrad Simonsen and his team trick an overly ambitious and rather despicable Copenhagen reporter into laying a
trap for the murderers. Harry Hole has no time for the Norwegian press, who return the favor by characterizing him at every
turn as the policeman who once shot a suspect in a foreign country. On the TV series *Borgen*, the prime minister's press secretary
eventually turns out to be the slimiest, most disloyal member of
her entourage, and the news programs on which she must appear at crisis moments invariably come off as rigged set-ups run
by superficial ratings-seekers. In *The Killing*, a journalistic pest
named Salin, bent on collecting trashy gossip about the mayoral
election, is last seen attempting to barge his way into a stroke
victim's hospital room. *The Bridge* features among its characters
a sleazy and ambitious internet reporter who is delighted when
the killer contacts him directly. And so on.

Even the novels that showcase heroic reporters also feature backstabbing colleagues, corrupt editors, smooth-talking
corporate administrators, and occasional items of planted or
otherwise suspect news. Journalism, in other words, is never
an entirely clean sport. But *The Girl with the Dragon Tattoo* and
*Burned*, along with all their sequels, do allow Mikael, Henning,
and their ilk to represent and defend the public good. In their
persistent efforts to unearth the crimes that the more powerful
figures in society are perpetrating, these journalists are carrying out the most laudable function of the press in a democracy.
That they are doing so through vehicles that essentially did not
exist a few decades earlier—a subsidized investigative magazine
on the one hand, an internet news site on the other—does not
disguise their affiliation with centuries of brave pamphleteers in
the tradition of John Milton and Thomas Paine.

In any event, if the press is suspect for its excessive interest
in murder and gore, then so too are we, the readers of murder
mysteries. The fact that Scandinavian newspapers naturally focus on the latest killing spree does not differentiate them from
any other newspapers worldwide. If anything, they seem more
restrained than the American press and the American internet
(though a particularly horrific case, like the submarine murder
and dismemberment of the Danish journalist Kim Wall, can
drive even the Scandinavians into the gutter). What does differentiate Sweden, Norway, and Denmark from the American
case is the pure number of news outlets that are evidently available to their citizens. Oslo alone appears to have five newspapers: *Dagbladet*, *Aftenposten*, *Verdens Gang*, *Dagens Naeringsliv*, and
*Dagsavisen*. Copenhagen has its own version of a *Dagbladet*—
*Dagbladet Information*, often shortened to *Information*—as well as

other daily newspapers called *Berlingske Tidende* and *Politiken*. (My list is no doubt incomplete, in that it includes only those periodicals which have been explicitly named in the mystery novels.) Stockholm, too, must have at least half a dozen printed news outlets, given the number of journalists hounding the various homicide squads from Martin Beck's time to our own. When you add in the fact that a Dane can apparently understand a Norwegian newspaper or a Swede decipher a Danish one, and when you further count in all the television stations, current-events websites, regional newspapers, and weekly or monthly magazines, it would appear that the amount of news coverage available to the Scandinavian citizenry is considerable.

Whether it is all helpful or accurate is another matter. But to judge by the relatively benevolent role it plays in the more recent murder mysteries, the press is increasingly seen as a force for good rather than ill in these countries—perhaps even as an effective crime-solving force, unburdened by the limitations of the traditional police. After all, its reporters are practically hackers, in terms of their internet abilities. They can find any piece of information with a touch of their laptop keys, and can instantly send documents and photographs to colleagues all over the country by text. There is barely any need for plodding investigatory work anymore, when just about anything can be found, or anyone found out, from a journalist's chair.

Still, I sorely miss those old policemen, Martin Beck and Lennart Kollberg and their cronies. It's not just their thoughtful, clear-eyed humanity I long for in the present, though that is valuable in itself. It's their pace: that slower, more cautious march toward the truth that came before mobile phones and email and internet search engines and digitized archives and everything else we now take for granted. That leisurely process was essential to, and almost synonymous with, the kind of exhaustive procedures that prevailed in their line of work, procedures that in turn underlay the whole idea of police procedurals. It was a new form that filled a contemporary need, and those books made sense—remarkably satisfying sense—in the world they sprang from. Perhaps that's why I find myself constantly returning to them.

Something else seems to be operating here as well: not only my need to recapture a lost past, but also a more pressing sense that these books and others even now have something to tell me. Fictional they may be, and outdated to boot, but the Scandinavia they portray feels important to me, perhaps even essential, in ways I can't fully account for. In part because they are so aware of themselves as fiction, these mysteries have managed to ally themselves with the part of my brain that, in sorting out the difference between existence and imagination, reality and dream, often comes up slightly confused. Is there a firm line separating the two? And how obliged am I to ferret it out? It seems more important than ever, for reasons of public morality as well as private, to be able to draw a distinction between things that are made up and things that are true. And yet I'm also aware of how dependent I've become, in these difficult times of ours, on the kinds of insights that only novels can offer.

Armchair contemplation, though delightfully comfortable, comes up against these questions, these concerns, and is forced to confess its own limits. To find out whether there is any such place as the Scandinavia I've been imagining, it appears I will actually have to go there.

And that means you, in turn, will have to come with me.

I must warn you that we are about to leave the black-and-white world of the printed page for the all-color universe inhabited by living beings, and everything will be different from here on in. Among the other things that will change will be your own role in this narrative. Up to now, I've pretty much laid things out for you, accurately or not, but now it will become partly your responsibility to determine the relationship between the schematic arrangements of fiction and the more complicated truths of reality. Like Dorothy making her journey from Kansas to Oz and back, you'll need to draw for yourself the connections, if any, between the people and events of the monochrome realm and those of the many-hued one. And like a detective on an investigating team, you'll also be asked to share in the job of weighing clues and figuring out explanations. I will not, on my own, necessarily have the last word, because I and the other people we'll be meeting along the way will all become characters in the unfolding plot.

# REALITY AS FICTION

She does not have a Scandinavian bone in her body, and yet the first time she sees Stockholm, she feels she is coming home. There is no accounting for this. Granted, she has a history of falling in love with foreign cities (Edinburgh in her early twenties, Berlin in her early fifties), and Stockholm, it turns out, is even lovelier than she expected it would be, especially in the gorgeous summer light. Built on a series of islands, some hilly, some flat, and all closely connected by bridges and ferries, it has a charmingly preserved skyline of whimsical turrets, onion domes, church-like spires, and other fanciful rooftops. It is much cleaner and neater than the cities she is used to, and everything seems to work remarkably well, from mass transportation and urban engineering to public health and public welfare. There are few if any visibly homeless people on the streets or in the subways. The buses and trains, which take you quickly wherever you want to go, signal their impending arrival with clear digital signs. Inviting green parks frequently interrupt the built landscape. Just about everyone appears to speak English, and the young people speak it nearly without an accent; the level of education is obviously very high.

All of these good things and many others no doubt come into play, but at the root of her response is something much less rational. It is that she feels instantly comfortable. *I could live here*, she says to herself, even though that is probably not true.

Partly, this is the result of a self-fulfilling prophecy. Having decided, based on the descriptions in the novels, that Stockholm would be the best place to base herself, she has found an apartment in Södermalm, a short-term rental that will be hers for the duration of the trip. So one reason she feels at home here is because she *is* home, in a way that she could never be in the hotels of Oslo, Copenhagen, and the other places she plans to visit.

Even in making this relatively uninformed choice, she has lucked out. Not only is Södermalm a great neighborhood, with its varied restaurants, its cliffside views across the water to the rest of Stockholm, and its lively street life, but the apartment itself is a dream. Located on the fifth floor of an old building on Folkungagatan, it faces inward toward a vast tree-filled courtyard, so the city noise is completely cut out even as the busy street's excellent transportation network lies just outside her front door. She is amused to note that her borrowed apartment has the same five rooms as Martin Beck's Gamla Stan place: a hallway, a kitchen, a living room, a bedroom, and a bathroom. But she is sure the decor in hers—white surfaces, pale wood, and gleaming metallic fixtures—is much nicer and more modern than Martin's was. And he had no outdoor space, while she has a large, awning-sheltered balcony, furnished with a pillow-covered sofa, a table, and two chairs, where she and her travel companion (who is also her life companion) can have breakfast on the sunniest summer days.

Before they leave on their own lengthy vacation in Spain, her hosts show her how the apartment works. The waist-high refrigerator and freezer are hidden behind the same white cabinet doors as the ones that house pots, pans, and cleaning supplies; she would never have known to look there if they hadn't pulled out the drawers for her. The stove-top lights up with a reddish glow at each of the burner locations, which are otherwise invisible in the glassy dark surface. The "kettle" is one of those English-style jobs that heat up the water in about thirty seconds flat. And even the French-press pot, though it follows the same general pattern as her similar device back home, is somehow more elegant and streamlined than the functional coffee-maker she is used to.

The bathroom, too, is an engineering marvel that is simultaneously a work of decorative art. Inside the partially walled shower compartment, the floor slants ever so slightly toward the drain, insuring that no water leaks out into the rest of the bathroom. As soon as the shower water begins to get hot, a fan starts up just above the nozzle, so there is never any condensation on the mirror. The wall opposite the sink is a span of uninterrupted white tile, save for the chrome towel hooks, and this—together with the fact that all personal items can be hidden behind the mirror over the sink—lends the bathroom the same clean, empty lines as the kitchen. The room as a whole feels so light, and so reflective of light, that it will take her days to register that it has no window.

The apartment owners now take her downstairs to the communal laundry room and show her how to reserve time there. Each flat in the building has its own laundry code, and this number must be tapped into the digital screen on the ground-floor wall to sign up for a two-hour period in the laundry room. You can reserve up to two visits at a time; when you have used one of them, you can then book another, so for laundry-doing purposes, at least, you need to be able to plan your life a bit in advance. And now she understands, as if in a blinding flash,

why Kurt Wallander was always missing his time in the laundry
room. Only the most well-regulated lives can easily fit in with
such an orderly system, and Wallander's existence, with its in-
tensive overtime and its last-minute apprehension of killers, was
anything but well-regulated. She is so thrilled by this revelation,
and so charmed by the newfound parallel between her life and
Wallander's (though his apartment building's sign-up, she realizes, must have been handwritten rather than digital), that she
almost fails to take in her hosts' instructions about how to use
the laundry room's washer and dryer. She does notice, though,
that there is one strange device she has never seen before, and
when they tell her it is the mangle, she is charmed again. She has
not heard of a mangle, she tells them, in anything more recent
than a nineteenth-century English novel. As she says this, she
vaguely recalls that Sloppy, in *Our Mutual Friend*, was associated
with a mangle, and this reinforces her sense that she has now
begun to live in the world of her favorite books. Perhaps that is
partly what she means by feeling at home.

That afternoon, after her hosts have bid them goodbye, she
and her companion explore the immediate neighborhood. Two
blocks away on Folkungagatan are a well-stocked ICA super-
market and, just across the street from it, a branch of the state-
run liquor store. Far from being the dank, forbidding institution
she has imagined, the liquor store is a light, airy, welcoming
venue, with wide aisles, a huge selection of wines, beers, and
hard liquors, and an extremely friendly staff. These branches of
the Systembolaget, as it is called, are all over the place—there
are two just between her flat and the nearest subway station,
and another tucked into the nearby Södermalm food hall—and
though they are closed on Sundays, they otherwise make the

purchase of liquor an easy and pleasurable chore. The cost, too, seems comparable to prices in America: perhaps a little more for a bottle of Crème de Cassis, a little less for a good Grüner Veltliner. So much for restricting the population's intake, if that was indeed the intention.

Later, toward evening, the two of them find their way to the cliffside that marks the edge of Södermalm, a five-minute walk from the apartment. All of Stockholm, it seems, lies spread out before her, like a three-dimensional version of the map she has been studying at home. The green expanses of Djurgården stretch to her right, the museum island called Skeppsholmen lies directly in front of her, the old town of Gamla Stan and the tall Riddarholm Church stand slightly to the left, and Östermalm, Norrmalm, and Kungsholmen are all visible in the middle distance. The waterway that divides her from the city center is called Saltsjön at this point; closer to the bridge at Slussen, it changes its name to Strömmen, and then, on the other side of the Central Bridge, it becomes Riddarfjärden, leading out to Lake Mälaren. She knows from her experience of other coastal regions—the San Francisco Bay Area, the five boroughs of New York—that there must be a shift from salty to fresh somewhere along this stretch, but from her present perspective, up on the cliff, it all appears to be a single body of water. As the sun begins to sink gradually over Stockholm's glistening rooftops and spires (it is ten o'clock already, and just beginning to get dark), she thinks to herself that she has never seen anything more invitingly beautiful. Part of the beauty, for her, lies in the city's extreme legibility, the way it allows you to locate the different parts so easily and therefore know at any moment exactly where you are.

It is still not dark out when they go to bed, and to prevent the morning's bright sunlight from waking them too early, she lowers the bedroom's blackout blind and pulls the heavy curtain across the French doors leading to the living room. Still, she wakes up intermittently. Shortly after midnight, she gets out of bed and goes out onto the balcony, where the night sky is a dark, faintly glowing blue that never quite reaches full blackness. At about 2:15 in the morning, half-asleep still, she hears the birds begin their dawn-greeting song. At 3:30 a.m., now fully awake, she gets up to write something in her notebook. So as not to disturb her companion with an indoor light, she again steps out onto the balcony, where there is more than enough daylight for her to write by. Only after she has completed this task can she fall deeply asleep until morning.

I t is not jet lag, precisely, that keeps her awake, for she has already been in Scandinavia for the better part of a week. Back in America, she had decided, for reasons that now seem arbitrary—the cost of airfares, the length of flights, the timing of the opera season—to start her trip in Norway. All those reasons proved basically correct, but the real reason to begin any Scandinavian journey in Oslo is that it is the easiest place in the world to arrive.

Gardermoen Airport actually *is* as efficient, modern, and shiny as the Harry Hole novels have led her to expect. The restrooms are indeed brightly lit (some even feature live plants growing in a square on the wall) and the spacious public areas are even nicer, with high ceilings, wood-covered walls, spotless floors, and perfect signage. The passport check and baggage pickup are so fast and easy that they leave no permanent impression on her memory. And, just as Harry always did, she can take the airport express (amusingly named Flytoget, though that's not at all how it's pronounced) from the terminal into town. A uniformed man fluent in English helps her buy her ticket from a machine, using her American credit card; the trains leave every fifteen or twenty minutes, as advertised; and the trip to the city center takes only about twenty quiet, comfortable minutes, most of it through pretty, sparsely settled farmland.

At the National Theatre station, which serves as both a train station and a subway stop, she goes into one of those little below-ground stores that sell snacks and sundries. These, she knows from her experiences in Berlin, are likely to sell subway cards— and indeed, the young man at the cash register (again, fully fluent in English) helps her calculate that it is worthwhile investing in the red plastic "travel card," which covers ferries, buses, and trams as well as subways, even if she will not be in Oslo for a full week. Like Berlin's transport card, which she has always loved, this one need only be carried and shown on demand— there is no turnstile to go through, either before or after. And like the airport-express ticket, this weekly pass can be bought on credit. In fact, throughout the entire time she is to spend in these countries, she is never to touch the actual cash versions of Swedish kronor, Danish kroner, or Norwegian kroner, because everything, even the tiniest purchases in a corner store, can be put on a credit card. In this respect, the future has already arrived in Scandinavia.

Walking to her hotel in St. Olavs plass, about a ten-minute amble from the subway station, she is struck by how empty the streets seem. Karl Johans gate—which is the main shopping street in town, stretching from the royal palace grounds at one end to the parliament building and beyond—is fully pedestrian-ized for most of its length, so that explains the absence of cars there. But even the surrounding streets are largely empty of traffic, and, more importantly, of people. This is a capital city that is utterly without crowds. You might see a stream or two coming out of the subways in the morning, or strolling along near the outdoor cafés in the late afternoon, but for most of the day each city block will have no more than two or three people on it, and often entire blocks appear deserted. In a way, this gives her the creeps. At the same time, she realizes that a Norwegian plunked down suddenly in the midst of Manhattan would find the sensory overload maddening, and with good reason.

Even in that short walk, she glimpses several major locations from the novels. There is the National Theatre itself, where Rakel and Harry attend an important opening night (though Harry, as usual, has to rush off early to solve a crime). There is the *Aftenposten* tower that Harry mentions at one point, visibly rising above the other downtown buildings. There are the Palace Gardens, and Karl Johans gate, and the Rådhuset, or city hall, all of which feature in the Sveen, Enger, and Nesbø books. And there is the tall-columned university building housing the city's grandest and oldest auditorium, where Harry exposes the villain in the climactic scene of *The Thirst*.

Dropping her bags at the hotel, she strolls out again in search of Harry Hole's own apartment. This turns out to be a mere ten minutes in the other direction, through Holbergs plass (another scenic location, where the SAS hotel was featured in the *Redbreast* plot) and past a number of buildings that are obviously newly built university housing. Nesbø has always described

Harry's neighborhood as ethnically mixed and somewhat downtrodden—to emphasize, perhaps, the difference between his mundane existence and Rakel's fancier one—but Sofies gate, like just about every place she walks to in Oslo, turns out to be a quiet, clean, and almost featureless neighborhood, again with not another soul on the street. She dutifully takes a photo of 5 Sofies gate, Harry's exact address, but there is nothing special to look at here. Despite the regularly conducted Harry Hole Walks that she has seen advertised on the VISIT OSLO website, which promise that they will take you to "Sofies gate, where Harry lives," no one has bothered to signpost this small, undistinguished apartment building in any way. In contrast, on the way back along Pilestredet, she encounters a blue plaque marking the spot where Edvard Munch lived for seven years during his childhood. (The building has now, apparently, become some kind of radical center, since it bears banners and graffiti saying things like "No Sexism, No Racism, No Homophobia, No Transphobia, No Hard Drugs, No Nazis," "Solidarity from Oslo!" and "1,000,000 Dead Cops," all written in English.) She is somewhat relieved to find that the real Edvard Munch still overshadows the fictional Harry Hole.

Back at St. Olavs plass, the room is still not ready, so she and her companion have lunch in the hotel's outdoor café, facing out toward the highly abstract but nonetheless rather gruesome metal sculpture that dominates the plaza. When it comes time to pay, she asks their waiter what the tip should be.

"Oh, any tiny amount is fine," he says. "Just round up to the nearest number. We are already paid well enough."

She has never in her life heard any waiter—any employee, for that matter—say anything like this, and it reinforces her sense that she has truly arrived in a new kind of place. It makes her think of Oscar Wilde's "The Soul of Man Under Social- ism," an essay she has always loved for its unusual combination of humanity and acerbity. Both qualities appear as early as the opening sentence, where Wilde announces, "The chief advan- tage that would result from the establishment of Socialism is, undoubtedly, the fact that Socialism would relieve us from that sordid necessity of living for others which, in the present con- dition of things, presses so hard upon almost everybody." This, it turns out, is no joke—or rather, it is a joke that is also a very practical truth.

The local tipping strategy is confirmed that evening by Alix, a high-school friend of hers whom they meet for dinner at a waterside restaurant called Louise's. She and Alix have not seen each other since they were teenagers, when they avidly partici- pated in folk-dancing sessions every Wednesday, Thursday, and Friday night. She herself has long since given up the practice, but Alix (who still looks very much the same, with her straight brown hair and her sardonic smile) now dances five nights a week in Oslo. Alix has been living in Norway since the late 1970s, when she parlayed her engineering degree from Berkeley into a series of highly paid jobs with computer start-up indus- tries. Now, after two long-term relationships with Norwegian men—the first ending in divorce, the second in his death—she lives alone and works part-time.

In between tastes of crab, shrimp, salmon, and other fresh seafoods, along with sparing sips of white wine ("Alcohol is in- credibly expensive in restaurants," Alix warns), there is a crash course on Norwegian habits and traditions. Their expatriate host summarizes the history of the current royal house, pointing out that the first modern Norwegian king was actually a prince borrowed from the Danish line after Norway won its independence from Sweden in 1905. She describes the two languages that have been battling since the late nineteenth century for primacy: "book" Norwegian, which derives heavily from Danish, and "new" Norwegian, which seeks out more local roots in folk vocabulary and rural dialect. She brings up the 2011 mass murders by Anders Breivik, noting that he first killed eight people with a car bomb in Oslo's city center before heading for the island of Utøya, where he shot more than five dozen teenagers a few hours later. In smaller asides, Alix tells them that the Norwegians mainly read mystery novels at Easter, when people are stuck for a week in their newly opened summer cottages but it's still too cold to go out; that November is truly horrible and dark, but that things get better once the snow begins to fall; that the sidewalks in Oslo all have heating pipes installed underneath them, so that they remain clear of ice and snow in winter; that the center of the city is practically carless ever since parking was eliminated downtown and a toll imposed on those driving into the center; and that there is a firm class division between the wealthy neighborhoods of western Oslo and the immigrant-filled neighborhoods of the east.

"No one is poor in Norway," Alix observes, but she goes on to describe the relative hardships suffered by the waves of immigrants, starting with the Pakistanis in the 1970s and extending up to the recent influx from the Middle East. "It's hard for people with immigrant-sounding names. They don't get jobs, they don't get apartments. Here at least they're citizens"—in contrast, she means, to Germany, where generations of Turks have been kept on the margins of society—"but the press refers to them as People of Foreign Origin, and that's true even if one parent is Norwegian and they were born here."

Alix mentions the recent political move to the right, with an anti-immigrant party that has now earned an official place in parliament, having exploited a certain amount of widespread prejudice even among the general population. The Norwegians, she says, get especially worked up about the few foreigners who can be seen begging on the streets—all of whom, according to Alix, are Romanians who come in the summer months to pick up money they can send home. ("Romanians" is the word repeatedly used by the Norwegians to describe these visitors, but after looking closely at some of the people in question, she and her companion decide that what they really mean is Romany, or the Roma. It's remotely conceivable, she supposes, that all the Roma in Norway come from Romania, but it seems more likely that something has been lost in translation.)

"And what's with the graffiti?" asks her companion, who has noticed it on the sides of buildings and remarked on its strange contrast with the rest of Oslo's orderliness.

"It drives the Norwegians crazy," Alix says. "That's not anything connected to the immigrants—it predates the massive waves of immigration—but the older Oslo inhabitants are really upset about it, and they don't know how to get rid of it."

On a quick trip up to Holmenkollen the next day, she confirms with her own eyes the class divisions in Oslo. No one is poor, perhaps, but some people are infinitely richer than others. Up in the area where Harry eventually moved in with Rakel (and where there turn out to be many "dark-timbered" houses—Rakel's would certainly not have been the only one), the dwellings are enormous, the plots of land are large and well-landscaped, and the views of the Oslo fjord and the sea beyond it are stunning. It takes about half an hour to travel by subway from the middle-class neighborhood at Majorstuen, where the train emerges from underground and graffiti is still visible along the sidings, to the Holmenkollen station, which lies a short walk from the Ski Museum and a massive ski jump that marks the local skyline (both prominently featured in the denouement of *The Snowman*). As in the city center, there are almost no people on these wealthy, suburban-feeling streets. But cars, most of them recent expensive makes, are much more common here than they are downtown, and they swoop by her as she strolls up and down the curves of Holmenkollveien.

She quickly tires of the place (no wonder Harry chooses to be either indoors or elsewhere) and catches the train back down to Frogner Park—or Vigelandsparken, as the guidebooks call this part of it. There she dubiously eyes the hundreds of naked human sculptures, cast in bronze or occasionally carved in stone, that the artist Gustav Vigeland made to line the grand allée running up the center of the park. There is something very odd about this country's attitude toward the human body, she decides. It is at once celebratory and grim. Vigeland's adult figures are all heavy with muscle, and whether it's men intertwined with women or adults holding on to children, the stronger figures appear to be overwhelming the weaker ones in a seriously unpleasant way. The most disturbing statue, perhaps, is a bronze in which a dancing naked man appears to be flinging three babies off his shoulders as he kicks a fourth one with his foot. But they are all upsetting to one degree or another. When it comes to local art, she infinitely prefers the two-dimensional work displayed in the National Gallery, where she encounters, among other things, a roomful of marvelous Munch paintings as well as some lovely canvases by an unfamiliar artist named Harriet Backer.

That evening she attends a long-awaited and much-anticipated performance at the new but already architecturally famous Oslo opera house. Designed by the local firm of Snohetta and built on what had previously been warehouse-occupied land down by the water, the 2007 opera house rises from its surroundings like a white sail or a snowy glacier. The distinctive slanted roof, which is open to the public, functions at all hours as a kind of urban park where people can sunbathe or picnic or just take in the view. Made of white marble and white granite, the sloping surface appears uniform from a distance, but when she walks on it, she discovers that it is actually sliced across by a series of tiny, uneven steps, so that a slight rise or drop suddenly appears beneath one's feet, marked only by a shift from rough to polished granite. She cannot decide if this is a fun-filled game or a malevolent trick, but in either case, caution is warranted. A small sign at the entrance to the roof announces that skateboards and bicycles are not allowed, and that visitors proceed at their own risk. That, however, is clearly part of the allure in this overwhelmingly safe nation.

Inside, the decor shifts to wood and glass, with a few gestures in the direction of cracked, frozen ice on the walls of the ground-floor restrooms. Possibly the most unusual feature, at least to an outsider, is the wide-open cloakroom. Lying just beyond the restrooms, it features row upon row of numbered hooks, all completely unattended—yet another example of the pervasive honor system. She looks at her ticket and discovers that Garderobe number 1304 has been assigned to her seat. If it were winter, rather than a seventy-degree summer night, she would be able to hang her coat there and retrieve it herself at the end of the performance, all without fear of theft.

The auditorium itself is modern in style but warmly welcoming, with slatted wooden walls, comfortable seats, good sightlines, and terrific acoustics. And the prices too are welcoming: her excellent orchestra seat came to only about $70 (as opposed to the $250 or $300 it would have cost in New York or San Francisco). Unfortunately, the opera itself is nothing much to write home about. An English production of *Don Giovanni*, it features some senseless directorial tampering and a terrible Leporello—a casting flaw which, as the Swedish woman sitting next to her quietly observes, pretty much wrecks the whole thing. But the music is well-played and the experience of being there is certainly pleasant overall. Perhaps the best moments occur at the intermission, when the glass doors between the indoor lobby and the harborside walkway are flung open, and well-dressed opera patrons mingle outside with skateboarders, parents wheeling strollers, random tourists, and teenagers on their way to a night out. Like the roof, the opera's outdoor terrace is a public space, and there is no barrier whatsoever preventing anyone from going in or out. Is this ease of passage attributable to egalitarianism, or to cultural orderliness, or perhaps to simple honesty? In Norway, they can be hard to separate.

Months before coming on this trip, she had made contact with both the Norwegian and Swedish embassies in Washington, where two extremely nice women—named, respectively,

Urd and Linda—had together offered assistance in a number of practical ways. Among other things, they volunteered to put her in touch with Scandinavian writers and literary organizations.

"I don't actually need to meet writers," she had answered. "But what I could really use are police officers, and particularly homicide detectives."

"Well," said Urd, "I do have a cousin in the Norwegian police."

As it turned out, the cousin had moved on to a different kind of police job. But at practically the last minute, three days before her flight from America took off, Urd forwarded her the name of a contact—Sølvi Glendrange, senior communications advisor for the Oslo police district—who readily gave her an appointment for the first Thursday morning of her visit. In the friendly email she received from Sølvi, she was invited to show up at the Oslo police district headquarters, Grønlandsleiret 44, at 9:00 a.m. "We can take a little tour around in our main building," Sølvi wrote, "and visit our Intelligence and Investigation Department," including "the Violent Crime Section, where all homicides and attempted homicides in our police district are investigated."

And now that Thursday morning has arrived. Anxious not to be late for the appointment, she emerges from the nearest subway station, Grønland, with at least twenty minutes to spare. She has not been this far east in the city before, and immediately upon coming up from below she perceives that she has entered a different Oslo from the western area in which her hotel is located. The neighborhood is pleasantly mixed and even somewhat crowded, with lots of young people heading off to work on bicycles and on foot, but also with many more black, Asian, and Muslim residents than she has seen elsewhere. The smell of curry and other spices fills the air, as women in headscarves—with and without small children—hurry past her on the sidewalk or stop to buy things at the shops.

She walks east on Grønlandsleiret and eventually ends up at number 44, which turns out to be a large, glassily modern building set back in parklike grounds. Men, women, and children are heading up the winding path that leads from the street corner to the building, and she is so struck by the number of families that she asks one woman with a child if there is a daycare center inside. "No," the woman laughs, "they issue passports here." (Later Sølvi will tell her, "Oh, yes, at this time of year it can get very crowded with families. Sometimes we have to go down with lollipops.") She calls Sølvi on her cell phone to say she's arrived, and Sølvi promises to meet her downstairs right away.

Inside, the place does not look like any police station she's ever seen in her life. There is a glassed-in atrium that rises up to the full height of the seven-story building, and incoming civilians are dispersing in all directions from the doorway she has just entered. A tall uniformed guard stands chatting with two people next to a cubicle to her left, so she goes up to him and says, "Hi, I have a meeting with Sølvi," to which he immediately responds, "Oh, you must be the American writer!" She asks if it's okay to take a picture of the luminous interior, and he instantly says yes. Then another uniformed man darts out of the cubicle and hands her a stick-on badge with her name preprinted on it, just as Sølvi, a round-faced, smiling young blonde woman, appears. As she leads her upstairs, Sølvi informs her that not all the citizens are there for passports; some are hunters getting their required gun permits.

They begin their tour in the sixth-floor press room, which is empty now except for the two of them, but which might hold as many as forty or fifty people when it's a big case. "There are not many homicides in Norway," Sølvi says, "so every homicide is a big case."

"And would any of them be serial killings?"

"We don't have serial killers, as far as my knowledge goes. We have serial rapists. And we have—there can be several killings in a row, but not with the indicators of a serial killer as you would define it." This leads Sølvi almost immediately onto the subject of the Anders Breivik case, which she alludes to with the shorthand "22 July," much as an American would refer to 9/11. That July date, now firmly engraved on the Norwegian psyche, was the day in 2011 on which Breivik first set off a fatal car-bomb in Oslo and then, on a nearby island, shot and killed sixty-nine people, most of them teenagers attending a Labour Party summer camp. All the evidence suggests he was acting alone, spurred on by a combination of hatred of immigrants, hatred of the Norwegian Labour Party, and a random accumulation of other right-wing attitudes. It was the most lethal attack to occur in Norway since the Second World War; a survey conducted afterward found that one out of four Norwegians said they knew someone affected by it. Like the Olof Palme murder in Sweden, it is the atrocity that defines the before-and-after versions of modern Norway—though in this case the crime resulted in the successful apprehension and prosecution of the criminal.

As they move out into the hallway, she and Sølvi happen to run into one of the prosecutors who worked on the Breivik case, and they stop to chat with him. His name is Pål-Fredrik Hjort Kraby, and like all the other police lawyers, he works right there in the building. There are other prosecutors, at the regional and national levels, who work elsewhere and are brought in on the biggest cases, but these ground-level police lawyers are the ones who work most closely with the investigation teams, handling their warrants, going to court to extend custody, and so on.

He loves his work, he tells her, in part because, before getting this job, he worked for six months, straight out of law school, at a "super-boring" job in the Treasury. Then he was lucky enough to be hired on at police headquarters, where he has now been a lawyer for what he says is "a long time"—though this hardly seems credible, as he looks to be only in his late thirties. "I had very high expectations for this job," Pål-Fredrik tells her, "and they were *more* than fulfilled." He particularly likes going to court as often as he does (at the Treasury, the lawyers never appeared in court), and though most of his cases involve sexual offenses like attempted rapes or adults having sex with minors, he did get to work on the Breivik case as one of the three in-house lawyers assigned to it.

Since Breivik was undeniably guilty of the crimes with which he was charged, the only way he could have gotten off would have been an insanity defense. Yet the defendant himself desperately wanted to be tried as sane, so as to broadcast in court his personal effort to "save Norway." Two court-appointed psychiatrists initially judged him crazy, but Pål-Fredrik, after interviewing him, thought he seemed extremely logical and not irrational. Eventually a woman known as "the best forensic psychiatrist in Norway" examined him, and she declared him sane, which satisfied both sides—Breivik because he thought it would allow him to air his opinions publicly, and the prosecutors because it would enable them to lock him away for a long time.

The maximum prison term in Norway is twenty-one years, and that's what Breivik got, but Pål-Fredrik is convinced he will be in for life, because the preventive-detention rule permits them to review his case every ten years and add to his term if he still constitutes a danger to society. At the moment Breivik is complaining about his prison conditions, which, although not otherwise harsh, involve his being kept in solitary confinement. But that, argues Pål-Fredrik, is for his own protection from the other prisoners, since "killing him would be like a super-bonus, you would be a hero in the prison."

Oslo is such a small city that the prosecutor and the criminal actually came from the same neighborhood. "We went to the same junior high school," says Pål-Fredrik. "He lived one minute away from me." But their paths had never crossed before the court case, and Pål-Fredrik feels their childhoods, though geographically similar, were actually quite different, in that Breivik had "a troubled single mother" and other early difficulties. Not that Pål-Fredrik is offering this as an excuse. "No one sympathized with his actions," he says, though he acknowledges there might have been a lot of Norwegians who "sympathized with his principles: blocking immigration, the right-wing parties."

For reasons no one understood at the time—or ever, for that matter—Breivik chose as his defense attorney a then-obscure lawyer named Geir Lippestad, a man who was known to be associated with the Labour Party. "We thought maybe he wanted to kill his lawyer," says Pål-Fredrik, "so all sharp implements, even pencils, were banned from the interview room." There was no further violence, though, and Lippestad ended up doing a superb job, working to represent Breivik to his client's satisfaction and at the same time managing to heal some of the painful feelings aroused by the murders.

"He was voted the most popular man in Norway after the trial," Pål-Fredrik says of Lippestad.

"But why?"

"Because of the way he did it," interjects Sølvi. "Very human."

"A very sympathetic guy," Pål-Fredrik adds. He notes that Lippestad eventually gave up the practice of law—even though his successful defense of Breivik had brought a lot of new business to his firm—and now represents the Labour Party as a member of the Oslo City Council.

Bidding goodbye to the prosecutor, she and Sølvi move down the hall to the office of a lead detective in the homicide division, Bård Dyrdal. A smiling, solidly built, middle-aged man, dressed in a red-and-white-striped polo shirt, black jeans, and black sneakers, he greets them warmly at the door and invites them in. His office is not large (the two visitors take up the only two available seats, besides his desk chair), but it's a pleasant work space, with a bright window looking out on the expansive view and pale-wood surfaces throughout.

Bård tells her that he began his training at the police academy in 1989 and, starting in the early 1990s, he was an ordinary police officer patrolling the streets. Then, in around 1995 or 1996, he began to work in investigations, and now he is the oldest detective in homicides. "If there is a Harry Hole in the Oslo police department, it would probably be me," he jokes, alluding to both his age and his high solve rate.

Oslo, he tells her, has only about twelve homicides per year (a number that strikes her as ludicrously low for *any* city, and especially for one that has generated so many fictional killings). But it has many more attempted murders, where people who have been shot or stabbed are rushed to the hospital in time to save their lives. Bård attributes the city's low murder rate in part to the excellent trauma centers that manage to keep these victims alive. "You may be less likely to be attacked in the provinces," he says, "but if you are attacked with a knife, you are better off here." Both nationwide and in Oslo, the majority of homicides are domestic cases. In Oslo they also have a number of gang-related murders, in crime waves that go up and down—up when a new cannabis-selling gang arises and impinges on another's turf, and then down when the police apprehend the latest criminals.

Bård, though, feels hesitant even to use the word "gang." "The media calls it a gang," he says, "but it is more complex: people who have been friends before, since their childhood. The main members might be twenty or thirty years old, but then they recruit younger people from the neighborhood, brothers, sisters." He acknowledges that "a lot of these 'gangs' tend to have a foreign connection: they might be born in Norway, but their parents might be immigrants." But that fact, he says, "has nothing to do with most of these people, nothing you can do by regulating immigration. That's just bullshit. What we can do is just take care of people more, make sure the youth has something to do."

He brings out a tiny tape recorder, halfway in size between a USB drive and a small cell phone, and places it on the table. "My main tool is this little thing," he explains. "We just sit down and talk about the problems." Then, getting up from his desk, he leads her down the hall to the actual room where he conducts the interviews (and where Anders Breivik himself sat in one of the two black armchairs that face each other at a slight angle). It is nothing like her television-inspired idea of a police inter-view room. The one-way mirror has long since been covered over with a homey curtain, and the interviewing officer relies instead on a steady sequence of information and questions piped in electronically from an adjoining room. The setting is at once soothingly domestic and extremely hi-tech.

The main change Bård has noticed over time, in the two decades and more since he became a homicide cop, is that the approach to conducting interviews is now much more scientific. A corollary of this is that the police leave their options open longer, instead of zeroing in right away on a suspect or a motive. "It also means being more aware of why we do things—more aware of the flaws," he adds, noting that they frequently study their old cases to see what mistakes were made.

"Do you study the Olof Palme case, too?" she asks.

"We do—in the police academy and elsewhere, we look at the Palme case to learn what not to do. But frankly, I don't think all those mistakes could have been done in Norway, because the policing here is not that political. I think we are way beyond them in investigations, and have a more scientific approach, and are more able to learn from mistakes in the past."

His point of comparison may be Sweden, but the discrep-ancy that really strikes her is the one between Norway and America. The Oslo urban area has twelve homicides a year; San Francisco, which is comparable in size, has more than fifty, and New York has around three hundred. Could gun control ac-count for part of the difference?

"Guns in Norway are more common than guns in America," Bård tells her, "because in Norway we have a long tradition of hunting. But it's rare in Norway for people to buy guns to 'protect themselves.' That's more like the criminal mindset."

"And do the police here carry guns?"

"We could, but we normally don't. We keep them locked in the patrol car. The police in Norway are officially armed and are given permission to use their guns in what they deem exceptional circumstances. But I never use my arms. I don't even do the shootings I need to do at the firing range to keep mine up." But then, he acknowledges, he doesn't apprehend suspects. His job is to run the investigation and do the interviews.

He takes her to one of the investigation rooms, where a large table contains seats and computers for the head of investigations—that is, Bård himself—as well as for two analysts, the legal advisor, the administrative organizer, and the logwriter keeping notes on the investigation. While he's showing all this to her, another team of four, containing one man and three women, is meeting at a smaller table.

"What's the proportion of women to men in your department?" she asks, remembering all those novels with one or at most two women on the murder squad.

"Fifty-fifty," he estimates. "The leader of the homicide division is female. My leader is a female, her leader is a female, and *her* leader is a female."

For the most part, he says, these higher-ups do not interfere with his investigations, though "of course" politics sometimes enters the picture, especially in terms of the allocation of resources. "There was one case where a young beautiful Norwegian ten-year-old blonde girl disappeared and it turns out she was murdered. That investigation got a lot of resources that would not be available for other crimes. Media attention has a lot to do with it." Bård's sympathies—which are not, he feels, necessarily those of his entire department—tend to lie more with east Oslo than with the whiter, wealthier west. "I would more recognize the problems from the east side" is how he puts it. Yet he himself comes from a comfortable background, growing up as the child of a banker and a teacher who lived just outside of Oslo.

She turns the conversation to alcohol consumption in Norway. Is that a big problem?

"Yes," he says. "Alcohol is the most normal drug affecting violence overall." And this is true even though the state heavily regulates alcohol consumption, an approach that he thinks probably cuts down on the crimes of passion. "Love and hate are the key reasons for murder—and alcohol, because it lowers self-control."

She asks about the few beggars she has seen in the streets and, like Alix, he describes them as Romanians. "Their main reason why they're in Norway is they have to make a living," he says of the poorly dressed, mostly elderly people who sit begging on public street corners. "It's a visible problem, but it's not a big legal problem." Apparently Norway used to have a law against begging in the streets, but it was lifted in 2005, and the result was that beggars came in from the outside. The locals complained a lot at first, but those objections peaked a few years ago.

"People need to feel that it's someone else causing the problems," Bård observes. "Before we had the immigration, all the problems in Norway were people coming from the north to work in the south. People like *us*, they are never the problem."

After thanking Bård profusely, she follows Sølvi back down the hall to the Sex Crimes division, a fifty-five-person unit led by Kaja Lid. Kaja, a tall, thin, somewhat worried-looking woman, feels uncertain about her English, so Sølvi translates what she says. The gist of her message is that sex crimes have gone way up recently because women in Oslo now feel more comfortable reporting rapes and other abuses.

There is also a relatively new crime to deal with, which she calls "internet rape." This year they had three hundred more cases of it than last year—an increase of forty percent—and she only has ten investigators working on it, whereas it could easily occupy her whole department. Kaja does her best to publicize the crime so that more people will report it; at the same time, she worries that all the publicity about how easy it is to commit internet rape will create new predators.

"But what, exactly, *is* internet rape?"

It turns out to be a crime that takes place entirely in cyberspace. The rapist contacts his victim—almost always a child—online, and then watches through the webcam as the child, urged on by the rapist, performs sexual acts on himself or herself. In one recent case that they investigated, a twenty-five-year-old man had abused fifty-two child victims over the internet, with sixteen of those cases counting as full rape. He ended up with a nineteen-year prison sentence—in other words, just two years short of Anders Breivik's maximum—though he and his victims had never even been in the same room.

Toward the end of their conversation, she asks how many of the sex-crimes investigators are women, and Kaja estimates it at eighty percent of the department. That figure would be even higher, but all ten investigators in the internet-rape division

happen to be men. "The internet is interesting to boys," Kaja
drily remarks, in English.

Their tour of Violent Crimes has already taken nearly two
and a half hours, but Sølvi has one more person to introduce
her to. Down on the ground floor, they meet with Håkon
Johannessen, a superintendent in the Crime Preparedness division, more commonly known as the first responders. Håkon—
a good-looking, crew-cut young guy in jeans and sneakers,
who pretty much resembles Hollywood's idea of a Norwegian
police officer—eagerly brings them into his office to watch a
PowerPoint about his department. A go-getter working on his
master's degree in criminal justice, he is filled with statistics
and self-confidence.

His unit, which is on call 24/7, is responsible for going out
to every crime scene as soon as the street cops call in a dead
body, a fire, or anything else that could signal a crime. "Okay,
so maybe a person is found dead in a river," Håkon says. "Our
mindset is that, okay, it could be a suicide, it could be a murder,
it could be an accident, it could be a disease. We work on hypotheses." Their methods, he announces, are derived from those
of the Metropolitan Police in London, but tailored to the Oslo
situation. His officers collect and consider the initial evidence,
including DNA, phone data, video, fibers, witness reports, and
all the other things that are at their most "dense" at the beginning of an investigation. "The Golden Hour principle," he
calls it, and this phrase, together with "the use of hypotheses," is
peppered all over his PowerPoint presentation. The people he
recruits for his unit, he says, must demonstrate innate curiosity
and the ability to work under stress, and Håkon feels he can
generally detect such qualities during the initial interview. All

his detectives, he adds, have at least a bachelor's degree from
the three-year Police University College, and all are fluent in
English—a language they often use to interview victims and
witnesses, since many of the newer Oslo residents do not speak
Norwegian.

By this time she has been at police headquarters for nearly
half a day, and though Sølvi offers to introduce her to more people if she likes, she feels her brain is already stuffed full with new
facts and ideas. So she politely makes an excuse about having an
appointment at the Munch Museum—which she does, though
it is only a loose sort of arrangement she made with her companion when she left the hotel that morning. She is satisfied, in
any case, with the amount she has already gleaned from the Oslo
police department, whose relationship with outside writers and
journalists seems almost as open and transparent as their building's atrium. Could it all be just a trick, an illusion, to make her
think well of them? It hardly seems likely that such a complete
Potemkin village of competence, efficiency, and reasonableness
could have been assembled in the few days between their first
email exchange and her visit to headquarters—and besides, she
is nowhere near important enough to warrant it.

She has one more interview to conduct before she leaves
Oslo, and that is with a young couple, Lisa and Emre, who
are relatives of a New York friend. Lisa is Norwegian, Emre is
Turkish, and they met each other in New York when they were
both living there. Now in their late thirties, they have settled in
Oslo with their little boy, who is just under a year old.

As she walks up the hill from her hotel into the attractive

neighborhood where Lisa and Emre have their flat, she ponders the fact that she has not gotten much use out of her transit card. Everything in Oslo is so close to everything else that she has only rarely had a chance to use the superb subway system. She did, however, examine the subway map in detail, looking for a station called Valkyrien—the title of a recently exported Norwegian TV series, supposedly named after the subway station under which the thrilleresque, bio-terror, medico-science-fiction episodes mainly take place. She is only half-surprised to find that the subway station itself, like everything else in that far-fetched plot, is made up.

Emre and Lisa welcome her into their large, thoughtfully decorated flat, serve her some baklava that Emre has managed to buy in Oslo (though he apologizes for the fact that it's not as good as the Istanbul version), and take turns playing with their son as she plies them with questions about life in Norway. She comments on the fact that it must be nice to be raising their child in such a safe, protected environment.

"It's very safe here," Lisa agrees. "Yeah, but it's very boring. With a kid, safe is good, but let's see for how long. Compared to New York, which feels so free . . . I miss New York every day."

Lisa was a graphic-arts student at Pratt Institute when she met Emre, who had come to New York years before, acquiring American citizenship in the process. He now holds dual Turkish and American citizenship, but not Norwegian, because that would require giving up everything else, as Norway does not allow dual citizenship. Their son, when he reaches eighteen, will have to decide which of his three possible citizenships he wants to choose. For the moment, they are just hoping he will grow up fluent in English, Norwegian, and Turkish.

"Istanbul is a long time in the past," says Emre, who left his birthplace in 2001. "Definitely New York was my home; Istanbul came second." But now he feels settled in Oslo and is reasonably happy there. "I think it's free here too, but everything is more . . . predetermined."

"The system here works very well as long as you follow the general path," Lisa explains. "With your life choices—if you do what everyone else does, it works. But if you choose something different, you can feel isolated."

"I personally think New York is a very lonely city," Emre interjects, "but you get distracted, so it's a different kind of loneliness."

Has he ever, she asks, experienced any anti-immigrant prejudice in Norway?

"Zero so far," he answers.

Lisa points out that her grandparents came from the far north of Norway, and they definitely encountered a form of prejudice when they came south, finding it hard to get a job, an apartment, and so forth. Norway is a provincial nation, she feels, and she senses this even in her job as a graphic designer. In terms of Scandinavian design, for instance, "Norway is like the youngest sibling there. It's more happening now, but it feels very young."

The three of them now start discussing crime in Oslo, and specifically sex crimes. She repeats to them what she learned at the police station: that rape victims are now treated respectfully and are therefore reporting it more. Lisa shakes her head. "My impression of how rape is treated in this country is that it is not treated seriously. I have two or three friends who were raped, and they were almost encouraged not to report it by the police.

A lot of people feel it doesn't get followed up. It becomes a report, but it's a dead report."

Lisa thinks rape is a bigger crime here, proportionally, than in New York. She tells one story about a seventeen-year-old girl who went to a party, got drugged with Rohypnol or something like it, and then got dragged to an isolated house by three guys who repeatedly raped her. When she woke up, she made her way home and then went to a hospital, because even though she couldn't remember much, she could feel that something was wrong. But when her case went to court—twice, in fact—all three men got off on the grounds that the young woman was partying and drinking, and therefore the sex must have been consensual.

Lisa takes pains to point out that these alleged rapists "were all Norwegian." Then Emre remarks that there are all kinds of immigrant populations in Norway, and the home cultures of many of them are quite conservative when it comes to judging the behavior of women. But Lisa insists, "I don't think it's an immigrant problem."

The conversation turns to the curious emphasis on child sexual abuse, as manifested both in Scandinavian crime fiction and at the real-life police station. Why do the Norwegians, she asks, get so incredibly worked up on this subject? Why does it feature so prominently in the mystery novels?

Lisa considers this for a moment and then says, "When I think about people's reactions to sexual crimes against children—people get extremely emotional. And Norwegians are not very emotional." Her theory is that it may be a way for the authors to tap into a level of feeling that would not otherwise be available to them.

Lisa also comments on the fact that, sexually speaking, Norwegians are far behind the free-and-easy Danes and even Swedes: "We're not there at all." Part of the reason for this, she suggests, might lie in this otherwise secular country's deep connection to its established church. "We're automatically part of the church when you're born, so you have to opt out," Lisa says. "Now you can do it online, but I remember I had to make, like, four attempts to opt out."

Emre takes this opportunity to bring up Black Metal, which has been an intense interest of his since he was a teenager in Istanbul. He describes Norwegian Black Metal, which first became widely known in the 1990s, as *the* form of acting out in a counter-cultural, against-the-grain way. Metal music had existed in England and elsewhere before that, but the Norwegians made it stronger and darker. "Black Metal is a unique kind of metal music, questioning norms more extremely than most," he says. "It will deal with religion itself, and anti-religion, including elements of Satanism and occultism. The music itself, in its chord progressions and so forth, is dark."

Her ears have perked up at the mention of Satanism (shades of *The Devil's Star*), and now Emre steps into the next room to dig out some ancient underground magazines. These are old Black Metal publications saved from his youth, which he keeps stored in one of their closets. "In the early 1990s in Norway, something was happening," he says, opening the pages to show her the portraits of pseudonymous Black Metal figures and their weird symbols. "These guys—ten, fifteen, twenty guys—burned down thirteen churches in Norway. No one knew what was going on. The police didn't have a clue. There were a few murders also, members of rival bands killing each other. When the police finally connected up the murders to the church burnings and discovered that Black Metal was the source of these crimes, Norwegian music boomed. Worldwide, people associated Black Metal with Norway. Even now, it's a trademark. Fish, oil, and Black Metal are the three big Norwegian exports."

Lisa mentions that a therapist she went to in her twenties said he was not at all surprised by the Black Metal crimes, because the intense degree of repression in the culture had to come out somehow. "The social norms are in your face if you're actually looking," Emre comments, and they both bring up a recent study suggesting that Norway is one of the top five countries (the others are South Korea, India, Pakistan, and Iran) with the strongest social norms.

Another Norwegian habit that Emre proves to be an expert on is snus. She is delighted when he brings it up, because she has totally forgotten to ask about this substance, although a number of mysteries had mentioned it. Reading the novels, she had assumed that the use of this chewing-tobacco-like stimulant was perhaps class-related, something that old people in the country or less educated people in the city would do. But Emre corrects her: it's common in all age groups, he says, and more frequently used than tobacco. Snus is also notably stronger than tobacco, and Lisa brings up the fact that one of her female bosses, an art director, used to bring a can of snus to meetings to show that she was as tough as the boys.

Emre gets up to fetch a couple of cans off the kitchen shelf. They are little round tins of the sort pastilles might come in, and at the moment, by Norwegian law, the tins bear no form of decoration or bright color. (He points out that this cosmetic attempt to discourage the use of snus, like the similar attempts to limit alcohol and cigarette consumption, has not really achieved its aim; if anything, the sales of snus have gone up.) Taking a pinch of the dark-brown substance out of the tin, he shows her how you knead it with your fingers and then stick it under your upper lip, against the gum. "Unlike cigarettes, snus is socially acceptable," he tells her. "You can do it in meetings. And it can be bought in corner stores. Norway and Sweden are the only countries in Europe where you can buy it." It comes in different levels of strength, and Emre uses either 2 or 3. Level 4, he says, is too strong for him.

This leads them onto the inevitable subject of alcohol and its role in Norwegian life. Culturally, they both say, Norwegians drink a lot of alcohol when they go out, and they get very drunk. Since it's cheaper to buy wine and liquor at the state liquor store, Vinmonopol, they often drink at home first—"It's called 'foreplay,'" Emre says—and then they go out and drink more. The government taxes liquor heavily and thus has a kind of financial investment in its continued use, but at least officially, alcohol consumption is discouraged in every way possible. A non-Norwegian friend of theirs who works in Oslo as a bartender is fond of saying: "In Norway, alcohol is a crime."

A week or two later, sitting on the balcony of her borrowed Stockholm apartment and drinking her usual kir, she thinks back to that conversation with Lisa and Emre. Even as a tourist, she now realizes, she was conscious of a bit of that Norwegian repression, that attempt to impose strict social norms. If something similar exists in Sweden, she cannot feel it to the

same extent. For one thing, the consumption of unhealthy sub-
stances is not as strictly controlled here. Snus, for instance, is
packaged in brightly colored tins (she saw them arranged at an
Arlanda airport shop under a huge sign announcing SNUS), and
alcohol, though sold by the state, is not particularly expensive
or difficult to get.

Still, Sweden does seem to have at least as much of a drinking problem as Norway. The main sign of it, in her own neighborhood, is the number of red-faced men and women—most
of them clutching a cigarette in the hand that is not lifting the
stein—who drink beer all day long out in front of the cafés and
bars of Folkungagatan. The high retail prices evidently do not
prevent people from consuming alcohol in restaurants, where
most Stockholmers seem to take wine or beer with lunch as well
as dinner and even, in some cases, with breakfast. Harder spirits
are celebrated (and, in the museum bar, consumed) at the pointedly named Spritmuseum on Djurgården, the only purpose-
built museum she is aware of which is devoted entirely to the
culture of alcohol consumption; among other things, it features
semi-poetic wall captions along the lines of "What would alcohol be without / intoxication? / Without the filter and the sense /
that anything's possible. / When things get a bit dizzy. / And you
can finally let go / of the cramp of daily life." This reinforces her
notion, derived from the novels, that part of the motive behind
the heavy drinking is a desire to throw off the constantly present, deeply ingrained sense of restraint. She doesn't actually see
any passed-out drunks on the streets: in that respect, at least, the
problem is more under control than it is in, say, London or Mos-
cow. But there is a pervasive sense that the free public-health

system, which is trying to keep people alive as long as possible, is up against a cultural tradition that involves slowly drinking oneself to death.

The Swedes also seem ripe for a skin-cancer epidemic. The women, especially, appear to think it's not possible to be too tanned. In this hot weather—reportedly warmer than any spring or summer for the past two hundred years, or perhaps ever, depending on whom you speak to—they don't even have to fly to tropical resorts to toast themselves. They can just loll around for hours on the decks of ferries, or in the grassy parks, or at the tables of the outdoor cafés. Sunscreen is readily available in the local pharmacies, where the salespeople have all taken two-year degrees in pharmaceutical counseling and can intelligently advise you on what to buy, but few Swedes appear to be applying it to their own skins. She understands that after the long winter they are desperate for the sun. This is only natural. But given the length and strength of every sunny day (which is causing even her own hair to lighten to the color it was in childhood), she fears for their dermatological futures.

They are, however, lovely people on the whole, and she enjoys living among them. She is doing her best to adapt to Swedish ways—taking off her shoes, for instance, whenever she comes into her own apartment, using the cushioned bench in the hallway that has been set there for just that purpose—and she can sense in herself an ever-developing tendency to contribute to the cleanliness and civility she sees all around her.

"It's a very civilized society, a very educated society," says Dorotea, a long-ago immigrant whom she meets a few days into her Stockholm stay. "The average Swede is a decent human being."

Having arrived in 1970 as a Polish-Jewish refugee, Dorotea is filled with praise for the Swedish bureaucracy that handled her family's immigration. Sweden, she notes, was one of only three countries in the world that were taking in the persecuted Polish Jews without requiring a visa (the others were Denmark and Israel), and when they landed at the port of Ystad, her family had nothing. "We felt that we came to a very welcoming country—welcoming in a practical way. From Day One we were learning Swedish, and there were people trying to help us find a job and a home." Dorotea was sent almost immediately to *gymnasium* in Uppsala, and her academically trained parents were given state-subsidized jobs at the university there. The government also supplied them with money to buy winter clothes (they had arrived in August) and even gave them a small allowance to cover things like her mother's cigarettes, or candies for herself and her brother. "There was someone who was thinking about everything," she observes.

Dorotea knows that this is not necessarily the experience of the more recent immigrants, whose vast numbers have overwhelmed the system. But her conviction about the intelligence behind the social arrangements persists to this day. "Sweden is an enormously practical country. It works. When we talk about everyday life, it's so easy."

This does not, however, prevent the average Swede from complaining all the time. "They love to complain about the weather, the trains, everything," says Dorotea. "People feel badly treated by the winter. They take it personally when the dark comes, every November."

One needn't, it appears, wait for November to see this tendency in action. The local habit of complaining about the weather is made clear to her during a conversation with another new acquaintance, a literary agent named Tor. She has just asked him, in his professional capacity, to comment on the dark quality of so much Scandinavian noir. Where does he think this comes from? "The darkness might come from the darkness," Tor answers. "We have many, many months of complete darkness. Eight months a year, we are longing for the sun. Icy cold—minus twenty degrees Celsius—and you know it will not be light for months."

She is to have her own opportunity, six months later, to experience something of this sensation during a quick trip back to Stockholm. The mid-December nightfall, as she learns on this later visit, really does come shockingly early. By 2:30 p.m., a deep-gray twilight has set in; at 3:00 it is fully dark, with all the streetlamps and car headlights long since turned on; and they are still on at 9:00 the next morning. Because she is only there for three days, the eighteen-hour night doesn't have time to depress her, but she is aware of looking at her watch every afternoon around 3:30, thinking it must surely be time for her evening vodka tonic. No wonder the poor things have a drinking problem.

It is still not very cold at this point—the waterways aren't yet frozen, so the ferries don't have to hack their way through the ice—but already the locals are moaning about the winter. Dorotea thinks they are all acting like babies. "People from the far north of Canada don't complain," Dorotea points out when they meet again in December, "and they have the same darkness, the same cold. Swedes should focus more on the cheerful things about winter. Like Lucia . . ."

The festival of Lucia—which is actually what has motivated

this brief winter trip—manifests itself in many forms, but the version she ends up witnessing is a special December 13 concert at the grand old St. Jacobs Kyrka. The one-hour concert announced for 6:00 p.m. has completely sold out in advance, so every pew is filled by the time the lights go down at 6:05. From her seat at the very front, she watches as fourteen young women and sixteen young men, all carrying lit candles to illuminate the darkened church, proceed up the center of the nave and the two side aisles, singing as they come. They are all wearing socks rather than shoes on their feet, so the procession is silent except for the unamplified, unaccompanied sound of their mingling voices. Both boys and girls are dressed in white: the boys wearing conical white hats, the girls with red sashes on their white dresses, symbolizing the third-century martyrdom of St. Lucy of Syracuse, who was killed for her faith.

About fifteen minutes after the singers have assembled at the front, when several more songs (none of which are familiar to her) have been performed by the full group, another young woman—this one bearing a crown of seven hotly burning candles on her head—proceeds up the center aisle and comes to rest near the front pew, facing the audience. This Lucia is brown-haired, not blonde, and she has a modest, self-effacing air; as she joins in with the other singers, she takes the harmonizing alto part rather than the melody-carrying soprano. But when it's time for her to perform her solo, her rich mezzo-soprano fills the church with its unearthly beauty. "Christianity has all the best songs," an atheist friend of hers is in the habit of saying, and at this moment, listening to that thrilling voice and watching the candlelight glow on the young singer's earnest face, she has to agree. The whole experience has utterly disarmed her usual resistance to religion. The final song in the concert, sung in full chorus, is the traditional "Santa Lucia" tune (this one she *does* recognize, though it is in Swedish rather than Italian), and only when that is over do the lights come on again. As she moves past the Lucia girl, who is now standing in mid-aisle, surrounded by congratulatory friends and relatives, she sees that the young woman's dark hair is filled with white streaks of candle wax.

The winter darkness is one thing, but the trains are quite another matter: she doesn't have to wait six months to understand the local complaints about them. In fact, her mild disillusionment with Stockholm's transit system sets in after only a few days in the city.

When she first arrives at the beginning of June, she can't imagine what there could possibly be to object to. Just as in Oslo, you can buy an affordable card that gets you onto all of Stockholm's subways, buses, and even local ferries, and while it's not quite like Norway's honor system (you have to place your card on a digital reader when you enter the subway turnstile or board a bus), it's still an easy flat-rate process with no exit payments. The trains and buses run frequently enough to make trip-planning simple, and they are clean, efficient, and quiet. Many of the subway stations are inventively decorated, too, as if a whole pack of artists had been unleashed underground (which, she gathers, is pretty much what happened). All throughout her first weekend in town, she wonders why Martin Beck was always going on about the horrible subways.

Then she takes a trip at rush hour on a Tuesday morning and she understands. The train is packed tighter than any subway she has ever ridden. Even after letting the first overcrowded train go by, she has to stand all the way, squished up against the other passengers. And there is no air-conditioning. No doubt it's not needed most of the time, but it definitely makes for uncomfortable rides on these warm summer days. Luckily, the bus system is so intelligently designed, with separate lanes and even special tunnels to speed the buses along, that she is largely able to switch over from subways to buses—something she has never managed to do in any other city, even or perhaps especially in America, where riding the M1 down Fifth Avenue can practically cause her to have a heart attack with impatience.

Just as Martin Beck's complaints about the subway suddenly come to life around her, so do other aspects of his ten-book existence. She locates Köpmangatan, the address of his bachelor flat in Gamla Stan, and notices that the cobbled, two-block street is so narrow that even if Martin lived on the top story, he still wouldn't have received much light in his apartment. Later, eating at a seafood restaurant called Melander in the Södermalm food hall, she is distracted from her delicious cold salmon and new potatoes by the thought of a pipe-smoking detective with an excellent memory. As she strolls through the rest of Södermalm and comes upon a major business street called Hornsgatan, she remembers that this is where the bank robbery took place at the beginning of *The Locked Room*. (On this same stroll she comes across Bellmansgatan, the lovely street where Stieg Larsson's fictional Mikael Blomkvist lived. But though she dutifully takes a picture of the street sign, it fails to move her in any way, for Blomkvist has not seeped under her skin to anything like the degree Martin Beck has.) On another day she takes a trip out to Tulegatan, just to walk down the street Rhea Nielsen lived on, though as she reaches the end that terminates in Vanadis Park, she realizes that all of the surrounding construction is relatively new, and must therefore date from the period after Sjöwall and Wahlöö.

She also, early on, makes a beeline for Kungsholmsgatan, the street where Martin Beck occupied an office, and where the National Police Headquarters was being built during his time. "Beeline" is perhaps not the right word for the meandering path she takes through the architecturally fascinating streets of Östermalm and Norrmalm, past the grand Dramatiska Teatern with its gilded statues in front, then up Biblioteksgatan to the imposing but very accessible National Library, and finally down Kungsgatan—literally, King's Street—which leads her across a short bridge to Kungsholmen. There she is at long last able to catch a glimpse of the enormous police building, a multi-story complex which fills the entire square block bounded by Kungsholmsgatan, Norra Agnegatan, Bergsgatan, and Polhemsgatan.

Her first impulse is to capture the building in photos, and she starts with the most picturesque part: a symmetrical yellow-painted edifice dating from 1909, with arched windows, a copper-domed tower, and an elaborately carved stonework door all facing out onto Polishus Park. She then works her way around to the Bergsgatan side of the building, which—though distinctly less attractive, and painted orange instead of yellow—is still constructed out of the same kind of plaster or stone, with regular windows punctuating its five or six floors. Beyond that, however, lies the new monstrosity, which she takes to be the "ultramodern colossus" that was rising out of a pit in the Martin Beck era. This part of the block looks almost like a downtown office complex, with its three matching rectangular boxes that alternate thin strips of reflective windows with wider metallic-brown bands. That is, it *could* be mistaken for a regular office, except for the coils of barbed wire on the metal fences surrounding the adjoining car parks. The signs posted on this side say things like "Kriminalvården/Häktet Kronoberg" and "Polisen/Beslag," but since they can't be read clearly from across the street, she approaches closer to take a better picture.

At this point a bald, puce-faced, thick-necked policeman (*Bulldozer Olsson brought to life!* she thinks) rushes out of the nearest guardhouse and yells at her to stop. He points to all the signs posted around the place saying that photography is forbidden. She explains that she doesn't speak Swedish, which isn't much of an excuse since, as she can now see, the signs all feature a little crossed-out camera. In somewhat broken English, the guard indicates that she is to trash any photos she has already taken. She holds her phone up and quickly flicks through her recent pictures, slowing down when she gets to the one she took from across the street. He watches while she deletes it. Then, with a glare that is clearly meant to intimidate her, he lets her go. It doesn't really matter that she has lost that one photo—it was only meant as an *aide-mémoire*, and she can always reconstruct the building in words—but it leaves a bad taste in her mouth in regard to the Swedish police, especially in comparison to the friendly and open Norwegians.

She has already tried, in fact, to make contact with the homicide department in Stockholm, since she is hoping for an interview along the lines of the one she got in Oslo. The first thing she did was to ask Sølvi to give her contact information for her press counterparts in Copenhagen and Stockholm. As soon as she arrived in Stockholm and set up her computer, she duly sent off the two emails, and the Copenhagen one was answered within a day or two. "You shall be very welcome in Copenhagen Police . . . I am head of homicide, serious robbery, fire, sex crimes, and human trafficking in Copenhagen. I am looking forward to seeing you," says this email from Jens Møller Jensen, who gives her an appointment on the Thursday morning of her prospective visit to his city.

From Stockholm she receives only a rather formal note from someone named Stefan Marcopoulos, a press secretary at the Swedish Police Authority, announcing that "due to high work-pressure we can't guarantee anything but we will try." That is the last she ever hears from him. She fruitlessly sends a few more emails to his address, and finally calls the phone number listed in his email, which is answered by a female voice. After a bit of confusion, she makes clear to the intelligent woman on the other end of the phone, whose name turns out to be Katarina Friskman, what she is looking for, and Katarina says that what she really wants is the Stockholm homicide department, not the National Police.

They exchange email addresses, and Katarina promises to copy her on any messages she sends to that department. At the same time, Katarina gives her the name and email of yet another policewoman, Ewa-Gun Westford—this one located in the Skåne region—who is famous among her colleagues for having written a book about working in Wallander's territory. That promising interview never materializes (Ewa-Gun, who proves to be quite friendly, will be away on vacation during her scheduled trip south), but through that connection she manages to make an advance appointment with Patric Nihlén, a community police officer in Wallander's own town of Ystad.

Meanwhile, she has been working on other approaches to Stockholm. A friend of a friend knows a retired police chief named Tommy Lindström, so she emails and texts him, getting no reply whatsoever. Three separate people offer to introduce her to Leif G. W. Persson, who, they assure her, is so well-connected that he will just be able to pick up the phone and arrange a police appointment for her. "He's so powerful in Sweden, you wouldn't believe," says Tor, the literary agent. He tells her that Persson is always appearing on TV: "Every time a murder occurs, they call him. He is probably one of the three most famous people in Sweden. He's huge." But something makes her resist this tack—not just her mild distaste for Persson's Palme trilogy (though that would certainly introduce a measure of bad faith into the process), but also her fear that such a forceful and opinionated broker would influence the nature of her results. So she turns instead to her Swedish landlady, Eva, who happened to mention, just before leaving for Mallorca, that she worked in human resources at the Stockholm police department. "If you need help making a connection, I can try," Eva had offered.

In the end, after days of long-distance research, Eva offers her a contact name: Varg Gyllander, the press officer for the Stockholm police region. She instantly writes to him and gets an auto-reply saying he is on vacation for the next three weeks. Around the same time, she receives an email from Katarina, who has reached out to an officer named Bengt Carlsson in the Stockholm police; apparently he will be writing directly to her. Then Eva emails from Spain again, letting her know that "Varg Gyllander has passed your question and email address to his colleague Bengt Carlsson in the City department." Clearly this is the person she wants—but will he get back to her? She can only wait and see.

Taking a break from all this finagling, she leaves Stockholm for an overnight visit to Visby. Visby is the largest city—if you are being strict about definitions, the only city—on Gotland, which in turn is the largest island in the Baltic Sea, located nearly halfway between Sweden and Eastern Europe. It is a very old city, with a ring wall dating from the thirteenth century, and it has been occupied over the years by Vikings, Germans, Danes, Swedes, and countless others. A member of the Hanseatic League, it was a crucial trading center for centuries, though it has now declined into a state of UNESCO-preserved picturesqueness, functioning mainly as a vacation resort for mainland Swedes. All this makes it a good spot for a little jaunt, but her real reason for going there is to visit the place described by Mari Jungstedt in her Anders Knutas series.

You can get to Visby by a three-hour ferry trip from the port an hour south of Stockholm, but to save time, she and her companion decide to fly from Bromma, Stockholm's second and smaller airport. This turns out to be an adventure in itself. Bromma is such a tiny airport that once you get through security—which is notably friendly and unintrusive—there is only one big room serving all seven gates. The room is empty when they arrive but mobbed by the time their plane takes off, and the people waiting for their various local flights are all milling around in clumps rather than lining up as, say, the British or the Germans would do. (Sweden is not a queuing culture, she has observed at bus stops and elsewhere, and that initial impression is confirmed here.) But eventually they walk out onto the tarmac and ascend the portable stairway leading up to their prop plane, where, during the thirty or forty minutes it takes to get to Visby's even tinier airport, they are served free soft drinks and free sandwiches—in all ways, a trip to the past.

The taxi driver who takes them from the airport into town is a crew-cut ex-army man (his hobby is pistol-shooting, he informs them) who has strong feelings about immigrants. He is particularly worried about the number of them getting taxi permits, because police records from their home countries are unavailable and many of them may, he suspects, have criminal pasts. To get him off this subject, she points at the ring wall and asks what that is. This gives him a chance to expound on local history, which by his account is extremely bloody. He mentions a medieval crime wave that was so extreme the German soldiers had to step in and extract the criminals ("All the bad guys got executed"), leaving only the monks in residence and resulting in many years of peaceful German rule. At the end of their ten-minute taxi trip, having taken them through the southern gate to the front door of their cute little hotel, the driver activates the credit-card machine and churns out a receipt that is nearly a foot long. "That's Sweden for you," he says in a disgusted voice.

It's about ten o'clock in the morning, and the mostly pedestrian streets of ancient Visby are deserted. Apparently the first cruise ship has yet to arrive, though the town is clearly ready for them, with gift shops that open at 11:00 a.m. and a vast supply of public WCs. She and her companion stroll around the cobblestone streets, entering and leaving the intermittent plazas and finding their way through numerous skeletons of churches.

Only the major cathedral, Santa Maria, which was originally constructed as a Catholic church but then converted to Protestantism after the Reformation, has been preserved intact for continued use; the rest of the churches have fallen into beautiful ruins which romantically punctuate the landscape. The old town is almost ludicrously charming, and aside from a few modern buildings located near the water—the Wisby Strand Conference Hall, the library, the Wisbygymnasiet—nothing mars the illusion of timelessness.

Outside the ring wall is another matter, though. There lies modern Visby, including the nondescript police station, which she duly snaps on her phone (though secretively, in case another Bulldozer Olsson lies in wait). For the most part the newer section of town is low-built and suburban, dominated by ugly buildings, rigorously straight streets, and huge parking lots, with a pedestrian mall that runs down its center and features McDonald's and other cheap corporate outlets. Architecturally and aesthetically, nothing could look less like ancient Visby, but this is obviously where the majority of people live and work. Do they envy the few who have homes and jobs within the ring wall, or do they feel somehow superior to these parasites of the tourist industry? Jungstedt's novels give her no clue.

In the course of the day, she pays an extended visit to the Gotland Museum, which is filled with fascinating things. The history it depicts ranges from the prehistoric to the much more recent, with an emphasis on the Viking and medieval periods. On display is, among other things, a nine-thousand-year-old male skeleton, still holding the sleeping position in which he was buried. The museum confirms that violence is as integral to the island's history as the taxi driver suggested it was. He had mentioned the deadly Danish invasion, for instance, and here it is, introduced by a wall that shows the date 1361 written in dripping blood. And though the talkative driver's medieval "criminals" turn out to be pirates, the story of their defeat by Teutonic soldiers is much as he described it.

Her favorite things in the whole museum are the picture stones dating from the seventh century and earlier. Visby has a huge collection of them in all sizes and designs, and she lingers for a long time among them, admiring the artful depictions of horses, humans, birds, dwellings, tools, and ships, along with some more abstract designs. "Picture stone imagery provides us with a unique insight into prehistory," the wall captions say. "Apart from religious beliefs, myths and legends, they convey details and realistic depictions of people's appearance, dress and activities, as well as the various constructions and uses of ships, houses and weapons." In that respect, she thinks—as useful evidence about the culture that gave rise to them—they are not all that different from modern Scandinavian mystery stories.

Next she drops in at the local art museum, which is only one street away from the Gotland Museum. The recent art displayed here is not as compelling as the picture stones, but then very little is. Because it is Ingmar Bergman's hundredth anniversary year, and because he spent most of his later years on Fårö, the smaller island just to the northeast of Gotland, the art museum is featuring his life and work in two out of the three current exhibitions. An assortment of contemporary artists have been invited to construct various forms of homage to him, and though one or two have done something interesting (she particularly likes the detailed architectural paintings based on Bergman's study), most of the results will probably never be shown again after the anniversary year is over.

That night, after an excellent dinner at a friendly, locally recommended restaurant, she and her companion wander down to the waterfront. The town of Visby, which is built on a steep hillside, slopes down to a harbor on the western edge of the island, so nightfall on a summer evening offers a spectacular sight. As the dying sun descends toward the horizon, reaching and then gradually disappearing into the seemingly endless expanse of the Baltic, its fiery intensity causes the undersides of the clouds to glow rose and the white building facades to turn bright gold. The setting seems like something out of a fairy tale or a dream, with the unearthly lighting effects augmented by the eerily quiet lapping of the waveless sea on the shore, and for once she feels she is experiencing something completely new. It is a good feeling, but also a faintly terrifying one—as if to suggest that there are more things in heaven and earth than are dreamt of in her philosophy.

The whole time she has been on Visby, she has been re-reading *Killer's Art*, a Jungstedt novel whose plot she had almost forgotten. She is pleased to be reminded that here too, as in so much other Scandinavian fiction, original artworks form an essential element—in this case *the* essential element, as the title suggests. The book places both the killer and the victim within the Swedish art world, and while moving between Visby and the larger Stockholm galleries, the plot also manages to go back in time to some of the famous artists of the early twentieth

century. One story in particular captures her fancy, and that is
the tale of a woman artist named Ellen Roosvaal von Hallwyl,
a noblewoman who left her first husband—the military attaché
Henrik de Maré, with whom she had one son, Rolf—to marry
her son's tutor, Johnny Roosvaal. In 1915 she and Johnny together built a dream house called Villa Muramaris on Gotland.
A painter and sculptor, Ellen Roosvaal decorated much of the
house and garden with her own work; of particular note was
the sandstone fireplace, framed with and surmounted by a series of iconic human figures. According to *Killer's Art*, Rolf de
Maré (who only outlived his mother by a dozen years or so)
was particularly attached to the villa and spent many summers
there, in the company of close friends like the artist Nils Dardel,
whose painting *The Dying Dandy* is one of the modern period's
emblematic works of homoerotic art.

Villa Muramaris turns out to be a real place, located only
about five kilometers from Visby in the approximate direction
of the airport, and though Ellen died in 1952, the house has apparently been preserved intact by the subsequent owners. Eager to see
this fragment of a fictional world that also belongs to the real world,
she directs the taxi driver to take them to Villa Muramaris on the
way to their flight back to Stockholm. But the taxi driver—a
brusque local woman with very poor English—informs her that
the house burned down a few years ago. Hinting darkly at her
theory that it was not an accident, but arson, the driver claims
to be the person who first noticed the smoke and called the fire
department to the scene.

Undaunted by this news, she still insists on going there,
and it turns out that the current owner is restoring the building and has nearly finished with the major renovation work. He

will, in fact, be holding a party there later that day, and because
the house is being opened anyway, he allows her to go in and
quickly see the place. Much of the detail still remains to be
done, but Ellen's fireplace has already been fully rebuilt, and
she is very glad to have seen its male and female figures brought
back to life. There is a lovely, slightly overgrown garden, too,
which is filled with sculptures that did not get destroyed in the
fire. Both the house and the garden overlook the nearby Baltic,
whose shore is accessible via a downward-sloping wooded path.
She does not take the path (she does not have time before her
flight back to Stockholm), but even from up here she can catch
glimpses of the dark-blue sea shining through the trees.

As she wanders among the oddly appealing sculptures sprinkled around the garden, she is struck by the intensity of the
human figures. Their poses, their expressions, are not wholly
realistic, but nor are they abstracted to the level of form. They
represent people whose emotions range from joy to sorrow to
somewhere in between, and whose gestures always express those
emotions. These are very different from the agonized statues in
Oslo's Frogner Park—they are much gentler and more good-
humored, for one thing—but they share with the Norwegian
work that sense of intense expressiveness. This, she now realizes,
must account in part for the Scandinavian attitude toward art. It
offers one way, in what is clearly a rather repressed or at any rate
formal culture, for people to experience and generate feelings
that might otherwise remain tamped down inside.

When she returns to Stockholm, she makes a point of visiting a museum that features some of the early-twentieth-century
artists mentioned in *Killer's Art*. The Thielska Galleriet, designed
by the prominent architect Ferdinand Boberg and initially

constructed as a private house, has been open to the public ever since Ernest Thiel, the original owner, went bankrupt and persuaded the Swedish government to take over the building in 1926. It still houses work by all Thiel's artist friends, including Prince Eugen, the king's brother, as well as Bruno Liljefors, Anders Zorn, August Strindberg, Edvard Munch, and others. (It does not, however, contain Nils Dardel's *The Dying Dandy*, which is owned by the Moderna Museet on Skeppsholmen, but luckily she has already been there and seen that.) Since the Thielska is located on the far tip of Djurgården, she takes a ferry to get there, an added pleasure—and a very common one, in Stockholm—that helps put her in the proper frame of mind for her immersion in this early-twentieth-century world.

The art, as it turns out, is only part of the attraction. It is the house itself and the arrangement of the artworks within it that account for the special feeling of the place. Some of the paintings, particularly those in the grand Munch salon, are terrific; others are of merely local interest, though even these have a certain appeal. About halfway through her stroll around the galleries, she comes upon a 1905 Bruno Liljefors landscape containing a single grouse in the foreground, and she is so struck by the parallel to old Mr. Wallander's art that she can't help snapping a photo of this relatively minor work. She is amused to see that just by taking the photograph, she has caused the nearby museum patrons to examine the Liljefors more closely, as if they hoped to discover something in the picture that would warrant this degree of attention.

Later, in a conversation with Tor, the agent who represents many of Sweden's mystery writers, she brings up the outsized role that original artworks seem to play in the novels. Tor looks surprised and even slightly chagrined when she asks if buying art is a common Swedish habit. "I buy art," he confesses. "Last year I bought two limited prints and a sculpture. I just love it when the arts are figured in books." But he doesn't feel that he, as a recently minted gatekeeper to mystery-series publication, can be held responsible for imposing his personal taste on the novels. After all, books like the Wallanders and even the long-ago Martin Becks alluded to the artworks found in Swedish homes and offices many decades before he became an agent. Instead, he thinks, the inclusion of these references has something to do with the function of art as an indicator of individual personality or social class. "I love all mentions of culture in books: what they are wearing, what they are eating, what they have on their walls. Do they have a Bruno Mathsson table or IKEA? It says very much about the main character."

She points out to him that very few American mystery readers would recognize the name of a specific furniture designer. Cars, yes; maybe couture-house clothing; perhaps even expensive watches—these class indicators would be recognizable in America. But artists? Not so much.

He counters by reminding her of Michael Connelly's Harry Bosch, whose given name is Hieronymus. She is a bit shocked that she's forgotten this example, and wonders how many others she's ignored. Perhaps, she worries, there are more analogies between American and Scandinavian mysteries than she had supposed. Maybe her whole belief in the distinctiveness of the form is built on an illusion. But then she remembers that Michael Connelly himself had described Maj Sjöwall and Per Wahlöö as among his primary influences, so he too might be said to come out of Nordic noir. She doesn't voice this theory, though, because she doesn't want Tor to knock it down.

One day, back in Södermalm, she decides to walk over to the mosque. It is a sign of how significantly Stockholm has changed, in the years since Martin Beck inhabited it, that there even *is* a mosque, especially one of this size. Founded in 2000, after years of discussion between the city council and the growing Islamic community of Stockholm, the Stockholm Grand Mosque occupies the old Katarina power station—a rather lovely brick structure which was originally designed (again by the ubiquitous Boberg) in a style the architect viewed as "Moorish." The building is located on a short street called Kapellgränd, and she approaches it from the direction of Katarina Kyrka, the largest and oldest church in the neighborhood, which is just around the corner from the new mosque. This allows her to admire the series of beautiful double-height arched windows—each outlined with a fan of radiating bricks—that line this side of the prayer hall, and there she can also read the engraved words "Stockholms Electricitetswerk Katarinastationen" that still remain over what was once the main door.

Now, however, the mosque is entered on the adjoining side, through a smaller door that leads directly into an anteroom. She waits there, aware from her experiences in India and Bangladesh that women are not always welcome in the prayer hall itself. An elderly man, clearly someone with official status at the mosque, approaches her with a questioning look, and she says she would like to see inside the prayer hall, if that is at all possible, and offers to take off her shoes. At first the elder shakes his head, but then he changes his mind and allows her to come to the open door of the worship space and stand there for a minute, without going in. From her post, she can see a vast room flooded by light from the arched windows and divided into sections by a few shorter walls. On the floor are numerous praying figures on their prayer mats, all facing east; even as she watches, more come in. "Ramadan," explains the elder, answering her unasked question about why there are so many worshippers in the middle of a regular weekday.

She knows, from talking to her new Stockholm acquaintances, that relations between the original Swedes and the more recent Muslim immigrants are not entirely happy. During the four years extending from 2014 through 2017, when waves of refugees fled the wars in Syria, Afghanistan, Iraq, Somalia, and elsewhere, Sweden took in over half a million immigrants—more new residents, relative to its population, than any other country in Europe. This sudden influx put tremendous pressure on the nation's health and welfare resources. In Stockholm's northern suburbs of Rinkeby and Tensta, in particular, the concentration of refugees and the absence of sufficient social services led to poverty, crime, and gang shootings. Schools there are still filled almost exclusively with immigrant children, with no way for them to learn Swedish from their peers, and the parents of these kids are largely unemployed. For a while the police and ambulances were even afraid to go there, and the residents suffered accordingly.

Things seem slowly to be improving in the northern suburbs, now that so much attention has been called to the problems there. But the political effects on the culture at large have meanwhile continued to worsen. Both in Stockholm and nationwide, there has been a definite move toward the far right, with the anti-immigrant populist party, who call themselves the Sweden Democrats, making major inroads among voters. In the 2014 elections they gained enough power, as the third-largest party, to force the weakened Social Democrats to tighten border controls and limit immigration. Now, in 2018, it is feared that the extreme right might become the official opposition—or, even worse, lay claim to the government—after the September elections.

"It's scary," Dorotea says about the new, brutal attitude toward outsiders. "I think it will switch again, because I know that the Swedes are not racists. They got scared. We were ten million people receiving 160,000 a year." Dorotea is particularly attuned to the problem, having witnessed the difference between the welcome her family received when they arrived from Poland in 1970 and what is happening now. "My father was in love with Swedish democracy. He always said it was democracy with a human face. But all of a sudden it collided with reality. The ability to change quickly is not there."

During the whole of this visit to Stockholm, she herself has witnessed only one outright example of Swedish racism. One afternoon, while riding the 76 bus from her neighborhood into the center, she became aware of an Asian family speaking what sounded like Chinese a few seats away. Hearing foreign languages on Stockholm public transport is not in any way unusual: on almost all her subway rides she sees headscarved Muslim women animatedly speaking into their cell phones in Turkish, Urdu, or Arabic, or young men chatting with each other in a mixture of some African language and Swedish. But on this particular bus there was also an elderly, prune-faced Swede who, passing the Asian family on his way out the back door, began jabbering away in his own imitation of Chinese. Every time the family members spoke to each other, he jabbered again, and his message was clear: *You are an intruder. Learn Swedish or go home to your own country.* She felt an intense desire to yell at this stranger—to express her anger at him viscerally, in a way that years of living in New York have trained her never to do—and only her sense that he was obviously a bit crazy enabled her to calm down.

It's true that she herself doesn't speak Swedish, so she may be missing all sorts of racist comments that are uttered *sotto voce.* But her sense of the culture, overall, is that she is missing less than she expected to. Before arriving, she'd realized that her access to Scandinavia through mysteries had been due entirely to the work of able translators, and in their absence she worried that she might feel utterly excluded, kept out by the impenetrable wall of language. This has turned out not to be the case, in part because of the prevalence of English, but also because her eyes can tell her things even when her ears cannot. She recalls hearing someone once say (though she can't remember if that someone was a psychologist or a theater director or simply an amateur observer) that if you watch television with the sound off, you can instantly tell the difference between a real person expressing himself normally and an actor playing a part: that is, the actor's gestures will ring false in a way that his words may not. Perhaps being in Sweden without knowing Swedish gives her a similar kind of blinkered, distant insight.

Leaving the mosque now, she catches the subway to Hötorget, where she emerges from underground only steps away from the spot where Olof Palme was assassinated in 1986. Near the corner of Sveavägen and Tunnelgatan, set flush with the sidewalk paving stones, is a brass plaque that announces (in Swedish, but even she can puzzle it out): "On this spot the Swedish Prime Minister Olof Palme was murdered on the 28th of February, 1986." Sveavägen is a very busy street, and pedestrians are rushing quickly along the sidewalk, ignoring the plaque and often stepping directly onto it. At one point two businessmen in suits carry on a long conversation during which one of them stands directly on the bronze rectangle without ever looking down. He is still standing there when she crosses to the other side of Sveavägen, where another side street, the extension of Tunnelgatan, has been renamed Olof Palmes gata. There are many such locations throughout the country—along with similar places named after Anna Lindh, another important politician who was assassinated in Stockholm in 2003—but it is clear that on a daily basis, in the very spot where he died, people are no longer thinking about this catastrophic murder.

The Swedish Parliament, over which Palme once presided (and where the pitched battles between his Social Democrats and their right-wing opponents are even now taking place), turns out to be located all by itself on a tiny island called Helgeandsholmen. The Parliament building lies just across a short bridge from Gamla Stan, and she only encounters it by chance when she happens to be on a walk there. She notices how imposing the building looks, which causes her to ask the guards in front what it is. They answer her politely, though clearly it is part of their job to keep strangers like her from barging in uninvited. (Swedish guards, she has discovered, are on the whole much friendlier than their British or American equivalents. When, early in her Stockholm stay, she found herself lost in front of the Royal Palace, she had asked the uniformed guard, who *looked* as formal as the famously unresponsive fellows guarding Buckingham Palace, "Are you allowed to talk to me?" Somewhat to her surprise, he answered, "Sure," and then, abandoning both his martial bearing and his post, came forward a few steps to take her map out of her hands and show her where she was.)

She never does manage to get inside the Parliament. But later she pays a visit to Stockholm's City Hall, a strikingly attractive brick building which was constructed during the early-twentieth-century reign of King Gustav V. This is where the Nobel Prize banquet is held every December, and the grand ballroom in which that event takes place—the Blue Hall, their tour guide calls it, though it is actually colored rose and beige—is suitably impressive. Even more beautiful, in her eyes, is the vast chamber devoted to the weekly City Council meetings, with its intricate wooden fretwork supporting a gloriously painted ceiling. On either side of the long room are high wooden galleries holding benches for the public and the press, while the elected council members sit in curved, concentric rows along the length of the room, facing a slightly raised president's podium that is in turn backed by a geometrically patterned wall. The left-wing parties, currently in the majority, traditionally occupy the left-hand side, while the right-wing parties sit on the right—and the woman who is leading this particular English-language tour takes pains to stress that this is left and right from *their*, the people's, point of view, and not from the president's. She also mentions that the current council of 101 members is pretty evenly divided between 51 men and 50 women. All this, of course, could change after the September local elections, which are held every four years, at the same time as the national elections.

The guided tour (from which one is not allowed to stray, for security reasons) next leads through a long corridor called Prince Eugen Hall, named after Gustav V's brother, who did the murals and the bas-relief sculptures that adorn that space. The murals are in the usual Scandinavian post-impressionist colors—greens, blues, pale ocher, and pale rose—and they depict a watery view that is meant to correspond to the actual view of Lake Mälaren one sees out the tall windows opposite. On either side of the window embrasures are bas-reliefs of male and female figures, naked and in semi-classical poses. These male-female pairs, the guide says, are meant to mirror each other across the window openings, just as the mural mirrors the view—and some people have even suggested that the male-female theme is picked up in the series of paired columns, one round and one square, that divide the room longitudinally. As the guide moves the rest of the tour group along, she lags behind to photograph the art and think about this notion of a mirroring that is not an exact mirroring. There is something useful here, in the idea of a paired asymmetry. After all, what is she herself doing but forging unmatched pairs out of such entities as Sweden and America, or fiction and life?

Emerging from this dreamy thought process, she sees that she has been left all alone in Prince Eugen Hall. So much for staying with the group. She races to the end of the corridor and, turning right, finds herself in the grandest space of all: a triple-height marble-floored ballroom, surrounded on all four sides by gold-colored mosaics and filled with small clumps of people. Going up to the nearest clump, she asks their leader where the English-language tour has gone. The man looks around and then says, "There," pointing at a small Union Jack held aloft by her original guide. She gratefully rushes over and merges with the group just in time to hear the history of the gold mosaics.

Designed by the artist Einar Forseth and installed under extreme time pressure in the last two years before the City Hall opened in 1923, the images on the walls pay tribute to various aspects of local, national, and general human history. Just under the roofline and above the stained-glass windows, for instance, is a long parade of figures meant to symbolize the life of mankind, from birth to youth to mature strength to the feebleness of old age. On the far wall is a single gigantic rendering of a wide-eyed, snaky-haired Queen of Lake Mälaren, holding a crown in her right hand, a scepter in her left, and what appears to be a reduced version of the City Hall in her lap, while another recognizable totem—a tiny image of the Statue of Liberty—peeks out from the lower-left corner of the mosaic square. Around on the other long wall, the one closest to the spot where her tour group is currently standing, is a fanciful series of birds, animals, and humans, with individual panels designed to honor specific heroes of Swedish history, including statesmen, scientists, artists, and so on. Drifting toward that nearby wall, she spots a Greek-garbed figure carrying a mask of comedy and accompanied by the inscription "Aug. Strindberg." She is pleased to note that even though Strindberg died as recently as 1912—less than a decade before the mosaics were designed—he was considered famous enough to join the immortals.

———

Strindberg has been dogging her footsteps in various ways ever since she got to Stockholm. He is not a writer she ever thought much about before, or if she did, she thought of him mainly as the author of painfully agonistic, somewhat schematic plays in which men and women said terrible things to each other. Here in the city of his birth and death, however, he becomes much more palpable, if not indeed ever-present. Since arriving, she has learned that he was not just a playwright, but also an accomplished novelist and—even more surprising—an excellent painter. She has looked at and admired his paintings in the Moderna Museet and the Thielska Galleriet, and she has been slowly reading his gloomy, satiric, rather clever early novel, *The Red Room*, over the course of her trip. Now, she decides, it is time to visit his house.

She has an ulterior motive for this visit, in that she is hoping to see a tile stove. This and the ubiquitous "Falun red" are the two items of traditional Swedish home decoration she had particularly wanted to witness in person during her time in Sweden. Falun red turned out to be easy. It is sprinkled all over the Stockholm archipelago (not to mention Norway's fjord landscape), and she now has many photos of barn-red country cottages stored on her phone. "Is this Falun red?" she asked Dorotea at their first meeting, showing her one of the recently taken snaps, and Dorotea nodded yes. A short lesson on the role of the color in Swedish history—its origins as an imitation of British and Continental brick, its nominal connection with the town of Falun, capital of the *echt*-Swedish district of Dalarna—soon followed, and that was that.

But the tile stove is proving more elusive. She has not penetrated to the interior of any Swedish dwelling except the one she occupies, and that flat is so modern that no heating system is visible at all. Perhaps the Strindberg Museum, located in the apartment the writer occupied during the last four years of his life, from 1908 to 1912, will have a tile stove.

Unfortunately, it turns out that Drottninggatan 85, the address of Strindberg's final home, was a newly built apartment building at the time he moved in, complete with all the modern conveniences, including radiators in each room, electricity instead of gas, and even an elevator just like the one in her Folkungagatan place. The building itself is still residential in appearance, with no signage on the outside except for the house number, and most of the apartments are occupied by individual residents or small businesses like lawyers' offices. Only inside the entrance lobby can one find a discreet sign announcing that the Strindbergsmuseet is on the fourth floor.

Before going into his "home"—the part of the museum that has been preserved exactly as he left it—she is asked to put on blue paper shoe-covers to protect the carpeting and the wood floors. Garbed in her paper booties, she can't help imagining herself as a forensic detective assigned to investigate the Case of the Dead Author. And in fact it does really seem as if Strindberg has only recently departed. His possessions, and especially his rather cluttered desk, with its quill pens, its brushes, its notebooks, its family photos, and even a pair of spectacles laid neatly across the blotter, have been preserved exactly as they were when he lived there.

She has always considered Strindberg, when she considered him at all, to be a severe misanthropist leading a lonely life of despair. She is surprised, therefore, to find that he had in his apartment not just one but *two* telephones: one to make calls within the building (including to the fifth-floor restaurant, from which he had all his meals sent down, since there was no kitchen in the flat), and the other for outside calls. A *Stockholm Telefon* directory hangs on a chain nearby, and just next to the phone is a scribbled list of frequently called names and numbers in Strindberg's own handwriting.

His drawing room, too, is a testament to his active social life. The largest and best-lit room in the flat, it has seating for eleven people, not counting the person on the piano stool. According to the museum handout, that pianist was generally his brother Axel, a skilled musician who often performed for Strindberg's "Beethoven Fraternity." As if to invoke their ghostly presence, Beethoven's death mask, carved in black stone, still hangs over the piano, while the score of his Op. 27, No. 2 sonata sits open on the rack above the keyboard. These intimate performances, accompanied by food, drink, and lively conversation, no doubt derived at least part of their convivial atmosphere from the room's elegant appurtenances, among which she notes some distinctive if idiosyncratic artworks, several items of antique-looking wooden furniture, flocked wallpaper in tones of burgundy and gold, and an ornate oval mirror.

It all forms a definite contrast with the monastic bedroom located just next to it, with its single bed, its small bedside table, and its simple assortment of wooden furniture, including a chair, a bookshelf, and a wardrobe. The bedroom's most appealing feature is its two full-height, side-by-side windows, one of which is actually the upper part of a door leading out to a private balcony. From this perch, on January 22, 1912, Strindberg greeted the torchlight procession of nearly fifteen thousand people who had assembled to celebrate his sixty-third birthday. "So that the procession will be able to identify my particular balcony," he wrote to a friend, "I shall place my most beautiful electric lamp there with its red eye pointing toward Tegnérlunden!" That, as it turned out, was to be his last birthday. He died of gastric cancer a few months later, in May, and an estimated sixty thousand people—a fifth of Stockholm's population at that time—lined the streets to watch his coffin being carried to the graveyard.

She does, in the end, manage to locate a few tile stoves: one a simple, square-cornered, white-tiled one, in the old Gamla Stan apartment being rented by friends visiting from San Francisco, and another—several others—in the nearby Royal Palace. Her American friends have suggested this visit to Stockholm's Kungliga Slottet, and even she, a resister of palaces in general, has to admit it's impressive, with its endless corridors filled with inestimably valuable goods. The tile stoves here, like the white one in her friends' flat, reach from the floor all the way up to the ceiling, with a little square door for wood at the bottom. But unlike the merely domestic one, many of the royal stoves are rounded in shape and encased in arched niches, and all are made of elaborately decorated colored tiles. They hardly seem big enough, though, to supply the heating needs of such grand rooms. Perhaps, she concludes, the royals of the eighteenth and nineteenth centuries were in the habit of dressing warmly.

It is here, in the Royal Palace, that she encounters yet another significant deathbed scene: the chamber where King Gustav III died after being shot in 1792. Now that she knows a bit more about Gustav III, she sees a certain irony in his manner of death—a gunshot wound received during a masked ball at the opera house—for this particular monarch was nothing if not histrionic. He often insisted on taking the lead role in his own private theatricals, which could go on for many hours at the Drottningholm Palace Theater (an eighteenth-century gem that had been built under the direction of his mother, Queen Louisa Ulrika). Then again, he made everything in his life into a stage set of sorts, including the pavilion he built for himself at Haga Park, as well as the original Royal Opera House, one of his many artistic commissions. As Mark Twain would say, he knew how to "spread himself." He was also an extreme autocrat, who fought against giving up any of his power even to the Swedish nobility, and who explicitly allied himself with other princes in an effort to defeat the French Revolution. It makes sense that he was the first cousin of Catherine the Great of Russia, in that their attitudes toward unlimited monarchical control and royal aggrandizement through cultural expenditure were remarkably similar.

The current King of Sweden, Carl XVI Gustaf, is a horse of an entirely different color. Genial and courteous, he rules—if that is the right word for a democratically overseen monarchy—with a light hand, presenting himself as someone who is essentially equal to his subjects, even if he happens to possess a lot of money and privileges that many of them lack. (In this respect he seems influenced by the widespread Swedish principle known as "the Law of Jante," a term that has been explained to her by one local informant as meaning "Everyone is the same, you're nothing special, don't put on airs.")

Though she is no fan of royalty in general, she has nothing against the king personally. Still, she finds herself intermittently put out by the monarchy's continuing hold over Sweden. There are even a few occasions when her own schedule has been inconvenienced by the royal family's activities. The weeklong pomp attendant on Princess Adrienne's christening, for example, prevented her from getting inside the palace on the day she was out at Drottningholm, and she had to content herself with a visit to the perfectly preserved (and still active) eighteenth-century theater. There was also the time, back in Stockholm, when the king's "Sweden Day" speech in the city center caused the 76 bus to suspend its service midway through June 6, thereby forcing her to walk miles to the subway station.

Such glitches, she admits, are minor, and they could easily happen—*do* often happen, in fact—when an elected American president makes an appearance somewhere. More irritating to her is the tiresomeness of encountering the Royal This and the Royal That wherever she goes. And most annoying of all is the grand style of architecture and design she has come to associate with the Scandinavian monarchs, Norwegian as well as Swedish. Standing in the gardens of Drottningholm Palace on a hot summer day, with wide gravel paths and clipped hedges extending practically to the horizon in all four directions, she decides once and for all that a little of this fearful symmetry goes a long way. Its effect, if not its intention, is to make the carriage-less commoner, the poor, bare, forked human, feel tiny and unimportant.


I t is only when she travels to Copenhagen that she has a sense of escaping from this mildly oppressive monarchical influence. This is not because Denmark is any more of a pure republic than the other two countries. On the contrary, it too has its royalty, presently embodied in Queen Margrethe II and her son

Crown Prince Frederik. But there is something about the urban landscape of Copenhagen—call it chaos, or disorder, or simply a substantial degree of irregularity—that undermines the sense of grand planning from above and makes everything seem chancier and more open.

This is not always a good thing. In fact, compared to Oslo or Stockholm, Copenhagen is definitely a bit grungy. The Central Station itself, a lovely old arched train station in the nineteenth-century European style, is much nicer than she had expected, but on stepping outside it, she quickly spots drug dealers, heavy boozers, and other insalubrious characters. The area around the train station is perhaps the least appetizing urban area she has seen since coming to Scandinavia (though it still doesn't begin to approach the homeless-filled sidewalks in downtown San Francisco, which one well-traveled young Norwegian sales-woman had described to her as looking "like a war," with all the bodies strewn around). On one side of the station lies bizarre Tivoli, a cross between Disneyland and Las Vegas. On the other side, blocks of tourist hotels sit cheek-by-jowl with purveyors of porn. Her own hotel, on a side street just off the busy artery Vesterbrogade, is located directly across from something called Lady Love, which boasts in English above its doorway, "Voted as the best strip club in Copenhagen." A block away from the hotel, she passes a shabbily dressed drunk sleeping in a doorway—something she has never seen in either Stockholm or Oslo.

As it turns out, her advance characterizations of the three capital cities, formed by reading escapist fiction from several thousand miles away, have proven to be surprisingly accurate. Oslo is indeed idyllic, though also a bit boring. Copenhagen is the grittiest of the three, exciting but occasionally unpleasant.

And Stockholm is, as she predicted, a splendid compromise, at once orderly and urban, magical and functional.

But though its capital may have won the beauty contest, there is one respect in which Sweden has become tarnished in her eyes since she actually got to Scandinavia, and that has to do with its behavior during World War Two. Neutrality proves to be a euphemism covering over some rather ugly practices. Not only did the Swedes sell their valuable iron ore to the Nazi war machine; they also allowed nearly two million German soldiers to pass through Sweden by train on their way to occupied Norway. That these facts are told to her by modern-day Swedes, and even emphasized in Swedish novels like Åsa Larsson's *Until Thy Wrath Be Past*, only slightly ameliorates her sense of betrayal. It also turns out that Sweden's great leap forward financially during the 1950s and 1960s can be tied back to its wartime position. Unlike the rest of Europe, the country had no military expenditures to make up for and no bombed cities to reconstruct, so it started the postwar period already rich and just got richer. Choosing to spend its accumulated wealth on creating a more egalitarian society was commendable, she still feels, but the means of accumulation now seem questionable.

What Sweden has lost in her eyes, Norway has gained— perhaps because, while in Oslo, she visited the Resistance Museum at the Akershus Fortress. She already knew from her mystery-reading that there *was* a Norwegian resistance movement, but until she walked through this large and well-designed museum, she had not been aware of its extent. There was the official military opposition, of course, headed up by the government-in-exile in London and aided by the British, but there was also substantial resistance on the part of individual civilians back in Norway. Teachers and preachers, standing up bravely against the new rulers, refused to disseminate Nazi lies in their classrooms and churches. The underground press, employing mimeograph machines and producing illegal pamphlets, kept the flow of information going among the resisters, who eventually constituted a sizeable portion of the population. All this activism was far from risk-free: the Germans ended up imprisoning about 45,000 Norwegians, many of whom were sent to concentration camps.

Even Norway's Jews are represented in the Resistance Museum, where one whole panel is devoted to their fate. "In October and November 1942," the panel informs her, "the Germans set on foot a nation-wide operation aimed at rounding up all Jews in Norway" (of which there were about 1,800 at the time). "A number managed to avoid arrest, and were assisted over the border into neutral Sweden. But between November 1942 and February 1943, 760 Norwegian Jews—men, women, and children—were sent to the extermination camps in Germany and Poland, where the gas chambers awaited them. Of these 760, only 24 survived."

Just a single flickering newsreel of Vidkun Quisling appears in the museum, and nothing is said about his ultimate fate. The exhibits end with the liberation of Norway in April 1945. But when she looks up the facts afterward, she learns that in October of 1945, after being tried for murder, treason, and embezzlement, Quisling was executed by firing squad. A few additional high-ranking figures were executed in the subsequent three years, and then, in 1948, a collaborator named Ragnar Skancke became the last Norwegian to be put to death by the state. Capital punishment had already been abolished once in Norway, in

1905 (it was Quisling, in fact, who brought it back), and it was now abolished again—so emphatically that even after the mass murders committed by Anders Breivik, a majority of Norwegians said in an opinion poll that they did not want the death penalty restored.

I n Denmark, she is not reminded of the Second World War at all. The Danes, she has heard from both Swedes and Norwegians, are an easygoing people compared to their Scandinavian neighbors, and one aspect of this ease appears to be a sense of the past worn lightly. It's not that Copenhagen lacks historic monuments. Indeed, they are sprinkled all over, starting with the huge and elegant Rådhus located in the center of town. (It is this charming brick city hall, with its distinctive clock-tower and its vast forecourt, that appears as the repeated establishing shot in all the "political" parts of *The Killing*'s first season.) Not far away is the cunningly designed Round Tower, where one walks up a broad spiral ramp—once traversed by horses—to reach a Baroque-era observatory and a series of terrific city views. The sixteenth-century astronomer Tycho Brahe has left his name on the planetarium that lies at the beginning of a lovely riverside walk, and the nineteenth-century storyteller Hans Christian Andersen is commemorated in one of the major boulevards running through town, as well as in the slightly kitschy Little Mermaid statue that attracts tourists to the harbor area. Still, for the most part Copenhagen feels tremendously up-to-date, like a cross between Amsterdam, say, and Hamburg. One sign of its eco-conscious modernity is the huge number of bicycles that appear on every busy corner at rush hour, in phalanxes of forty or fifty at a time, outnumbering both cars and pedestrians as they wait to cross with the light.

Bicycles are certainly the best and easiest way to get around town. The city does possess a limited network of underground trains, but it's not particularly functional (especially at the moment, when several of the stations are in the process of being heavily rebuilt). The local bus system turns out to be simple to understand, but even that useful network is less organized and more relaxed than the Stockholm equivalent. Bus stops here are not always well-marked, and they do not always carry digital information (or even *any* information) about arriving buses. She discovers this when, after obtaining a precious dinner reservation at one of Noma's well-regarded offshoots, she tries to catch the recommended 93 bus that is supposed to take her to the restaurant's neighborhood. She goes, as instructed, to the bus stop on Vesterbrogade, but the signage says nothing about any 93 bus, though two other buses are said to stop there. Just as she is about to go into panic mode and start searching for a taxi (though she has not seen one on the streets since arriving in Copenhagen), the 93 rolls up unannounced. "This would never happen in Stockholm!" she fumes to her companion, who has long since learned to put up with her bouts of anxiety in the face of the unexpected.

A different bus, the 14, delivers her the next morning to her appointment with Jens Møller Jensen, the chief superintendent in Copenhagen's homicide department. The office at Teglholm Allé 1 turns out to be a good twenty minutes from the center, in a neighborhood so obscure that the bus driver, seeking a way around some road-blocking construction, gets lost on the one-way streets until a local passenger puts him right. Deposited

on a nearly empty street in what her map tells her is the South
Harbor area, she quickly finds her way to the correct building, a
block-long structure of pale brick and dark glass. This is clearly
not the police headquarters she read about in the Danish novel
by the Hammers, the "monumental" one with "gray, dirty walls
of rough plaster" and "oversize golden morning stars." It is, in
fact, a new structure built within the last few years just for the
investigations division. As such, it apparently receives few visitors, at least compared to the Oslo police headquarters. When
she arrives, she is the sole person standing outside the locked
doorway, and it is only after she announces herself to a receptionist on the intercom that she is buzzed in. (But at least she
*is* buzzed in here. Later, attempting to make an unscheduled
visit to the older HQ on Polititorvet—which looks exactly
like its description in *The Hanging*, not to mention its exterior-
shot appearances in *The Killing*—she pushes the button labeled
"Information/Reception" and gets a brusque male voice telling
her, "It's closed to the public." Three men standing by a car in
the nearby parking lot suggest jovially that if she wants to get into
the police station, she should just break a car window and the cops
will come take her in. "Too hard," she grins, and they all laugh.)

The policeman who comes to fetch her from the lobby of the
investigations unit is not Jens Møller Jensen himself, but a jeans-
clad, crew-cut fellow named Jakob Rahbek Grell, a younger superintendent who works under the chief. When they reach the
second floor, Jens (a middle-aged man who is dressed slightly
more formally than Jakob, but still with an open-necked shirt
and no jacket) meets them and shakes her hand. He explains that
he invited Jakob to join them because Jakob's English is better
than his, and then leads her down the corridor to his office.

Just outside the closed door, he says, "You're not afraid of dogs, are you?" Bemused, she smiles and says no. It turns out that he has a big brown dog in his office—not his own pet, but one he is keeping for a friend and planning to return later that day. Because the temperature outside is so hot, he doesn't want to leave the animal in the car. The dog, which is bigger than a Labrador but smaller than a Great Dane, proves to be both friendly and well-behaved: after licking her hand in greeting, it lies back down on the floor and sleeps through the whole interview, sometimes snoring audibly.

Jens (whose English is in fact quite good) quickly explains the Danish system to her, pointing out the ways in which it differs from what she might find elsewhere in Scandinavia. Here the prosecutors do not lead the investigations. The police compile all the evidence on their own, though on big cases they might start consulting with the prosecutors early in the process so as not to waste valuable resources—he calls it "the citizens' money"—by going off on different tangents. "When we are finished, we deliver the case to them," Jens says. "At the same time, we are investigating for the defendant. If they have questions, we will look into it." In other words, the defense does not have to hire a private investigator here, because it is the police department's job to investigate for both sides.

"But how can the defendants trust you when it's your job to put them in jail?"

"That is not our job," he answers. "If something happened, it is our job to put them in jail, but if nothing happened . . . Our job is to find out the truth. The job is to enlighten the case. If we don't have a case, we can live with it and move on." He acknowledges that when they arrest a suspect, "the detectives will have some feeling against the perpetrators. But I always say to the detectives, 'Be sure you are listening to what he says now. We have to be objective.'"

As in Norway, there is a first-response unit that is on duty twenty-four hours a day. Whenever these officers find what they think is a homicide, they call Jens right away, and it is his task to assemble a team to handle it. For some crimes—those that take place in the middle of the night, and where the culprit has been immediately apprehended—he might decide to wait a bit. "If it is a man killing his wife, they don't have to wake up at night. That can wait until the morning. But if it's on the street and an unknown perpetrator, the team goes into action right away."

When she asks how many murders take place in Copenhagen in a given year, Jens and Jakob invite her to guess; and when she responds with a hesitant "Fifty? A hundred?" they burst out laughing.

"We barely have fifty a year in the whole country!" Jens tells her, and goes on to say that the average is twelve a year, though it can range from ten up to fifteen. So Copenhagen, despite its more sordid appearance, has a murder rate roughly as low as Oslo's. Most of the murders are family-related. (Two years ago, Jens remembers, a man killed his wife and three children, so that accounted for a substantial portion of the murders that year.) The others tend to be connected with gangs or organized crime, but that only accounts for two or at most four out of the dozen. People are, for the most part, killed by those they know. There are relatively few cases where the perpetrator is a stranger, and as a result the police are quickly able to solve about ninety percent of the murders.

The notorious exception to this familial rule—a case she now brings up—is the recent murder of the journalist Kim Wall, who was killed and then dismembered by a deranged inventor named Peter Madsen after she went alone to interview him on his submarine. The crime was so unusual that it occupied the front pages of international newspapers for days and even weeks. Jens and Jakob both agree that it was totally out of the ordinary for Denmark, much more like a murder-mystery case, of the sort they never confront in real life.

The investigation (as they proceed to tell her) started as a search for two people who had disappeared in a submarine. Kim Wall's boyfriend reported that she never came home after the interview—that was on Thursday, August 10, 2017—and when Jens went to his usual Friday-morning police meeting, it was described as a missing persons case that was being handled by another unit. Neither Madsen nor Wall, nor any sign of the submarine on which they were supposed to meet, could be found, and the police assumed there had probably been some kind of accident. They began to search with helicopters in the air and boats in the water, and at around 10:00 a.m. on Friday morning one of the helicopters finally spotted Madsen. At just that moment, when he must have seen that they now saw him, he answered his cell phone for the first time, having not responded to their calls in all the hours before. That was the first suspicious item of behavior on his part.

Peter Madsen was a figure already known to the police, though not because he had ever committed any crime. He was, on the contrary, a rather well-known personality on Danish TV, someone who was often brought in to speak about space travel and related subjects. He was considered a brilliant eccentric, but his eccentricities seemed harmless. ("You need to be a little crazy to be a rocket man," Jakob suggests.)

In the first interview the police conducted with him, Madsen told them that he had put Kim Wall ashore the night before, and that his submarine had then started to sink when he was alone on board. The area where he said he had let her off contained a few CCTV cameras, and she was not visible on any of them. Still, the investigators thought she might have gone ashore there, walked a short distance, and been attacked by a stranger. They searched but found nothing. There was no body, and the submarine lay at the bottom of the sea. That was how things stood on Friday evening.

On Saturday morning Madsen learned that they were planning to raise the submarine, and at that point he changed his story. He told the two police officers who were interviewing him that Wall had died in an accident on the submarine. He didn't see the accident, he said, but he heard her fall, and when he went to look, he saw her lying there on the floor with a lot of blood coming out of her head. After ascertaining that she was really dead, he buried her at sea. A captain is responsible for burials at sea, he insisted, and he was the captain of his ship.

Ten days after he was first detained, on Monday, August 21, two people who were riding their bicycles in a park near the water found Kim Wall's dismembered torso. (This part sounds so much like the opening of a *Law & Order* episode—or, for that matter, a Martin Beck tale like *Roseanna*—that even as she listens to Jens and Jakob telling the story, she can't help finding it unreal.) Madsen's response to this discovery was to say that Wall was too heavy for him to lift on his own, so he had to cut her up to get her body into the water. Then, on October 6, the investigators found the head and both legs. An examination of the head showed no injuries to the skull, nothing which could have caused the bleeding Madsen had described. Pathology reports suggested that she had either been strangled or had her head chopped off when she was alive. At this point Madsen stopped speaking to the police entirely, and he never did say anything further until after the guilty verdict was delivered on April 25, 2018, when he announced that he was going to appeal.

Part of the evidence against him, as it turned out, consisted of the type of pornography the police found in their search of his home. When they examined his computer, they discovered what Jakob describes as "materials showing an interest in violence in relation to sexual behavior." Some of it was animation, but there was also some live-action video. A number of the episodes involved women getting their heads chopped off, both with and without sexual assault beforehand.

Violent pornography of the sort Peter Madsen indulged in does not necessarily constitute a crime in Denmark. Child pornography, on the other hand, does. Possession carries a fine; distribution carries a prison sentence. Jakob, whose investigative area is child abuse, estimates that he "would find child pornography in thirty to forty percent of the houses, if I kicked the door in. You find it at all layers of the society." He gives the example of a school principal who took his computer in to a repair shop, where it was found to contain child porn. But despite the widespread consumption of such materials, the actual abuse of children is almost always confined to the family—or, if not to an actual family member, then to a trusted figure like a teacher or a sports trainer. Exhibitionism, Jakob says, is the only sex crime against children routinely practiced by strangers. In that respect, the terrifying novels about the abduction and exploitation of children are pure fiction.

She wonders aloud why murdered, threatened, violated women and children are such a constant theme in Scandinavian crime fiction, if it doesn't happen all that often in real life. Jakob thinks that's precisely *why* it appears in fiction: "Because it doesn't happen so many times here, so it's still a little bit scary." But he also acknowledges that rape is more common in Denmark than murder. Most of the rapes are drug-related rapes that happen in nightclubs ("There's been a campaign to report drug rape. We take it very seriously," he says), but some are stranger rapes, and these can occasionally get extremely violent. In the past year, there were two cases of rape leading to murder or near-murder in Sjælland, the larger region that includes Copenhagen.

Jens then recalls that "in 1990 we had several murders of a sexual nature—murders of young women, some with rapes. Four of them remain unsolved." Three years ago, in 2015, the Danes brought to trial a serial killer who was also a rapist—the only serial killer that either Jens or Jakob can think of, though they know there have been other serial rapists. This man's earliest murder took place in 1987, his latest rape in 2014, and in the end he was convicted of three murders and three or four rapes. He was also questioned about the 1990 crimes, but Jens is "rather sure" he didn't do them.

She brings up the crime of "internet rape" that she first heard about in Oslo. Neither Jens nor Jakob has dealt with it—that's the province of a different department—but they know it's prosecuted in Denmark, though here it's called "livestreaming rape." When she asks what the prison sentence for it would be, they say they have no idea. Jens goes online to find out, while she continues to talk to Jakob about the kind of "grooming" that perpetrators do on websites visited by children and teenagers.

"You won't believe what I'm getting here when I put in 'livestreaming rape,'" Jens says, shaking his head and raising his eyebrows at the porn sites that have appeared on his smartphone. He decides instead to call up a journalist friend who is likely to know about the sentencing for such convictions. (Their department has very good relations with journalists, Jakob tells her while Jens is making the call.) When Jens gets off the phone, he reports the case of a seventy-year-old man who recently got twelve years for livestreaming rape, which was knocked down to eight years on appeal.

They have life imprisonment in Denmark, she learns, and they also have a psychiatric sentence that comes without parole. They do not, of course, have the death penalty. And though the Danish police are allowed to carry guns, and are in fact required to if they are working outside the building, it is difficult for criminals to use guns because the laws governing them are so strict. A criminal might be able to *obtain* an illegal gun with about a week's notice, at a cost of roughly a thousand dollars, says Jens. ("I wouldn't know how to do it, but they do," he adds.) But if someone carries a gun in public, he risks being picked up for that crime alone. Even if you have a gun license—if you belong to a shooting club, for instance—you need to take the gun to the club in a locked box, with the ammunition stored separately. Anyone found carrying an automatic firearm will get a minimum four-year sentence, and that increases if the gun is loaded, if it's carried in a public place, or if the carrier is a gang member, all of which can bring the sentence up to ten years.

"What's your image of America here?" she asks, expecting her question to lead to a reasonable critique of gun-craziness in the United States. But instead she gets a surprising response from Jakob.

"I grew up watching these movies where you're not allowed to take this or that because it's not in the warrant," he says. "If we kick in the door, we're allowed to take everything. We can pretty much do whatever we need to do for our jobs." Like most of her own compatriots, it seems, he has derived his knowledge of the American legal system mainly from TV shows and detective films.

When she asks Jens and Jakob about their stereotypical view of Swedes, they first come up with "A drunk." (For years, apparently, Sweden's stricter control over alcohol has meant that its citizens mainly came over to Denmark to drink.) Then Jakob adds, "Nothing is allowed in Sweden. Everything is forbidden. Denmark historically was where porn was allowed, more liberated about alcohol, more liberated in general. We're more free, maybe." He pauses and adds scathingly, "They make plans for everything."

"We love to hate each other," Jens points out about the Scandinavian nations. "But if we are in Greece, we just love each other."

In the past, they tell her, there has often been no passport control between the three Scandinavian countries. She mentions to them that on the flight from Arlanda to Kastrup, no one even bothered to check her ID, and they think this sounds normal. But they also remark that in some cases temporary border controls have been reintroduced because of refugees. This leads into the usual conversation about immigrants, and neither cop is hesitant about mentioning their role in the rising crime rate.

"It's not a secret that the gangs are heavily immigrant," volunteers Jens.

Jakob notes that the immigrants have mostly ended up living in high-crime neighborhoods. "That's how Denmark was shaped in the last ten, twenty, thirty years. Unfortunately they were born and raised in what we call ghettos today. We haven't been able to give them the same opportunities to—whatever would make them think differently."

She wonders about that phrase "what we call ghettos," and later she looks into the word's current meaning in Denmark. It turns out that terms like "ghetto" and "integration" have been given a new twist by the Danish anti-immigrant movement. In a package of laws just then in the process of being passed by the Danish parliament, twenty-five "ghettos" within Denmark have been defined as having such high proportions of Muslim residents that special laws will apply to people living in those areas. Children born in these ghettos must all, upon reaching the age of one year, be sent to mandatory preschool, where they will be separated from their parents for at least twenty-five hours a week and inculcated in "Danish values." To prevent any backsliding or "re-education," parents who take their children back to the home country for lengthy visits can be punished by four years in prison. This effort to "integrate" Muslims into Danish society is premised on the idea that their own culture offers nothing of value—that they are, in the words of one Danish citizen quoted in the newspaper, "300 to 400 years behind us." The fact that only ghetto residents would be subjected to these rules—which, if all the laws pass, could also include an 8:00 p.m. curfew for every minor (even law-abiding ones) as well as harsher-than-average penalties for those who commit crimes in the ghetto—does not seem to bother the Danish legislators, who have apparently forgotten a similar approach taken by Germany toward the ghettos of another ethnic group. Jakob is far too young to know much about the Third Reich, but his casual acceptance of the new ideas suggests that Danish education, however good it is in many respects, may lack a certain historical perspective.

Jens, on the other hand, seems less sanguine about the current approach. He interrupts Jakob to comment, "We have a lot of immigrants who are doing very, very well, that we don't hear a lot about." He predicts that "we will see many foreign people in public areas—for instance, as police prosecutors—in the coming decades."

Both police officers are agreed, though, that the large influx of immigrants in the past decade has led to an intensification of right-wing politics. The shift began with a man named Mogens Glistrup, who in the early 1970s founded a libertarian-style party for the purpose of combatting high taxes. Later he converted his Progress Party to an anti-immigrant agenda; eventually his racist, anti-Muslim statements became so virulent that even his fellow party members abandoned him. One of them went on to found the Danish People's Party in 1995, and it is this group which represents the right-wing populists in Denmark today. Its basic agenda, according to Jakob, consists of "kicking out Arabs."

She wants to know whether what she has read in the novels is true—that a newcomer to the country can't get permanent

Danish residency even by marrying a Dane. Yes, they tell her, it's true, and that is definitely the doing of the Danish People's Party. The law in Denmark used to be the same as the law in America: you could get the equivalent of a green card by marrying a Danish citizen. Now, however, you have to prove a long-term "connection" to Denmark in order to live there. They seem mildly gleeful about the fact that this stricter law has backfired on the man who introduced it, since that politician's son ended up marrying an Israeli and now has to live in Israel.

They also confirm her sense that prostitution is legal in Denmark in a way that it is not, strictly speaking, in Sweden and Norway. That's true, at least, if you are talking about an individual prostitute who conducts her own business and pays taxes on it. In such cases (which they admit are pretty rare), neither the prostitute nor her client is violating any laws. But pimps and brothels are illegal, and that accounts for most of the prostitution in the country, with many women being brought in from Eastern Europe and Africa. It's hard to catch the criminals responsible for this, because as soon as the illegal apartments containing these women are on the verge of being discovered, the pimps move them to another country. Recently the Copenhagen police have been in conversation with the Oslo police about how to stop this kind of human trafficking.

When she asks where in town the prostitutes are located, Jakob takes her map and circles the area directly south of her hotel, a fact she wryly comments on. "If you keep your eyes open," he tells her, "you will see Eastern European prostitutes in the daytime and African prostitutes at night." Neither man seems unduly concerned about this; they view it as "not a big problem, but a problem." Whenever the hotels complain too loudly, the police do a roundup and things improve for a little while, but then they go back to the way they were before. "It's less of a problem in the winter, more in the summer, but here all the time," says Jakob. "It's like drugs. If there is a demand for it, it will be there."

Just before leaving the police station, she remembers that she still needs to find out about those pastries and cups of coffee with which Scandinavian civilians allegedly greet any visit from the police. So she asks Jakob whether people serve him coffee when he comes to their homes during an investigation. He seems surprised at the question, but he answers readily enough. "It depends on their relation to the case. Witnesses, yes—they will often offer coffee."

That very evening she decides to visit Christiania, a place whose name had come up during her lengthy conversation with Jakob and Jens.

"What's Christiania?" she had asked when they mentioned a police operation that took place there.

"I can't believe you've never heard of it," said Jakob. "It's our biggest tourist attraction, after Tivoli and maybe the Little Mermaid. I thought the murder books might mention it, as the place where the body is found or something." (Later, when she checks, she sees that Christiania was indeed cited in two of the novels, one by Jussi Adler-Olsen and the other by Lotte and Søren Hammer, but in neither case was it described fully enough for her to understand what it was.)

Jakob explains that Christiania was set up as a social experiment in the late 1960s or early 1970s—at any rate, sometime before he was born. A small, walled-off neighborhood within Copenhagen, it's a place with its own special rules, where the residents govern themselves, and where you can openly buy drugs on Pusher Street. Uniformed cops are not welcome there, and even investigative cops wearing their yellow jackets would have to tread carefully, though the citizens of Christiania would probably help them solve a murder.

"Kind of like Hamsterdam in *The Wire*," she suggests.

"Yes, but less organized," Jakob says. He recommends that she go there and see it for herself. She won't find it at all dangerous, he assures her, though he warns that if she tries to take a picture there, they will grab her camera and throw it away.

But even this, she discovers when she gets to Christiania, has changed since the advent of smartphones. In fact, several of the ancient hippies she sees there are posing in front of their craft shops for photos taken by tourists. Since the World Cup trials happen to be on and Denmark is one of the competing teams, quite a few of Christiania's denizens can also be found clustered in large tents sprinkled here and there, watching the game on large-screen TVs and drinking beer in cups ferried to them by little blond children.

The whole encampment strikes her as possessing both the grimy picturesqueness and the nonconformist conformity one generally finds in such enclaves. She concedes that some things about the place are mildly appealing. The extraordinarily well-maintained graffiti on the long street-side wall is spectacular, and a number of the odd dwellings scattered throughout the compound have a handmade sweetness to them. But for the most part the environment reeks of purposeful squalor. It reminds her of the Haight-Ashbury, which she once or twice had occasion to

visit in her youth, though present-day Christiania has an added
air of the outdated and the left-behind. The few residents she
speaks to clearly feel superior to the rest of Denmark, seemingly
oblivious to the fact that the despised state is providing their
power lines, their social-welfare checks, and just about everything else that makes their "experiment" possible.

During the balance of her Copenhagen stay, she encounters several more examples of the Danish willingness to tolerate
what the Swedes would consider disorder. Even the trains run
erratically, as she discovers when she takes the one-hour journey
out to the Louisiana Museum of Modern Art, which is located on
the coast just below Helsingør. On the outward trip, the train de-
parts from the Central Station about twelve or thirteen minutes
late and then skips a number of stops in the middle, an omission
that is not announced until the passengers are on board. On the
return trip, the destination sign near the Louisiana stop says
nothing about Copenhagen; she has to ask some locals which
is the right train to take. Throughout both trips, the use of English in the announcements is intermittent rather than regular.
Sometimes there is no English at all, sometimes the recorded
voice just says, "Mind the gap," and sometimes there is a full an-
nouncement of the next station along with the words "We kindly
ask you to keep your belongings in your possession."

She has wanted to visit the Louisiana Museum for at least
twenty-five years, ever since reading about it in an essay by
Lawrence Weschler, and it proves to be no disappointment in
the flesh. At its core is a fine old house which has been augmented with several different kinds of modern wings, from fully
enclosed outbuildings, with their windowless walls and multiple
floors, to structures that are merely glassed-in corridors. The

whole complex sits on one of the most beautifully designed landscapes she has ever seen. From the café terrace, one can look across the water to Sweden, which seems practically near enough to swim to at this point. If you turn in the other direction, you face the museum buildings, which are surrounded by tall trees, grassy lawns, steep hills, shady dells, and winding pathways, all punctuated at intervals by remarkable sculptures. A Richard Serra pair of rusted metal walls serves as a natural-seeming gateway to one dell; a tall, brightly colored Calder mobile stands at the center of the largest lawn; and works by the likes of Henry Moore, Jean Arp, Max Ernst, and others surprise the wandering visitor at every turn.

It is easy to get lost in the museum—the wings do not seem to connect up in predictable ways, and you are always having to go outdoors to get inside again—but that is a great part of the pleasure. In fact, there is a purposeful feeling of haphazardness to the layout, as if you are being offered an unexpected encounter between art and nature, say, or between cultivated nature and the wild. A lawn as green and smooth as a carpet suddenly gives way to a small woodsy area. A path leads down into the unknown and opens onto a gorgeous Japanese-style vista, complete with weeping willows surrounding a tiny lake. You may have to go through the whole complex twice to be sure you have seen everything, and even then you might be confused about how the different sections relate to each other, but it is an eye-opening rather than anxiety-producing kind of confusion. She can't help feeling that this invigorating experience vindicates the Danish preference for the unplanned, or at least the *seemingly* unplanned, which at its best can provide a kind of delight that the Swedish and Norwegian love of symmetry cannot.

Back in town, on her last morning in Denmark, she realizes that she has not yet interviewed any regular citizens, only
policemen. She resolves to have at least a brief conversation on
the subject of murder mysteries and Danish culture with the
young barista who works at Hyggestund, the place where she
and her companion have taken to eating their breakfast. A tall
young man with a pleasant face, a brown ponytail, and the kind
of dark gray-blue eyes she has noticed in many Danes, he readily agrees to speak with her while he is wiping off the outdoor
tables. She explains her project and asks if he ever reads these
murder books.

"No, I don't read them," he says. "But I did write a paper
in high school on the connection between Danish despair of
the Kierkegaardian kind and the interest in crime fiction—you
know, wanting solutions where none exist in real life."

She notices that her mouth has fallen open and hastens to
close it.

"I got a very high grade on that paper," he muses, with a
reflective rather than a boastful air.

"I bet," she says.


And now it is time for her to cross the Øresund Bridge,
something she has been looking forward to since the trip
began. Flying into Kastrup airport, she could see The Bridge off
in the distance, its tall sail-shaped towers and pale supporting
pillars spanning the distance between the Danish and Swedish
shores. Driving a car across is prohibitively expensive, and the
private bus companies that make the crossing are not all that
easy to locate, so she decides to go by train, which is fast and

cheap. The whole trip from Copenhagen to Malmö, departing from the Central Station and passing right by the airport, takes less than forty minutes and costs about eleven dollars a person.

There is a brief moment of terror when she learns, from a downward-swooping arm gesture made by the ticket-seller at the station, that the train will be running *under* the bridge, which she assumes means underground. So much for glimpsing one of the major sights of her Scandinavia visit. Luckily this turns out to be the kind of train that runs on the underside of the bridge's roadway, like the subways that cross the East River on New York's Manhattan Bridge, well above the water itself. So even though she cannot see the elegant sail-towers from up close, she still gets a view of the underlying pillars and the approaching landmass—a view that is truer, in a way, to the series *The Bridge* than the more scenic route might have been.

The time spent on the bridge itself is only about ten or twelve minutes, and once the train has reached the Swedish side, it stops almost immediately at the Hyllie station. A flock of passport officers in chartreuse vests passes through each carriage, examining everyone's documents closely. It is easy to get from Sweden to Denmark, apparently, but much harder to go back the other way. Later, at her Malmö hotel, she is told by the receptionist that this level of border control has only re-appeared in the past two years, in an effort to control illegal immigration. She also learns that Sturup—the small airport that lies about forty minutes' bus ride from Malmö, through which she will eventually return to Stockholm—is not the airport used by most local Swedes, who prefer to take the train to Kastrup, only twenty minutes away. It's an odd setup the bridge has brought about, with the two countries now finding themselves closer together in terms of travel time yet more divided than ever by bureaucracy.

In Malmö, she is staying at the historic Savoy. It's quite a nice hotel, and it sits just across the canal from the Central Station, at a convenient walking distance from almost everything. More importantly, it still closely resembles the place where Sjöwall and Wahlöö set their *Murder at the Savoy.* Wandering around town, she has found a few other local echoes of the Martin Beck series, including the fact that many of the Malmö street names—Skeppsbron, Slussen, Kungsgatan, Drottninggatan, and so on—mimic their counterparts in Stockholm. This parallelism, she recalls, accounts for a crucial plot point in *The Locked Room,* where the final and successful bank robbery occurs in Malmö while the police are waiting for it to take place in Stockholm. But that's a tiny reverberation, compared to the extent to which the physical details in *Murder at the Savoy* (which she is re-reading at this very moment) exactly correspond to the present appearance of the hotel.

The Savoy has changed hands since then, and certain superficial arrangements have been altered in the lobby. But because the hotel is a landmarked building, and because it is in fact extremely proud of its connection to the mystery tale, the Grill Room, where the titular murder took place, has been left almost exactly as the novel described it. Large windows face out onto the adjoining street corner, and though they are now sealed shut, and perhaps always were, they are certainly big enough for an escaping murderer to climb out of. The bar with its barstools, the pale-green pillars separating the dining room into sections, the screened-off prep area and the large door into the kitchen all remain as they were in Martin Beck's time. (She finds she can't help thinking of it as "then" and "now," as if the fictional past and the real present existed on a continuous temporal plane.) Even the inconsistent clocks, with the round-faced clock over the kitchen door reading 5:03 while the grandfather clock in the lobby says 4:49, are just as they were then, when the incompetent Backlund, the first officer on the scene, wasted crucial hours trying to ascertain the exact time of the shooting.

All of these correspondences give her a degree of pleasure she would not have expected, and it is heightened rather than diminished by the huge poster, or perhaps fresco, which appears to have been painted directly on the Grill Room's most prominent wall. "A Martin Beck mystery," it proclaims in big gold letters, next to a noirish rendering of the Savoy frontage. Below that, in small white type, are the names Maj Sjöwall and Per Wahlöö, followed by a large "Murder at the Savoy." It is only some hours later, back in her room, that she realizes how odd it is that the sign is in English and not Swedish—as if it has been waiting all these years for her arrival.

The rest of Malmö, it is clear, has not stayed back in the 1970s. Though there is a traditional Stortorget, or main city square, flanked by an impressive city hall, a beautiful old apothecary shop, and some other architectural gems, the square's main draw on a Sunday night in June is the Shawarma King. Lending some life to the otherwise deserted public space, this tiny counter-restaurant serves kebabs and spicy vegetable dishes that can be carried to a number of outdoor tables, where catchy Middle Eastern tunes play from radios and people of both sexes converse animatedly in Arabic with their friends. Elsewhere in the city, too, there turns out to be a large immigrant population that fills up the open-air market on weekdays. Riding the buses or walking along the shopping streets, one sees many more women in hijabs than in either downtown Stockholm or downtown Copenhagen, and there are quantities of Africans and Asians mingling with the Lebanese, Syrians, Turks, and, of course, native Swedes. She has read a few news stories about shooting deaths in Malmö caused by immigrant gangs, and about the various reactions on the part of the city—some bad, some good—to its large influx of recent immigrants. Yet there doesn't, at least to the superficial observer, appear to be a lot of anxiety or stress associated with the cultural mix.

"Malmö is so much more laid-back," says the hotel receptionist, who has recently moved down here from the capital. "In Stockholm you have everything and more, but there's so much stress. In Malmö you can walk everywhere and enjoy it. People aren't running for the train. In Stockholm everything has to be this way"—and she gestures with her hands as if putting things into separate drawers, slotting them into place—"but here it's a little more laid-back." Hearing the young woman say these words, she thinks back to the slow-moving, slow-thinking Skåne characters who occupy the edges of the Martin Beck stories, figures of mild derision in the eyes of the sophisticated Stockholmers. And then she recalls what she has recently learned in Stockholm: that Per Wahlöö himself came from Skåne, so all those jokes about southerners were at his own expense.

I t is with a blend of excitement and trepidation that she sets out one morning for Kurt Wallander's hometown of Ystad. Will the correspondences between the fictional world of the past and her actual encounters in the present continue to be as moving as her

Savoy experiences have been? Or has Henning Mankell got it all wrong, and will she find his version of Ystad unrecognizably different from the real place she is about to see?

The problems start as early as the Malmö train station, where she learns that she will be unable to buy a roundtrip ticket to Ystad. For reasons that are never made clear, she has to purchase a one-way ticket and then get her ticket back to Malmö at the other end. This is unnerving enough. But when, after a fifty-minute ride through rolling farmlands and occasional vistas of the sea, she debarks at the Ystad station, her anxiety increases tenfold. There *is* no Ystad station, it turns out, only a faintly marked crossing on the train tracks, next to a small, rather dirty-looking plastic and metal shelter. She crosses the road and looks for a ticket booth, but none is evident. Then she asks a bystander, and he directs her back across the tracks to the nearest Pressbyrån—a kind of Swedish version of 7-Eleven, where one can buy magazines, candies, and sundries. She goes up to the cashier, who admits that they do sell tickets to Malmö, but only within two hours of departure time. He is not positive about the schedule, but vaguely thinks the trains go once an hour on the half hour.

On her way into town she stops by the local library, which is also the local tourist office, and there she gets her first whiff of the lethal virus. She is able, as she expected, to pick up a map of the town, but also on display—on walls, on shelves, even on the counter between her and the information-givers—are posters, leaflets, and booklets about Kurt Wallander. Not Henning Mankell, mind you, the real-life author who indirectly brought all this fame and prosperity to the town. No, it is his character, grown larger than life, who has taken over everything.

As she leafs through *Ystad's Best Guide to Wallander* (offered in English, Swedish, and at least two other languages), she learns that forty-four Wallander films have been shot in Ystad since 2004. Five different actors, including four Swedes and Kenneth Branagh, have taken on the part of the homicide detective. The film studio built to produce these movies and television episodes is still the largest to be found anywhere in Scandinavia, and all together the films have brought the Skåne region an estimated 250 million Swedish kronor (nearly $28 million at current exchange rates). A British survey conducted in 2014, the booklet announces proudly, "estimated the PR value of Wallander in social media at SEK 210 million. The name Ystad has become known globally and has seen a large viral spread thanks to the Wallander films."

She understands that this is not *her* Kurt Wallander—that quiet fellow who misses his laundry appointments, regularly monitors the outside temperature, and spends hours thinking about his cases—but a grotesque cinematic avatar. Despite his fictional origins, this filmic Wallander has apparently grown so real that his "locations" in the city are presented as part of the visible, and visitable, geography. His house on Mariagatan, the café where he regularly drinks, the place where he buys his opera CDs, the bookstore in the town square where he shops for books, even the street where he parks his old blue Peugeot: all are cited with exact addresses in the Wallander guide and marked with prominent dots on the tourist maps.

The situation brings to mind a passage from a novel she has just read recently, Eric Ambler's 1959 *Passage of Arms*. There's a scene in it where a couple of American tourists on a worldwide cruise are being taken around Saigon:

"That café there." The driver pointed. "That was where Quiet American made bomb explosion. Many killed."

They were coming to a square now. Greg looked from the café to the driver.

"But *The Quiet American* was a novel," he said.

"Yes, sir. That is café back there. I was near at time of explosion. Was very bad."

"But it was fiction," Dorothy said. "It didn't actually happen."

When Ambler wrote this winking tribute to his colleague Graham Greene, Greene's prescient 1955 Vietnam novel had only been out for a few years, and both authors were still very much alive. What was gently satiric in that context becomes much more ghoulish here in Ystad, with Henning Mankell already dead and his fictional creation dancing ever more heavily on his grave. For the first time ever, she begins to sympathize with Mankell's expressed desire to get rid of Wallander, an effort that finally ended (though only on the page, it seems) with his giving the character terminal dementia.

The town of Ystad was probably a quiet, pleasant place once upon a time, with its winding, cobbled streets and small pastel houses leading down to a working harbor. Now, however, it is at least as touristy as Visby, though without the dramatic setting or the ancient ring wall to justify the number of day-trippers. The old city center resembles a well-preserved stage set, a back-lot version of its former self, with a Stortorget catering largely to tourists and a pedestrianized row of shops purveying useless and often Wallander-related items. She is relieved, in a way, to emerge from this deadening cuteness into the real-life suburbia that surrounds the old town. There she makes her way along a nearly deserted traffic corridor until she reaches the long, two-story, window-filled building that constitutes Ystad's actual police station. (Resembling as it does an unobtrusive office complex, it is nowhere near scenic enough to have served as the televised police station, which apparently moved over the years from a set inside the film studio to a disused railway-station building and thence to an abandoned handicraft factory.)

Patric Nihlén, the police officer with whom she has an appointment, comes down to greet her in the small lobby, where she has been sitting among numerous families who, as in Oslo, are at the police station to get passports. A portly middle-aged man dressed in partial uniform, he leads her up to his office on the second floor, mentioning as they climb the stairs that she is the second writer to come asking about Wallander in a ten-day period. Just last week, a colleague of his had an interview about Wallander and Mankell with a Stockholm journalist.

Patric is not a homicide specialist. The town of Ystad is far too small to require its own homicide department, and when an unusually high number of murders took place in the district—five within an eight-month period, back in 2014 and 2015—they had to call in outside help. "We don't have the capacity to solve it on our own," Patric tells her, "so we have to have help from Malmö." But he has been present as part of the first-response team at a couple of murders that took place just outside of Ystad. One of them involved a son killing his father, probably over drug-related matters; in the other, a husband shot his wife. Though he had been working as a policeman for years at that point, he still found the sight of the dead bodies shocking. "It didn't seem real," he says.

In the case of the wife-murderer, he and his partner had just finished one job and were eating burgers in their car when they got the call. "In a small, small town outside Ystad, a woman was killed by her husband. He shot her. And we were the first ones there, me and my friend"—or rather, they arrived at exactly the same time as the ambulance team. What most upset Patric was seeing the wife's body, before it was taken away. "A small woman lying just inside the main door of the house, shot in the back. It's hard to describe how you feel. Afterward me and my colleagues always sit talking, because it's not normal to see dead people in this way."

At that time Patric was a sergeant heading up a team of five men and three women. Now he is a community relations officer, responsible for monitoring Ystad's nightclubs and pubs. He regularly works with these liquor-purveying establishments in an effort to reduce the number of assaults. "In common assaults, eighty to ninety percent are related to alcohol," he points out. They might have only one murder a year in Ystad, but they are likely to have three assaults a week, particularly on weekends. "Sweden is kind of special in that way. The drinking problem during the weekend is when the assaults outside the pubs happen. Sometimes it happens inside, but not very often."

"Do the number of assaults go up on holidays, like Walpurgis Night and Midsummer's Eve?"

"Sometimes an increase in crime is related to those special occasions, but then the next year it's down again, so that is not consistent."

She tries to find out whether any of the other crimes resemble the extreme events depicted in Wallander novels. They have very little problem with rape in Ystad, apparently. As for child abuse, "We have it like in every district, not higher or lower than any other part of Sweden." Two women officers who work downstairs from him handle those crimes against children. There is some smuggling at the port ("We know that a lot of things stolen in Sweden pass out of the country through Ystad port, mainly to Eastern Europe"), but not much of it is connected with violence. As for serial killers, he cannot recall a single one in the immediate Ystad neighborhood. But he knows of at least one from Malmö, a few years back, and he is pretty sure there have been others in Sweden. The Malmö serial killer, who was convicted in 2012 of crimes that took place in 2009 and 2010, was a native-born Swede who was killing people of other nationalities—"dark-haired people," as Patric puts it. "Yes, a racist."

Suicide is something he has had to handle locally, and what makes him sad is that it so often involves young people—"young love that was broken," he hypothesizes. A few years ago there was a rash of teenagers jumping in front of trains, and more recently there were three young guys who killed themselves, two of them related to each other. "There was some connection between them, but we never did find out why," he says. The suicide rate in Ystad isn't as high as in the big cities, but it rises near Christmas and in the summer, he tells her.

"Why the summer?"

Because there are higher expectations in the warm, light months, Patric thinks. People feel they should be happy then, and if they're not, they become especially distressed.

She wonders aloud why Henning Mankell chose Ystad, of all places, as the setting of his Wallander novels.

"I think he knew someone. I think he did know one person

inside this police house." Patric says he is just guessing at this, but other people at the station have come up with the same theory. "Many of the things about this character Kurt Wallander fits this person here. He had a similar personal life: divorced, lived alone, two children. Drank a bit, as most Swedes do. And he was a very good police officer, very clever."

The man was named Kurt Ingvar Wald—not all that different, Patric points out, from the fictional character's name—and he was always put in charge of the bigger crimes. "He was a man who could answer many questions. If you had a problem on a case, you could go to him and he had good answers. He also had a good humanity, both inside and outside the police station. A very kind person." Patric asserts this with a certain authority, since he himself knew the man, who retired only about ten years ago.

"Is he still alive?" she asks.

"Actually, I saw him yesterday, walking with his dog."

They start to talk, then, about the effect Wallander's fame has had on the town. Some of it seems a bit laughable. About a decade ago, Patric tells her, a German tourist actually came to the police station wanting to meet Wallander, and they had to inform him that the detective wasn't real. Even now, if Patric is downtown wearing his uniform during the summer, at least two or three tourists a week will come up to him with questions. "They often ask about Wallander. And they ask about his house—where he lived."

She remarks on how strange this seems, with these two parallel existences, the real-life police force and the filmed Kurt Wallander, both occupying the same place. He agrees, and then goes on to tell her about other things that have changed in Ystad

because of Wallander. There used to be an annual summer cele-
bration every July called the Monks' Festival, named after the
monks who inhabited the town centuries ago. People would
dress up as monks and party together in the streets. And there
was also a race called the Monks' Race—not marathon-length,
but shorter, with one race for adults and one for children. Now
the former is called the Wallander Festival, and the latter the
Wallander Race. And even the café where the movie-Wallander
drank, which used to be called Fridolf's, has now been renamed
the Wallander Café.

As she wends her way back through the tourist-filled town
toward the train station (where she does, indeed, succeed in
buying a ticket at the Pressbyrån, and where the train to Malmö
comes, as predicted, at half past the hour), she thinks to herself
that she has rarely felt so desperate to get away from anywhere.
*If I had to live in Ystad*, she muses, *I'd drink too much, too.*

Back in Stockholm, she realizes that she still has two day-trips
to make to complete her Mystery Tour. One is to Sandhamn,
one of the outermost islands in the Stockholm archipelago,
where Viveca Sten has set her Nora Linde/Thomas Andreas-
son books. All through the two-and-a-half-hour ferry ride that
takes her there, she worries that she will find another Ystad, a
place devastated by its thriller success. Luckily, the six or seven
Sandhamn novels published to date have not yet achieved the
worldwide fame of the Wallander books. Perhaps this is because
Sten is nowhere near as good a writer as Mankell. More likely,
though, it's because the televised versions of these novels haven't
reached a mass viewership outside of Sweden. Either way, she

is relieved to find that their stamp on the charmingly down-at-heels village and its surrounding rural beauty is minimal. The island is still an unspoiled summer retreat, with its west side facing back toward the other 25,000 islands of the archipelago, the east looking outward onto the open Baltic.

In the whole afternoon she spends there, walking from the harborside town to the beach at Trouville and back again through the light-filtering, path-filled forest, she runs into just two tourists who refer to the Viveca Sten mysteries. This pair of Englishwomen—one of whom is short and rather conservative, the other tall and left-leaning—are not actual fans; they only know about the series because their little hotel has given them a map of the places where the books' murders occurred. She advises the two Brits not to bother with the Sandhamn novels for now, but instead to go straight to the Martin Becks. To encourage them, she spells out the first and last names of the authors so they can look them up when they return home. "Madge," says the taller woman, attempting to fix Maj Sjöwall's name in her memory.

The one other day-long trip she makes is to the town of Uppsala, which lies only fifty-five minutes by train from central Stockholm. Uppsala has much to recommend it besides the Kjell Eriksson series. As the books accurately convey, it is an old university town with a strong town-gown division—in this case a literal, geographical division marked by the Fyris River. On one side lies the university, as well as the old castle, the cathedral, a number of large parks and gardens, and some extremely nice housing. On the other side is everything else a city of about 150,000 could need: the city hall and its public square, the train station and its plaza dedicated to Olof Palme, a food hall, a theater, a large number of retail businesses, and an even larger number of affordable flats and houses. Both sides are attractive, but only the university side is beautiful.

She spends most of her time there at the Gustavianum Museum, which was built in 1625 and describes itself as the oldest surviving university building in Sweden. (Uppsala University itself predates the museum, having been founded in 1477.) The Gustav being commemorated in its name is not, thank heavens, the everlasting Gustav III, but an earlier king, Gustavus Adolphus, who donated the money necessary for the building's construction. Its distinctive cupola, however, dates from about a half-century later, when an Uppsala professor of medicine known as Olof Rudbeck the Elder commissioned the anatomy theater that rises from the structure's top floor.

Ever since seeing Bologna's masterpiece in the genre, she has considered herself an admirer of seventeenth-century anatomy theaters, and this one is no exception. Like the interior of the Drottningholm Palace Theater, the Gustavianum's anatomy theater is made of wood painted to look like marble. Unlike the Bologna auditorium, which features wooden benches for the anatomy students to sit on as they watch the dissection taking place down below, this one has only narrow spaces for standing observers, and the steps up to those viewing areas are so high as to suggest that the medical students were all quite tall as well as very thin. The high, rounded cupola that is visible from outside the building arches over the otherwise octagonal room, the top two layers of which are encircled by clerestory windows, so that the whole space is both light-filled and extraordinarily vertical in its feel. It is as if one's attention were being lured upward toward the light, even though, as an anatomy student, you were required to direct it downward instead, at the procedure taking place on the wooden table in the center of the room.

On the level below the anatomy theater, the museum consists of two darkened rooms, both devoted to the history of the university's science faculties. One room exhibits various scientific instruments in the fields of astronomy, chemistry, physics, chronometry, spectrometry, and other specialties she knows nothing about—all old, all beautiful, and all extremely functional at one time. Across the central corridor, in the other darkened space, she finds a series of even more valuable treasures, including the Augsburg Art Cabinet, a kind of marvelous dollhouse of precious and unusual things that was given to King Gustavus Adolphus by the German city of Augsburg in 1632. That room also contains a number of displays celebrating various prominent Uppsala professors, most notably Carl Linnaeus, whose enormous achievements in botany and biology are conveyed in several vitrines. She is filled with a sympathetic pride in Sweden's long scientific history, which clearly makes up a significant part of the nation's character. It explains, to a certain extent, why things still work as well as they do here—not only technically, in regard to engineering and infrastructure, but also in terms of how carefully the social welfare system is planned out. Perhaps this even applies to police procedures: the plodding, day-by-day investigations of a Martin Beck or a Kurt Wallander, which do in the end yield superlative results, could be the modern inheritance of the Linnaean tradition.

Early Swedish science clearly had to break away from the influence of medieval Christianity in order to make the progress it did, but this is not made explicit in the wall captions. The schism comes up, though, in a talk given by a young man who is just then guiding a group of English-speaking tourists around the museum. She runs across them outside the Linnaeus room, from which she is emerging and which they are about to enter. The pony-tailed guide, who is just getting going on his anti-clerical, pro-science speech about the brave Uppsala professors, starts by alluding to the monastic tradition as the "earliest" period of education. He then pauses and reconsiders. "Well, obviously there has always been education," he adds in a gently self-correcting tone, "as long as there was an older person and a younger person."

This simple, true remark, delivered in such a reflective manner, somehow strikes her as typical of this nation and its people. It is as typical, in its own way, as the courtesy shown her by a kindly, white-bearded guard earlier that day, when she initially approached the Gustavianum from the wrong side. Rather than making her go around to the front door, as any normal English or American guard would have done, he let her in the back door with his key card and told her how to reach the front lobby from there. *This is truly the human face of bureaucracy*, she thought then, and she thinks it again when she hears the museum guide's thoughtful clarification. It is based, she suspects, on a degree of mutual trust and mutual respect that barely exists between strangers in America anymore.

Ever since arriving in Sweden—ever since getting to Scandinavia, in fact—she has been pondering the question of why there is so much emphasis in the mystery novels on terrible things happening to children. As the police forces have assured her, child abuse by strangers is no more common here than it is in America; if anything, it is even less common, though the thrillers would suggest otherwise. When she asks Tor, at one point, why so many mysteries have harped on this theme, he answers, "Probably because it's the worst crime thinkable. What's the worst thing a person can do, what's the most evil a person can do—your main character fights against the most evil." But this, it seems to her, simply begs the question. Why do the Swedes (and Danes, and Norwegians) feel such a need to contemplate repeatedly this particular "worst"? What is it about the children in these countries that sets them up as potential victims of horrific crime, when in reality they are perhaps the least likely to experience it?

The fictionally induced fear, she notices, is also at severe odds not only with police statistics, but with the behavior of Scandinavian and particularly Swedish parents. Time after time, at beaches, airports, parks, museums, and other public places, she has witnessed small children engaging in risky behavior that a hovering American parent would instantly put a stop to. Three-year-olds wander far from their parents' sides and are left to their own devices among crowds of other people. Tiny little girls wave to their mothers from the tops of high parkland hills, while boys of the same age jump from boulder to boulder as their fathers look on from a distance. Nobody seems at all worried that a stranger is going to run in and snatch the child, but even more pointedly, no one seems worried that the child will injure *herself.* From an early age, these children are given the sense that the world is a secure place in which they can afford to have their own little adventures. Their physical safety, the parental behavior implies, is pretty much up to them.

It is not until Midsummer's Eve that she finally works out the link between these two opposing parental attitudes, the real-life lack of anxiety and the fictional fear. The Midsummer holiday itself—which she has, in a way, planned her trip around—is something she's been longing to see ever since reading about it in various mysteries. Despite her best efforts, though, she hasn't managed to get herself invited to any of the private celebrations, which mainly take place out in the countryside, and this is a bit worrisome, since it is clear from all the signs and websites in Stockholm that the whole city will be closing up for that Friday and Saturday. Luckily Skansen, the huge Stockholm park devoted to the history of Swedish life, will be holding a day-long series of events on Midsummer's Eve, and they are all open to the public.

Friday the 22nd turns out to be one of the few rainy days in June, and she wonders if the Skansen celebrations will be rained out. By noon, though, the skies have mainly cleared, so she heads for Djurgården, where Skansen is located. As she walks across the bridge from the nearest 76 bus stop, she is surrounded by people wearing wreaths in their hair—men, women, and children, all headed toward the same place she is going.

It seems to take forever to get around to the front gate of the vast park, where there is a long though fairly rapid line for admission. After she has paid, and has been given a map and a list of the afternoon's activities, she still has to take an escalator to get up to the right level of the park.

But now at last she finds herself at Tingsvallen, the large grassy area where the maypole has been set up, and where the sound of amplified singing greets approaching visitors. Once inside the maypole area, she moves around the crowd to get close to the bandstand. On its raised stage, a traditionally costumed woman and two accompanying singers, all backed by a folk-music band, are performing the lyrics of the dance tunes—and there before her eyes, in concentric circles around the tall may-pole, at least three or four hundred people are dancing.

The maypole is perhaps a bit less festive than she expected it to be (there are no streamers, just a very tall, birch-leaf-wrapped stick with some wildflowers stuck on here and there), but the dancers more than make up for it. The adults clearly know the dances from their childhoods, so even though the lead singer ex-plains everything beforehand in both Swedish and English, her rather schoolmarmy instructions are not really necessary. Every-one appears to know when to run to his left, or reverse to her right, or shake hands with the nearest neighbor, or crouch down on the still-soggy grass. When the songs invoke animals like pigs or cows or cats, the dancers snort or moo or meow in the right places; they particularly seem to enjoy the froggy moves that go along with a tune about frogs. There is one set of lyrics allud-ing to weekly washing rituals—including, she is delighted to note, the mangle—and again the dancers gesture appropriately. Another dance imitates a village priest who drives his car into a ditch. Still another requires the whole group to bow down facing the maypole and then salute it with a collective whoop. It would appear that in this one place, at least, Christianity and pagan nature-worship can mingle companionably together, as if there were no inherent conflict between them.

The dancing is not *good* dancing, in the sense of being skilled or difficult to execute, but it is thrilling to watch. Much of it involves simple running, as people hold hands or link arms with those on either side of them. Family groups dance next to to-tal strangers, with parents carrying the smallest children while the older kids prance alongside. People drop out of the dance briefly to greet recent arrivals with hugs and kisses, showing off new babies and exchanging the latest news, and then they jump back into the circle at a different place. A surprising number of teenagers are dancing with groups of their friends, and there are many, many young couples and singles. More than one woman wears a hijab, and at least one elderly man has a long gray braid down his back. A man with two adolescent boys who have Down syndrome passes by her in one direction; a few minutes later, after the circle turns counterclockwise, they come back the other way. She spots Indians, Pakistanis, Asians of all kinds, dancing with the same rhythms as the blond Swedes, using the same arm gestures, uttering the same sounds. Everyone's dancing is joyful and unabashed, as if there were nothing unusual in behaving this way in public.

Standing and watching from just outside the outermost circle, she feels her eyes filling with tears, and she is glad to be wearing dark glasses so that people don't wonder what is wrong with the crying woman. Nothing is wrong; it's just that she finds the whole thing unbelievably touching. Partly this is because she is always moved when people dance together in this natural, unchoreographed way (a remnant, perhaps, of her high-school folk dance years). But partly it is something more specific to this Swedish summer afternoon. She has a momentary sense that the culture is finally opening itself out to her in ways she would never have expected. It is baring its soul, or at least a part of its soul, and suddenly it becomes clear to her where the obsession with childhood comes from.

It is not just their own children's innocence the adults are guarding from imaginary crimes and violations, but the innocence of the children they once were. Childhood is evidently a period these Swedes recall with tremendous fondness—a time, as they truly or falsely remember it, when everything was joyful and fun. (Perhaps this feeling applies even more strongly to those who did not have a happy childhood, but who feel, for various cultural and conventional reasons, that they *ought* to have had one.) It's oddly touching to see these otherwise rather prim and withdrawn people dancing unashamedly in front of total strangers and making all the silly gestures and noises they learned as young children. No wonder the holiday is so beloved. On Midsummer's Eve they can return to being children again, all together and without embarrassment, as their own children join in and acquire the same history, the same habits. And her tears, she now realizes, must somehow be connected to this concerted yet effortless act of regression, in ways she can only begin to guess at.

At long last, just as her time in Sweden is approaching its end, she gets the appointment she has been waiting for with the Stockholm police department. Bengt Carlsson has written to her ("Sorry for this late answer," he apologizes, "but I've been extremely busy because of new murder cases from last Tuesday"), and he has set the last Thursday of her trip as their meeting date.

She goes, as instructed, to the Bergsgatan entrance, located on the side of the building that is neither quaintly old nor intimidatingly modern but somewhere in between. As in Ystad, she is surrounded by people in the waiting room who are mainly there to acquire passports, though it is obvious that a certain amount of other police business is taking place at the same time. At the reception desk she is issued an ID badge containing both her name and Bengt Carlsson's. Then she sits down to wait.

Bengt, when he arrives to fetch her, turns out to be a tall, gray-haired, blue-eyed man, informally dressed in a long-sleeved shirt, black jeans, and sneakers. He has a kind face and very intelligent eyes, the kind of glance that actually *sees* you. Unlike the other detectives she has dealt with, he does not take her to his personal office, but to a conference room instead, and though he gestures down the corridor toward the second-floor incident room, he says he cannot show it to her. Allowing her to choose one of the six chairs lining the sides of the conference table, he then sits down at the head, right next to her, and makes a joke about establishing his authority.

The first thing he tells her is that they are still in the midst of a massive police reorganization which began in 2016—the third biggest transformation since 1965, when the police were nationalized after having been run by the local municipalities. (That, she remembers, was the change that caused Martin Beck, or rather his authors, to feel that the police system was on its way downhill.) Bengt himself has been a policeman for forty-one years, and has been a detective since 1982. He joined the homicide division in 1987–88, though he tells her that is not actually what his department is called.

"We don't have pure homicide units. We call it *grova brott*, crimes that carry the higher penalties: homicide, arson, black-mailing, kidnapping, sex crimes like rape, and heavier drug crimes." His title, he says, would translate into something like team leader—literally, head of group. He tells her that his own ten-member investigative team is one of two on that floor, and of these twenty detectives, only four are men. All the "chiefs" except Bengt are women. He prefers, he says, to work with female colleagues. "Very sharp knives," he calls them, and adds that for some reason it is easier to recruit competent women these days. Two of the women on his team, in fact, are not even trained police officers, but social workers he has hired from outside; they cannot carry guns, so they have to stay in the car or at headquarters during dangerous operations, but Bengt insists they are "very, very good at the work."

Once again, she is struck by the discrepancy between the actual numbers of women detectives and their few paltry counterparts in fiction. Why have Scandinavian mystery writers chosen to downplay the fact that fifty percent or more of murder investigators are women? Surely the authors themselves must know this, if she has been able to find it out so easily. She presumes they must have some ulterior motive for presenting their female officers as isolated and beleaguered, but it doesn't make any sense to her. Still, this ancillary literary problem is hardly Bengt's concern, so she doesn't bother to bring it up now.

Instead, she asks him about the homicide rate in Stockholm. He answers by giving her the figure for Sweden as a whole, which he estimates at 100 to 120 murders a year. This is surprisingly high, compared to Denmark and Norway, and she later learns from a reliable internet article that Sweden has one of the higher murder rates in the European Union, mainly because of large numbers of gang killings in Malmö and the Stockholm suburbs. (On the other hand, as that same article points out, the Stockholm murder rate was only 1.3 per 100,000 in 2016, as compared to 29 per 100,000 in Chicago or 59 per 100,000 in St. Louis.) When she presses Bengt about the Stockholm numbers, he mentions that he is working on 32 cases now. This may or may not be intended to veil the actual numbers, which the internet puts at 50 Stockholm murders in 2017, about double the 26 that occurred in 2016. However you count it, her dear Stockholm is clearly a more dangerous place than Oslo or Copenhagen. But dangerous for whom?

"The one you have reason to be most afraid of is the one you live with," says Bengt, confirming that familial murders still account for the majority of cases. "The most dangerous place is your kitchen, and the most dangerous weapon is the knife you cut your bread with." He acknowledges that the recent statistics show a rise in gang murders and a slight decrease in domestic murders. But this does not mean that there has been an increase in stranger killings. "The most common killing is between people that know each other," he observes. "You never get as mad as at the people you live with or have a relation with."

"What are your citizens actually afraid of?"

"Old people are afraid of everything, including the dark. Young women are afraid to be attacked by rapists. And those who really should be afraid and take care—young men—don't know to be afraid. You have a mix of alcohol, testosterone, and tensions between people. My experience is that people often don't have realistic expectations of what to be afraid of."

He says that though there have been serial killers in Sweden, they are not all that common. The most famous case he can recall was a murderer named John Ausonius, whose crimes were committed in the late 1980s and early 1990s. "I actually worked that case," he tells her, and mentions that during the investigation the killer was known as the Laser Guy because "surviving victims and witnesses reported they saw this laser dot before the shooting. He used a small caliber, a .22, at close range."

That brings her back to the question of guns. Yes, he tells her, Swedish police officers all carry guns; it became mandatory in 1965. "Guess what they carried before that? Sabers!" he says, and mimes pulling a long saber out of a scabbard.

As for the general population, he does not think it's difficult to acquire a gun, even for criminals. "We have always had weapons here—hunters, shooting competitions. And then the National Guard used to be able to store their guns at home. I remember when I was a boy, a National Guard used to live next door, and on New Year's Eve he shot off his gun." He gives a brief, wry grin at the memory. "So we have a tradition of weapons. But using weapons in killings . . ." That, he thinks, is a recent development.

She raises the subject of the Olof Palme case, and Bengt's expression darkens. "It has become more and more history, but it was alive for a very long time. It was a trauma. I was very young: thirty years old when he was shot. I knew his son—we went to school together." For him, that crime was one of the "keystones" in the changing society. "I became a police officer in the old society," he notes, but then "the society changed from the old society to something very different." When she wonders aloud what those changes included, he answers, "Understanding that we must be more organized, better prepared. They didn't bother to use experts. They invented new wheels. If we had Palme again, we could handle it." He cites the quick solution to the 2003 Anna Lindh murder, and also to a "terror crime" that took place last year. "We are doing a good job," he insists.

She asks if he has read the Leif G. W. Persson novels about the Palme investigation, and he responds, "Of course." But he doesn't think those are necessarily Persson's best books. The ones he likes are the first three (which, she later discovers, have not yet been translated into English). "The first three books, I could identify myself. They were a mirror of what I call the old Sweden. In those days, a guy like me was the most important, telling everyone what to do every minute. It's not like that today, and I'm glad about it. We have a completely other way of thinking."

"Have you read any of the other mystery novels set in Sweden, the ones I'm writing about?"

"I've read all of them," Bengt says.

She asks which he likes best.

"What made me apply for the police was Sjöwall/Wahlöö. It made me enough interested that I applied for work here."

How perfect, she thinks—and how amazing. "What did you like so much about them?"

"The books describe the society, what it was like: the old society. And they managed to create those figures: Martin Beck . . ."

"Kollberg, Melander," she chimes in.

"Gunvald Larsson," he adds. "A brutal guy—he would never be in the police force today—but I kind of like him as a character." They agree that Larsson's habit of thumbing his nose at authority can be immensely appealing, and Bengt suggests that some of that tendency would be useful here and now. "They made a good decision in how they chose their characters," he says of the Martin Beck authors. "And in a pedagogic way, they explained a lot."

"How do you think they knew so much about the police?"

"From Ed McBain," he answers with a smile. "They started out as translators of Ed McBain." And now she recalls noticing that in *Murder at the Savoy*, the murderer himself was reading an Ed McBain novel—a weird tribute, perhaps, but then, he is a particularly sympathetic murderer.

"But they were also both journalists," Bengt goes on. "And journalists often had good police connections." (That "had" may be a bit pointed, since he has already told her that the Stockholm homicide department goes out of its way not to publicize its murder investigations. "We are not that good at going to the press with this," he mentioned in regard to the recent gang shootings. "We don't want investigations going out into the media, and they don't even write about it." And indeed, from her own brief experience, she would have said that the Stockholm police were intensely media-averse, compared to their counterparts in Oslo and Copenhagen.)

But she is anxious to get back to the literary discussion. Which of the modern mystery writers does he like?

"I really like Henning Mankell's books. They are the most realistic in my eyes, when they describe how it's done and how it feels. The plots are not realistic—they are ridiculous, all those killings in a small village. But the feelings . . ."

She brings up the Lars Kepler and Arne Dahl series, and he shakes his head. He doesn't like novels like that because "the police guys are super-special"—in other words, possessed of amazing intuition, cleverness, and physical skill that allow them to outwit criminals of an almost sorcerer-like malevolence. But when she mentions Jo Nesbø's books, he lights up. "I really love them. But Harry Hole, the character, he would have been kicked off a long time ago."

He doesn't object to unrealistic crimes, because he thinks those are inherent in the genre. What he dislikes most are unrealistic characters. "Most people, even politicians, get an idea of what things are like from these books," Bengt says. "They think the police environment looks like it does in movies." Whereas really, he explains, the environment is mostly just huge stacks of paper. "If you look at how we deal with things, it looks like bureaucracy. But we are very thorough. We get things done. We always have our eyes and feet in the courtroom when we work." He pauses and looks at her. "Do you understand what I mean by that?"

She realizes that she doesn't, and shakes her head.

"We're not looking for Truth. We are looking for what we can prove. To be able to do that, you have to go through a huge pile of papers"—and here he gestures with his hands, indicating a stack two or three feet high. "You have to know everything: who did it, how did it happen . . ." He describes their current investigation into the shooting that took place two weeks ago. They had the two people responsible for it in custody within half an hour. After that, they embarked on a full-scale investigation, with up to fifteen detectives involved in the early days. Now two to four detectives will continue to work on it full-time for three to six months, until it is ready to go to court.

In this respect and others, he believes, *The Terrorists* is the weakest of the Martin Beck books. Dispensing with much of the plodding detail, this last volume in the series is the least accurate in its representation of police procedure, the most openly satiric. "But he had become very sick by then," he offers as an excuse, alluding to Per Wahlöö's cancer, "and perhaps he had become bitter."

"Well, but *The Terrorists* did uncannily predict Olof Palme's assassination," she points out.

"That's not prediction," he says. "I don't believe in that. It's a fiction that came true."

Switching gears now, she asks him about his impression of America, and for the first time since she has arrived in Scandinavia, someone is willing to speak critically about her country's violent image.

"The States are not always respected in that regard," Bengt begins tactfully. "We have traditions—you know, during the Vietnam War . . . We think the system in the States is strange. Just looking at the weapons, and the lack of your ability to do anything about that."

He asks her, gently, what she thinks accounts for this.

"I think it starts a lot further back than policing," she says, warming to her subject as she starts to speak. "I think the causes of crime in America have a lot to do with the extreme differences between wealth and poverty. And if poverty is the root source of crime, then nothing in the justice system, nothing to do with the police or jail terms or crime prevention, will ever really affect it. And everything is of course getting worse and worse under this horrible administration."

She thinks about how angry and helpless she's felt whenever she read the news over the past year or two, and she knows something of that desperation is apparent in her voice and on her face. "And now this latest terrible thing," she adds, "with the migrant children being ripped away from their parents—"

At this Bengt winces, as if she had jabbed him with something sharp.

"We the police cannot solve the problems in society," he

agrees. Perhaps in an attempt to make her feel better, he then turns to the situation in Sweden. "Today we are paying the fines, in our suburbs, for the segregation of society." He himself, he points out, lives in a de facto segregated community of white people, who are all there because they have enough money to buy housing in a nice place. What leads to crime is "living in a bad environment," he says, and that is society's fault, not the individual's.

And there it is again—that measured, humane perspective, the very thing she has crossed the ocean to seek out. She has heard echoes of it before, in the words of Oslo's Bård Dyrdal and Copenhagen's Jens Møller Jensen, but here in the Stockholm police station she finds it in perhaps its purest form. At once empathetic and skeptical, fair-minded and restrained, it is the viewpoint she associates with Martin Beck and his team. The world which created those fictional policemen may be long gone, but something of her imaginary Scandinavia, something of its decency and thoughtfulness, still exists. There remains a realistic alternative, apparently, to the dangerous befuddlement of her own unhappy country.

But now Bengt suggests that in Sweden, too, things are about to get worse.

"We have our election in September, and I think our political landscape will be remodeled. I don't like populism. I've always been a left-wing guy, as perhaps you can tell. I am sixty-two years old, and when I say left-wing, my younger colleagues don't understand what it stands for."

Still, he believes the modern-day police force—a force so selective that he himself might not have been admitted if he were applying now—has many good things about it. "My younger colleagues are clever. They work to change things. We don't have an outspoken racism culture. And between men and women, it's also kosher. I vote for the younger generation. Nowadays, I don't even try to influence my colleagues with my point of view, which was rooted in 'Those were the days.' I trust them. The codes have changed—left-wing, right-wing—it's a new landscape. I trust the younger generation because they got a good education, good training."

She brings up the fact that the younger generation of both their countries is more in touch with the rest of the world, through the internet and possibly through the fact that so many people now speak English. Maybe it will be harder for the next generation of Americans to assume as blithely that their own children are more important than Mexican children or Honduran children. "Things seem so bad now, as if they've gone too far ever to recover, but look at Germany," she says. "I've spent a lot of time in Berlin."

"So have I," he interjects, and she nods in confirmation.

"Then you know what it's like. And if *they* can come back from *that*, then maybe we can too. It's so hard to say." She stops, and then goes on. "My husband is an old-style lefty, and he's pretty pessimistic about the way things are now. He thinks it will only get worse. But my son, who's a local politician and an activist in New York, thinks that his generation will manage to change things. And I'm caught between them. I don't know whether to be hopeful or to give up hope."

"You must never give up hope. That's the most important thing." Bengt is looking directly at her with those piercing blue eyes, and she feels herself intensely wanting to believe him—to believe that he does indeed have some kind of authority, however much he may joke about it. "I hope that democracy has grown strong enough to resist. As a police officer, I think of myself as a guard of democracy and its values. And there might be bad days, things that go wrong," he acknowledges. "But I am a proud police officer."

Their time is up. The interview has lasted much longer than either of them expected, and he urgently needs to get back to work. Bengt shows her out of the building, guiding her through the complicated exit arrangements that will lead her to an out-side door. ("It's hard to get in. It's even harder to get out," he teases.)

And now, as she walks down Bergsgatan toward the fancifully cavelike interior of the Rådhuset subway station, she starts to mull things over. On the face of it, the conversation she's just had was filled with depressing elements. Yet the overall emotion she finds herself left with is, strangely enough, a sense of enormous contentment. She's been aware of feeling something like this in a peripheral way ever since arriving in Stockholm, but it has gradually grown stronger over time, and her encounter with this mensch of a policeman has brought it to the fore. It's not simply a matter of having her preconceived ideas about Scandinavia satisfyingly confirmed or fascinatingly contradicted; that now seems relatively unimportant. What she's sensing in herself is the exuberant relief of knowing that, somewhere in the world, there's a respite from the circumstances she's been struggling with back home. If she weren't afraid of sounding so naively American, she might almost be tempted to call it a feeling of happiness.

# APPENDIX

## AN ANNOTATED LIST OF MYSTERIES AND THRILLERS

This is necessarily an incomplete list, since I've read just a fraction of the ever-growing body of Scandinavian mysteries, and among the ones I *have* read, I'm describing and recommending only a selected portion. The list is ordered in terms of my preferences, though it also includes a few books toward the end that I did not like but that you still might want to read. Whether you are new to the field or an old Nordic-noir fan, I hope you will find more than enough recommendations here to keep you happily reading for the foreseeable future.

**Maj Sjöwall and Per Wahlöö: the Martin Beck series.** As you will already have gleaned from the previous pages, these ten books are my top recommendation, now and for all time. It is essential to read them in order, as follows: *Roseanna, The Man Who Went Up in Smoke, The Man on the Balcony, The Laughing Policeman, The Fire Engine That Disappeared, Murder at the Savoy, The Abominable Man, The Locked Room, Cop Killer,* and *The Terrorists.* You may find the early books slow, but keep going; if you are not won over by the time you finish *The Laughing Policeman,* I guess you can give up, but you will have missed something terrific. The effect of the series is cumulative rather than singular, and the whole thing bears re-reading at, say, twenty-year intervals. Avoid, by the way, most of the television or film versions based on these characters: they have virtually nothing to do with the characters, plots, and feelings in the books themselves. (I have heard from other people that the Bo Widerberg film from 1976, *Mannen på taket*, is remarkably faithful to *The Abominable Man*, but since it can't be obtained in America at the moment, I've not been able to verify that myself.)

**Henning Mankell: the Kurt Wallander series.** This is my first runner-up, and I recommend these books almost as highly as I do the Martin Becks. Again, it is best to avoid the filmic renderings (particularly the ghastly Branagh series), but don't despair: even if you have already seen the TV versions, you can still get a huge amount out of reading the books. Though each novel can be enjoyed separately on its own, they are best read in order, starting with *Faceless Killers* and proceeding through *The Dogs of Riga, The White Lioness, The Man Who Smiled, Sidetracked, The Fifth Woman, One Step Behind, Firewall*, and *An Event in Autumn*. (I think the "prequel" volume, a set of belatedly published short stories called *The Pyramid*, can safely be ignored.) If you are like me, you will be unable to resist reading the last book in the series, *The Troubled Man*, even though it is not quite up to the level of the rest—but it does bring the Kurt Wallander story to a conclusion. I do not particularly recommend Mankell's stand-alone mystery involving Linda Wallander, *Before the Frost*, but I rather like his final novel, *After the Fire*, which is not a mystery, but a thoughtful contemplation of old age.

**Jo Nesbø: the Harry Hole series.** Among those writing today, Nesbø is my favorite Nordic-noir author, though in his
case I don't necessarily recommend going through the whole
series, unless you turn out to be a complete addict (as I am)
and need the additional fix. The best place to start is not at the
beginning—though feel free to go back to *The Bat* and *Cock-
roaches* afterward, if you like—but with the trilogy that starts
with *The Redbreast*, goes on to *Nemesis*, and concludes with *The
Devil's Star*. Each has a plot that completes itself within the volume, but there is a larger plot that runs through all three, and
you won't be able to put the books down until you get those final
answers. The novel that follows this trilogy, *The Redeemer*, is also
very good, and *The Snowman*, which comes after that, is possibly
Nesbø's most thrilling, though it is also the one where the Grand
Guignol theatrics begin to intrude. The books get more violent
and more implausible as they proceed; only you will know when
to quit. Since I have never ceased to appreciate the clever plotting and the good writing, I have not been able to quit at all, and
I buy each new Harry Hole installment as soon as it appears. I
am also a big fan of Nesbø's standalone mysteries (*Headhunters*
is especially good), and I think his rewrite of *Macbeth* is nothing
short of brilliant: you can read it with pleasure even if you know
nothing about Shakespeare's original, but the better you know
the play, the more you will appreciate the ways in which Nesbø
has adapted the plot into a credible version of late-twentieth-
century Scotland.

**Lotte & Søren Hammer: the Konrad Simonsen series.** This is
the point at which it gets harder to rank the books against each
other, and I would simply suggest that from here on in this list,

you read one in the series and decide for yourself if you want to go on. In general, the first volume in the cycle is the best, and that is certainly true with regard to the Hammers, whose *The Hanging* remains my favorite of their books. But I also have an enduring affection for Simon, the Countess, and the other characters who make up this Danish homicide team, and I would recommend all the others in the series, up to and including *The Night Ferry*. In addition to providing good plots and believable police teamwork, these books do an excellent job of conveying the social and political atmosphere in contemporary Denmark.

**Mari Jungstedt: the Anders Knutas series.** This, too, is a series in which I've enjoyably read everything, which so far consists of nine volumes translated into English. You can really begin anywhere—and if you don't mind starting in the middle, I recommend the artful *Killer's Art*—but if you start at the very beginning, with *Unseen* and then *Unspoken*, you will get a better sense of the developing relationships among the characters. The plots are compelling, the police work is good, and the evocation of the town of Visby (not to mention the island of Gotland as a whole) is so enticing it persuaded me to make a special trip there.

**Thomas Enger: the Henning Juul series.** These ones are a bit formulaic, but I have to admit that I couldn't put them down until I had read all five. Set in Oslo and using a crime journalist as the central character, they absolutely must be read in order: *Burned*, *Pierced*, *Scarred*, *Cursed*, and *Killed*. The end is somewhat unsatisfying, but that is almost predictable in a connected series that whets the appetite without filling it along the way.

The insights into the relationships between journalism (especially present-day online journalism) and crime are particularly interesting.

**Gard Sveen: the Tommy Bergmann series.** Here's another Norwegian, with a central detective figure who is simultaneously sympathetic and off-putting. (Tommy's marriage broke up because he was a wife-beater—not something that an American mystery writer would allow in a main character.) There are only two volumes translated into English so far, and the first, *The Last Pilgrim*, is the better one; it includes a detailed rendering of the Norwegian Resistance along with an intertwined modern-day plot.

**Jussi Adler-Olsen: the Department Q series.** I have very mixed feelings about this series. I absolutely loved *The Keeper of Lost Causes*, the first volume, which I read the minute it came out in English, and I have followed the Department Q team ever since. But each book, it seems to me, is weaker than the last, and the portrayal of the characters (particularly the bizarre rendering of the Arab helper, Assad, but also the craziness assigned to the female assistant, Rose) definitely stuck in my craw when I went back to re-read these books. So quit as soon as you're not enjoying them anymore. And above all, do not pay good money for Adler-Olsen's inept political thriller set in America, titled *The Washington Decree*.

**Arne Dahl: *Misterioso*.** This Swedish author (whose real name is Jan Arnald) has written several whole series, but the only novel I can highly recommend is the first volume in his

Intercrime cycle, *Misterioso*. Everything about it is great: the detective characters, the complicated crime, the jazz-inflected background, the satisfying solution. Naturally I went on to buy others in the series, but found the sequel, *To the Top of the Mountain*, so disappointing that I gave up on any further Arne Dahl reading. You may have better luck, because I have certainly not read most of his work.

**Roslund & Hellström:** *Three Seconds*. This pair of writers does actually have first names (they are Anders and Börge, respectively), but they publish under last names only, linked by an ampersand. Again, there is only one book in their voluminous output that I can recommend, and that is the gripping *Three Seconds*. It combines a sordid, high-level government conspiracy, excellent police work, and some terrific "tradecraft" in the elaborately worked-out plot. I was so delighted when I finished it that I immediately bought their more recent *Three Minutes*, which turned out to be one of the most boring thrillers I've ever read—proving, I guess, that it's not always a good idea for writers to perpetuate their main characters in subsequent volumes.

**Lars Kepler: the Joona Linna series.** Lars Kepler is the joint pseudonym of a married couple, Alexandra and Alexander Ahndoril, whose Stockholm detective is a Finnish transplant named Joona Linna. Despite their wild improbabilities, I enjoyed these books, especially *The Hypnotist*, which came out first. I recommend you read them in order, not only because Joona's life changes drastically as the series goes on, but also because the quality of the narrative declines somewhat, as is unfortunately the case in so many detective cycles.

**K. O. Dahl: the Frank Frølich series.** This Dahl (unlike Arne) is a Norwegian, and Frank is one of those irascible, rebellious, but still somewhat appealing male detectives who thrive in Nordic-noir police departments. The books are a tad formulaic, but not bad. I recommend starting with either *The Fourth Man* or *Lethal Investments*; if you like them, then by all means acquire the rest.

**Åke Edwardson: the Erik Winter series.** Edwardson's Gothenburg-based series features a chief inspector whose last name, Winter, suggests something of his gloom-filled personality. Erik has a family life of sorts, but he is excessively devoted to his work, something about which his companion, Angela—who is also the mother of his children—is always complaining. I didn't feel strongly enough about these books to buy more than one (*Room No. 10* is the volume I own), but I happily checked a few others out of the library.

**Håkan Östlundh: *The Viper*.** Östlundh has written a whole series about the Gotland policeman Fredrik Broman, only a few of which have been translated into English. However, the book of his I recommend most is actually a standalone called *The Viper*, featuring a complicated plot that is very cleverly (and very unobtrusively) based on *The Oresteia*. Try to forget this fact when you are reading the book, or I will have spoiled the ending for you.

**Steffen Jacobsen: *Trophy*.** Start with this one, which is quite good, and if you like the main character, a private detective and security consultant named Michael Sander, you will want to continue with *Retribution* and *When the Dead Awaken*. I found these less satisfying than *Trophy*—and Jacobsen's emphatically stated political attitudes begin to wear a bit thin—but all three are well plotted.

**Lene Kaaberbøl & Agnete Friis:** *The Boy in the Suitcase.* This pair of Danish authors went on to produce a number of Nina Borg books, of which this is the first and by far the best. Nina, a nurse by profession, is a rather haphazard and extremely neurotic detective figure, and I got a bit tired, after a while, of reading about her problematic home life. (When you find yourself sympathizing with the put-upon husband as opposed to his sleuthing wife, something is definitely wrong.) Still, the plots are reasonably interesting and the grungy Copenhagen atmosphere well-described.

**Leif G. W. Persson:** *The Dying Detective.* Here is where I part company with most Swedes, who appear to adore Persson's novels. The only book of his I can wholeheartedly recommend is his latest, *The Dying Detective*, which puts an end to the police detective Lars Martin Johansson—an appealing character who, with his partner and best friend, Bo Jarnebring, apparently featured in Persson's first three (as yet untranslated) novels. I truly wish I could read those, because they might help me understand Persson's popularity. I did not enjoy his trilogy about Olof Palme's assassination (rather grandiosely titled *Between Summer's Longing and Winter's End*, *Another Time, Another Life*, and *Falling Freely, as if in a Dream*), and I so thoroughly hated the character Evert Bäckström—who appears in a subordinate role in all the Persson novels I've read—that I did not have the stomach to pursue him through his own separate series.

**Kjell Eriksson: the Ann Lindell series.** Set in Uppsala, these books convey a slightly different Sweden, one where professors and regular townspeople live side by side as if in two separate universes. Once again, we are forced to contemplate a female detective's bad luck with relationships—a tiresome and, I would hope, nearly used-up theme in Scandinavian mysteries—and Lindell herself is only a so-so character. But the police teamwork in these books is impressive and the plots are pretty good. Try *The Cruel Stars of the Night* and see what you think.

**Åsa Larsson: the Rebecka Martinsson series.** Here we have yet another female protagonist with serious psychological afflictions, which makes the series problematic for me—as does the extremely rural setting, in the far north of Sweden. However, if you can get around those barriers, I recommend these books for their political and historical insights. *Until Thy Wrath Be Past*, for instance, conveys the Second World War background to a contemporary crime, while *The Black Path* skewers internationally successful (and exploitive) Swedish businesses. And we do get a good female police detective—the smart, reliable Anna-Maria Mella, who is paired with prosecuting attorney Rebecka Martinsson on her homicide investigations—so all is not lost in that regard, either.

**Alexander Söderberg: the Sophie Brinkmann series.** Only two of these—*The Andalucian Friend* and *The Other Son*—have so far been translated from Swedish into English, and they might be better classed as adventure tales rather than pure mysteries. But the plots are exciting and well-constructed, and the characters, though perhaps a bit too heavily involved with international criminals, are emotionally appealing.

**Christian Jungersen:** *The Exception.* This is a standalone Danish novel about a human-rights organization and the people who work for it. The writing is not particularly good and the political information sometimes feels undigested, but the mystery is compelling enough to keep you going, and the implied facts about Denmark's past and present are pretty interesting.

**Stieg Larsson: the Lisbeth Salander series.** Speaking of undigested information. Larsson was an intelligent and resourceful journalist, not a fiction writer, and his mysteries contain wads of unintegrated stuff that you will just want to page through. But despite their serious shortcomings as novels, these thrillers are sufficiently gripping to keep you reading nonstop, once you have started. It would be remiss of me not to list the Millennium Trilogy—*The Girl with the Dragon Tattoo*, *The Girl Who Played with Fire*, and *The Girl Who Kicked the Hornet's Nest*—since these three books opened the door to so many other Scandinavian mysteries. If you become strongly attached to Lisbeth Salander, you may wish to continue with the three additional novels written after Larsson's death by David Lagercrantz, who perpetuated the series at the heirs' behest.

**Malin Persson Giolito:** *Quicksand.* This novel, by a Swedish lawyer, is unusual in that it takes place largely in the courtroom. The murder plot—a school shooting—is perhaps overly topical and not terribly pertinent to Sweden, but the psychological aspects of the plot's unfolding are plausible and compelling.

*Quicksand* is Giolito's first book translated into English, and it makes me curious to see what else she'll do.

**Håkan Nesser: the Inspector Van Veeteren series.** These are good mysteries, and I've read just about every one that I can get my hands on. The only caveat is that they are set in an imaginary place—a made-up city in an unnamed country that seems to be somewhere between the Netherlands and Scandinavia—and this deprives the novels of a certain gritty realism, or perhaps just appealing reality, that I have come to expect from Nesser's fellow Swedes. You can start at the beginning of the series, with *Mind's Eye* or *Borkmann's Point*, or just drop in anywhere in the middle; the mysteries are all self-contained, though the character and his personal life develop somewhat over time.

**Karin Fossum: the Inspector Sejer series.** Most readers, and especially Norwegians, would rank this series higher than I do. The plots are generally compelling, and Inspector Sejer himself—a widower deeply attached to his dog—is an appealing character. But the savagery of Fossum's sadism has turned me away from these books time and again, and whenever I return, I always regret it. It is not her characters who are her worst victims, but we, the expectant readers, to whom she is always shockingly cruel.

**Gunnar Staalesen: the Varg Veum series.** Here is another Norwegian writer, this time from Bergen, where he sets his novels featuring the private investigator Varg Veum. Each novel is perfectly good—I have read three of them, out of the dozen or so he's written—but they are not, as a group, very memorable. I would recommend starting with either *The Consorts of Death* or *Where Roses Never Die.*

**Viveca Sten: the Sandhamn series.** We're now moving into the territory where I'm not actively recommending books, just dutifully mentioning them, sometimes for reasons that may be extraneous to their worth as mysteries. In the case of the Sandhamn novels (which I've referred to several times in the preceding pages), the main and perhaps the only reason to read them is their enticing setting in the Stockholm archipelago, which is evocatively rendered in the books. The plots grow ever more tedious as the series progresses, and the main character, Nora Linde, is a bit of a drip. Start with the first and best book, *Still Waters*, and then decide if you want to go on.

**Helene Tursten: the Irene Huss series.** This Swedish series is set in Gothenburg—again, a good reason to read it, since it's a very different Sweden from the one in the Stockholm novels, and Tursten is good at evoking place. But I found the police officer, Irene Huss, to be such an irretrievable ditz that I didn't want to read more than a single novel, *The Glass Devil.* Perhaps Tursten herself is beginning to feel that way, for she has recently started an entirely new series featuring a very different female detective, Embla Nyström.

**Anne Holt: the Hanne Wilhelmsen series.** A friend recommended these ten Oslo-based books to me, but I never made it past the first one in the series, *Blind Goddess.* The author has excellent police department credentials, but I found the writing clumsy and the characters flat. Still, I gather Holt is a big success

in Norway, so I'm including her books in my list just in case you
have a different reaction.

**Jenny Rogneby:** *Leona.* In this, her first mystery, Rogneby's
central character is a female police officer who—rather like the
narrator of Stein Riverton's genre-originating novel, *The Iron
Chariot*—turns out to be singularly unreliable. As a former investigator herself, Rogneby is good at describing Swedish police
procedures, but in this case both plot and character are a bit too
far-fetched. It remains to be seen how this writer will develop.

**Erik Axl Sund:** *The Crow Girl.* This enormous novel is by a pair
of Swedes, Jerker Eriksson and Håkan Axlander Sundquist, who
jointly write under the Sund pseudonym. They have produced
four books to date, but I have read only this one and have no desire
to sample their other wares. *The Crow Girl* goes beyond even the
Stieg Larsson novels in its depictions of male sadism and female
vengefulness; it also focuses so heavily on child sexual abuse as to
make it, at times, truly unpleasant reading. The multiple villains
all turn out to be interconnected in the mystery's ludicrously complex solution, which is arrived at through almost no serious police
work, even though a sympathetic female homicide detective lies
at the heart of the plot. The only reason I am listing it here is that
it has proven enormously popular among mystery fans, not only in
Scandinavia but also in Germany and the United States.

And now, for those of you who, like me, enjoy watching Scandinavian thrillers as well as reading them, here are a few TV
shows to look for:

***The Bridge.*** This Swedish-Danish co-production is wonderful in every way, and should certainly be at the top of your viewing list, if you have not already seen it. Beware of imitations: the American version (also called *The Bridge*) is nowhere near as compelling, and I strongly doubt that the French-English one (announced as *The Tunnel*) is up to the standard of the original, either.

***The Killing.*** I might possibly rank this excellent Danish series even higher than *The Bridge*, except that it's so hard to get in the United States. You do not want the competing American version readily available here, but the original (called *Forbrydelsen* in Danish), which is available from Britain with English subtitles. A warning: this show is exceedingly dark, and if you let it, it will take over your life, so you may want to consume the episodes sparingly.

***Borgen.*** This is not, technically speaking, a mystery series, but the story of the Danish parliament and the rise of a female prime minister is gripping at every moment of its three seasons. And given the back-stabbing and power-grabbing that occur in almost every episode, it certainly qualifies as Nordic noir.

***Nobel.*** A Norwegian program that focuses on the life of a soldier who is married to a political functionary, this series contains great acting, astute politics, and enough thrilling moments to keep anyone stuck to the screen for its duration. Its tender portrayals of comradeship and multi-generational family life balance and mitigate the darkness at its core.

*Occupied.* Again, this can only be peripherally viewed as a thriller, since it is not a police procedural or an account of a murder investigation. Instead, it is an extremely well-done portrait of what would happen if Russia—with the unspoken sanction of the European Community—took over Norway and proceeded to set up a puppet government there. Based on an idea by Jo Nesbø, this is essentially World War Two reimagined, but with Russia standing in for Germany, and Sweden (rather than England) housing the government in exile.

*The Protectors.* Not to be confused with a terrible English-language show put out under the same name, this Danish series follows the secret service officers (both male and female) who are assigned to protect a variety of political leaders and other important figures in places around the globe. The politics are intelligent and the characters excellently portrayed; best of all, the episodes come in delightfully predictable pairs, so that you only have to watch two hours each evening to get each plot's solution.

*Valkyrien.* This Norwegian show is more of a medical science-fiction thriller than a true mystery, but it is sufficiently compelling (despite its grotesque scientific implausibilities) to be one of my definite recommendations. A certain amount of pointedly political Oslo reality manages to seep into the imaginary plot and setting, and the scripts (from what I can tell in subtitles) seem particularly smart.

*Borderliner.* Also Norwegian, this is a gripping eight-episode noir that focuses on the personal and professional travails of

Nikolai Andreassen, a closeted gay cop who comes from a law-enforcement family. Though Nikolai is basically a sensitive, effective, honest officer, family obligations pressure him into a certain amount of corrupt behavior, which he then has to think his way out of. The characters are richly portrayed, the relationships are enormously appealing, and the plot is good up to the very end, when it mistakenly opts for inconclusiveness.

*Department Q.* A few episodes made from Jussi Adler-Olsen's books have made it over to American TV, and I can recommend them—more highly than the books, in fact, since the overt racism embodied in the Assad character has been eliminated in the television version. The plots are recognizably drawn from the novels, but the enlivening performances make them seem new.

*Bordertown.* I am breaking my self-imposed rule against Finnish mysteries by including this, but the series—set, as its title suggests, on the border between Finland and Russia—is really worth watching. The main character, an eccentrically creative homicide detective who has recently moved his family from Helsinki to this far-flung location, is played by an actor whose physical presence is so fascinating that I have looked in vain for other shows starring him. He is not a young man, but he moves as gracefully as a dancer, and the way the character moves turns out to be central to the way he thinks.

*Deadwind.* Another good Finnish series, this one featuring a female detective and her younger male sidekick, who together solve an extremely complicated murder while exposing some serious corporate crime. The twelve-episode plot is impossible to predict and at the same time nicely coherent (it's always re-warding when you get those loose ends thoroughly tied up), and the relationship between the two central detectives is appealing.

*The Lava Field.* Again, this mystery show technically falls outside my field, since it comes from Iceland, but the plot is excellent and the scenery, though quite real, is beyond belief. The mini-series is worth watching for its visual qualities alone, but it is also a good and well-solved murder mystery.

## ACKNOWLEDGMENTS

For financial and other support during my visits to Scandinavia, I would like to thank the Swedish Academy in Stockholm, the Norwegian embassy in Washington, D.C., and the Swedish embassy in Washington, D.C. Linda Zachrison of the Swedish embassy and Urd Berge Milbury of the Norwegian embassy have been particularly kind and helpful to me in all sorts of ways. I also owe tremendous thanks to Barbro Osher, the Swedish consul in San Francisco, who offered me excellent advice from beginning to end.

Many of the people who helped me in the course of my on-the-ground research are listed by name in the pages of the book; some appear anonymously or semi-anonymously, and I am equally grateful to them. As for those who assisted me behind the scenes, I need to thank Peter Galassi for his very useful advice about what to see and do in Stockholm; Paul Duguid for equivalent insights into Copenhagen; David Hollander and Todd Pearson, who greatly enhanced my visits to Sweden and Norway by overlapping my travels with theirs; and Nick Rizzo and Jessica Edmiston, who thoughtfully gave me Scandinavian reference books and Nordic novels during the years I was working on the project.

The seed for this book grew out of a lunch with my friend Brenda Wineapple, and though I can no longer remember who first mentioned Scandinavian mysteries, I know I would not have thought up the central idea without her. Ileene Smith, the world's best editor, helped me refine and improve the project at each stage. As usual, everyone else at Farrar, Straus and Giroux—Gretchen Achilles, Mitzi Angel, Scott Auerbach, Tyler Comrie, Alice Dalrymple, Jonathan Galassi, Brian Gittis, Debra Helfand, Jackson Howard, Na Kim, Devon Mazzone, Jeff Seroy, Lisa Silverman, NaNá V. Stoelzle, and untold others—lent their outstanding skills to making this book into the best possible version of itself.

Due to the unstinting generosity of Barbara and Martin Bauer, I was able to start and finish the book at the Katzbach Academy in Berlin, which is always my favorite place to write. This time, in particular, those Berlin stays were important to me in ways that only the Bauers can fully appreciate. Martin Bauer was also one of five early readers who helpfully commented on an unfinished draft of the book; the others were Bengt Carlsson, Lynn Glaser, Arthur Lubow, and Katharine Michaels. Huge thanks to them all. Finally, no acknowledgments would be complete without reference to my husband, Richard Rizzo— the unnamed "companion" of these travels, and of so much else besides.

## A NOTE ABOUT THE AUTHOR

Wendy Lesser is the founder and editor of *The Threepenny Review*. She has written one novel and eleven previous works of nonfiction; recent books include *Music for Silenced Voices*, *Why I Read*, and *You Say to Brick: The Life of Louis Kahn*, which won the Marfield Prize for Arts Writing and the PEN America Award for Research Nonfiction. A recipient of grants and fellowships from the American Academy in Berlin, the Cullman Center for Scholars and Writers, the Guggenheim Foundation, the Swedish Academy, and numerous other organizations, she currently divides her time between Berkeley, California, and New York City.